Behavioral Telehealth

Series Editors
Peter W. Tuerk
Medical University of South Carolina, Charleston, South Carolina, USA

Peter Shore
Oregon Health & Science University, Portland, Oregon, USA

This series is devoted to empirically based explorations of issues in the field of behavioral health and technology. A burgeoning area gathering increasing momentum, telemental health is currently not sufficiently served, lacking well-rounded, scientifically rigorous works upon which clinicians, administrators and researchers can rely. The Behavioral Telehealth series offers clinically relevant volumes that focus on key issues and replicable programs that take real life situations into consideration. The volumes are aimed at an audience of psychologists, psychiatrists and other mental health and primary care professionals who are using or plan to use this technological approach.

More information about this series at http://www.springer.com/series/10986

Peter W. Tuerk • Peter Shore
Editors

Clinical Videoconferencing in Telehealth

Program Development and Practice

 Springer

Editors

Peter W. Tuerk
Department of Psychiatry and Behavioral
  Sciences
Medical University of South Carolina;
  Mental Health Service
  Ralph H. Johnson VA Medical Center,
  Veterans Health Administration
Charleston
South Carolina
USA

Peter Shore
Department of Psychiatry
Oregon Health & Science University;
  VA Northwest Health Network (VISN 20)
  Department of Veterans Affairs
Portland
Oregon
USA

ISSN 2199-8604   ISSN 2199-8612 (electronic)
ISBN 978-3-319-08764-1   ISBN 978-3-319-08765-8 (eBook)
DOI 10.1007/978-3-319-08765-8
Springer Cham Heidelberg New York Dordrecht London

Library of Congress Control Number: 2014949796

Printed on acid-free paper

Springer is part of Springer Science+Business Media (www.springer.com)

Foreword

In the late 1990s on a lark I agreed to mentor a post-doctoral fellow who wanted to review the literature on the use of videoconferencing technology for direct provision of diagnostic and treatment services to patients with mental illnesses. At the outset of the effort I did not have much interest in the subject and did not see much potential for the concept to ever gain traction. While the fellow's attention soon waned, I found myself grappling with a new (to me) idea about how mental healthcare could be made far more accessible to people by bringing it to them where they lived.

As a concept, clinical videoconferencing—and there are many more or less specific terms, which are often used somewhat interchangeably—offered the hope of bringing clinical services to people who lived in rural areas, resided in prisons, worked in remote locations, or faced mobility or travel barriers that made it difficult for them to visit traditional mental health providers in their clinics and offices. The initial review of the early empirical research in this area surprised me. It suggested that clinical videoconferencing might just be a feasible and effective strategy for delivering much of the continuum of psychiatric services, including evaluation and diagnosis, medication management, and psychotherapy (Frueh et al. 2000).

That review led me and my colleagues at the Medical University of South Carolina and the Veterans' Affairs (VA) Medical Center in Charleston, South Carolina to begin a series of case studies and pilot projects to demonstrate the feasibility of the modality. From there we obtained research funding from the Agency for Healthcare Quality and Management to conduct a small randomized clinical trial with combat veterans suffering from posttraumatic stress disorder (PTSD). I left Charleston in the summer of 2006, leaving behind a single telehealth system and the notion that the concept was sound—that is, that clinical videoconferencing was "non-inferior" to traditional face-to-face care.

To my surprise and pleasure, my successors (Ron Acierno, Hugh Myrick, Peter Tuerk and many more) were far more ambitious and creative than I ever was. They developed the concept and expanded the services dramatically and now the PTSD clinic serves 14 VA facilities (i.e., medical centers and community based outpatient clinics) in three states, and has about sixty active home-based clinical video patients being treated at any given time by 20 clinicians. Moreover, a pilot study demonstrating that clinical video as part of standard care could be used to treat PTSD effectively has led to evidence-based trauma-focused treatment being offered to all patients receiving remote services with weekly clinical outcomes measures collected as part of typical "treatment as usual" and ongoing program evaluation.

Meanwhile, others around the country were also innovating, developing, and expanding. On the west coast, Peter Shore developed widely adopted practice guidelines and a Standard Operating Procedures (SOP) manual for home-based clinical video services. They demonstrated over a 95 % show rate and are now pushing out home home-based care and tablet use on an impressive scale. Out in Hawaii, Leslie Morland implemented several beautifully designed and conducted randomized clinical trials, bringing specialty PTSD treatment to veterans in the neighboring islands around Honolulu. In Arkansas John Fortney's creative vision and efforts led to telemedicine research and services for primary care patients and patients with severe mental illnesses in a largely rural state. Many, many others innovated and contributed as well.

Thus, the success of telehealth in the VA is a story of local clinical interest and local research efforts leading to larger successes—to numerous scholarly publications, federal research grants, federal service provision grants, national recognition, and ultimately to national policy development and a $12 million investment by the VA, almost entirely for dedicated clinical personnel.

Unfortunately, as with so many well-intentioned ideas, things often go awry when centralized planning initiatives take over. That is, when local efforts are superseded by top-down directives unconnected to local realities, and overlaid by competing agendas within a large bureaucratic system. Conflicting mandates and internal fragmentation have us seemingly going backwards in some areas as more and more security restrictions are forced into place and laws are mis- or over-interpreted to err on the side of protecting institutions rather than treating those in need. Even on a regional level, there is often great difficulty getting clinical managers to honor their facility-level service agreements with telehealth providers in their networks. Overall, it is good news that the VA and other large health networks are open to and are investing in clinical videoconferencing technologies; however, most meaningful and clinically effective telehealth programming is the result of the hard work of local champions pushing on clinical, administrative, bureaucratic, and logistical boundaries.

All this is to say that there is a tremendous need for a pragmatic how-to guide regarding methods to develop, implement, assess, and expand mental health services via clinical videoconferencing. This is what this volume represents. It is not a loose affiliation of chapters related to aspects of telehealth, or describing specific but not easily replicable research projects; it is a step by step, comprehensive resource for program development built on the scientific literature and the hard-fought failures and triumphs of those who contributed. I hope readers of this book will never have to discover a telemedicine system parked in a corner of a staff lunch room and

draped in a table cloth, as I did one time in the mid 2000s during a telehealth training visit to a clinic in rural Georgia.

Hilo, Hawaii   B. Christopher Frueh

Reference

Frueh BC, Deitsch SE, Santos AB, Gold PB, Johnson MR, Meisler N, Magruder KM, Ballenger
    JC. Procedural and methodological issues in telepsychiatry research and program develop-
    ment. *Psychiatric Services* 2000; 51:1522–152

Preface

When we were approached by Springer to edit a series of books regarding telehealth, our first thought was that the topic of telehealth was too broad for a series of books to cover. To our way of thinking it would be like writing a series of books on out-patient health services. The technologies and methods employed in what is called "telehealth," and its many pseudonyms, cannot be easily corralled or organized. If telehealth is defined by the transfer of health information electronically, than it is easy to understand why one book or series of books may fall short of that target. Accordingly, we made a suggestion for the series to focus on something more manageable and that we actually knew enough about to organize a helpful contribution—behavioral telehealth.

There are many good books on the market regarding telehealth, in and outside of behavioral realms. Quite often it is possible to learn a lot about many different aspects of telehealth from one expert resource, including telemental health models, asynchronous or store-and-forward technologies, or eHealth products conveyed over the web, etc. Given the many telehealth-related topics to cover in any one book, what is gained in breadth of knowledge is borrowed from depth and detail regarding any one particular area. Yet, implementation of telehealth programming is an endeavor that occurs almost entirely in dealing with, mulling over, guessing about, failing in, and working out highly-specific details. Accordingly, Springer's idea for a series was a good one. Against this backdrop, we noted that a comprehensive "turn-key" guide specific to clinical videoconferencing (CV) program development would be a helpful contribution for the first volume in the series.

Being familiar with the literature, we also noted that specific technical information regarding management issues was often mixed together with clinically-relevant information, obscuring the discernment or quick reference of either. In the past this mixing made sense as many of the early adaptors were also clinical champions. However, as telehealth programming continues to become more widely adopted in normative healthcare ecologies, the divide between the informational needs of the clinical and managerial realms is becoming apparent. Accordingly, this volume is divided into two broad sections; one geared for clinic managers and administrators, and one for clinicians. To avoid repetition of material, most chapters build on or reference others when appropriate, though each chapter can stand on its own for picking and choosing. All the chapters are structurally similar, with a focus on evidence-based and experiential pragmatic tools, (e.g., pros and cons of specific technology configurations, resources to plan for bandwidth, relevant CPT codes for billing in specific situations, boilerplate language to create local policy, templates for inter-facility agreements, informed consent templates, tools for knowing and navigating federal and state regulations, clinical protocol checklists for patient safety, checklists to overcome barriers to communication in the medium, etc.). Additionally, we tried to pay particular attention to thorough indexing to facilitate efficient referencing.

A few technical notes for clarification may be helpful, starting with the often obligatory telehealth discussion regarding nomenclature. While "telehealth" is a broad term, in many situations the meaning is rendered clear by the context of use and so there is little need to impose strict rules of vocabulary, especially when referring to the most common usage; i.e., interactions with a provider via a live video-feed. Having said that, we prefer the term clinical videoconferencing (CV) or "clinical video" for short, because it is more specific than others terms, such as "telemental health" (TMH), but not so specific as to be descriptively redundant, as perhaps "clinical video-teleconferencing" (CVT) now sounds to many. Regardless, in this volume the reader can assume that broader terms, such as "telehealth" or "telemedicine," were chosen purposely to refer to general practices, while clinical video is reserved for the more specific meaning.

We have been fortunate enough to have worked with experienced and extremely knowledgeable chapter authors on this project. In an effort to avoid unnecessary repetition of information among the chapters but also to capitalize on the authors' strengths and insights, they have agreed to a certain amount of lending and reorganizing of ideas among the submitted chapters, which we were grateful for. It is in that spirit of collaboration and cooperation that we all offer this volume.

Charleston, South Carolina   Peter W. Tuerk
Portland, Oregon   Peter Shore

Acknowledgements

(Peter W. Tuerk): I would like to acknowledge Ron Acierno and Hugh (Donald) Myrick for their mentorship, partnership, and unwavering dedication to improving mental health services for those in dire need. More generally, I would like to acknowledge my father, William F. Tuerk, for modeling a life dedicated to public service, veterans, and the greater good. I would also like to thank Keith Cox, Bethany Wangelin, Bridgette Niepoth, and Martina Radic for assistance with content and copy editing; each member of our telehealth clinic team, but especially Anna Birks, Carol Denier, and Justine (Tina) Irwin for keeping it going; and of course, Peter Shore, my friend and co-conspirator in this effort. We both would like to thank Sharon Panulla and Sylvana Ruggirello at Springer for their past and future guidance in helping us navigate this book series through to completion.

Dedication (Peter W. Tuerk): For Elena, Vivian, and Emma who make my world too, too sweet and just perfect.

(Peter Shore): I would first like to acknowledge David Greaves and Mark Ward for providing important early career navigation. I'd also like to thank Ken Weingardt for modeling an unwavering dedication to veterans despite the challenges of working within a complex healthcare system. To Jay Shore for providing ongoing mentorship; and finally a heartfelt thanks to Peter Tuerk for creating the opportunity to collaborate with some of the finest minds in telemedicine on this project.

Dedication (Peter Shore): For Vida, Lola and Caleb whose interlocking circle of encouragement, love, and humility has fueled me to achieve a rewarding life, and to my mother Mitzi, who worked tirelessly so I may pursue a higher education in service to others.

Contents

**Part II   For Clinicians: Clinical Standards and Protocols
              to Support Effective and Safe Intervention**

List of Tables and Appendices

Contributors

Ron Acierno College of Nursing, Medical University of South Carolina; Ralph H. Johnson VA Medical Center, Department of Veterans Affairs, Charleston, SC, USA

Sara Smucker Barnwell Department of Psychiatry and Behavioral Sciences, University of Washington, Seattle, WA, USA

Anna Hynes Birks Ralph H. Johnson VA Medical Center, Charleston, SC, USA

Thao N. Bui The Anxiety Center at EBTCS, Seattle, WA, USA

Ebony Butler Mental Health Service, VA San Diego Health Care System, La Jolla, California, USA

Nancy Cha Department of Veterans Affairs Pacific Islands Healthcare System, National Center for PTSD—Pacific Islands Division, Honolulu, HI, USA

Noah DeGaetano VA Palo Alto Healthcare System, Palo Alto, CA, USA; Stanford School of Medicine, Stanford, CA, USA

Lisa H. Glassman Center of Excellence for Stress and Mental Health, VA San Diego Health Care System, La Jolla, California, USA; University of California, San Diego, California, USA

Donald M. Hilty Department of Psychiatry, Keck School of Medicine at USC, Los Angeles, CA, USA

Michael A. Jenkins-Guarnieri National Center for Telehealth & Technology; Department of Psychiatry and Behavioral Sciences, University of Washington School of Medicine, Seattle, USA

Barb Johnston HealthLinkNow, Sacramento, CA, USA

Karen Kloezeman Department of Veterans Affairs Pacific Islands Healthcare System, National Center for PTSD—Pacific Islands Division, Honolulu, HI, USA

Elizabeth A. Krupinski Arizona Telemedicine Program & Southwest Telehealth Resource Center, University of Arizona, Tucson, AZ, USA

Brian E. Lozano Department of Psychiatry and Behavioral Sciences, Medical University of South Carolina; Ralph H. Johnson VA Medical Center, Department of Veterans Affairs, Charleston, SC, USA

Mary Lu Department of Psychiatry, Oregon Health & Science University; Mental Health & Neurosciences, Portland VA Medical Center, Portland, OR 97239, USA

David D. Luxton National Center for Telehealth & Technology; Department of Psychiatry and Behavioral Sciences, University of Washington School of Medicine, Seattle, USA

Lucy Moreno Mental Health Service, VA San Diego Health Care System, La Jolla, California, USA

Leslie A. Morland Department of Veterans Affairs Pacific Islands Healthcare System, National Center for PTSD—Pacific Islands Division, Honolulu, HI, USA

Sarah E. H. Nasatir-Hilty Department of Psychiatry, Keck School of Medicine at USC, Los Angeles, CA, USA

Michele T. Pato Department of Psychiatry, Keck School of Medicine at USC, Los Angeles, CA, USA

Larry D. Pruitt National Center for Telehealth & Technology; Joint Base Lewis-McChord, WA, USA.

Steven R. Thorp Center of Excellence for Stress and Mental Health, Mental Health Service, VA San Diego Health Care System; University of California, San Diego/San Diego State University Joint Doctoral Program in Clinical Psychology, San Diego, California, USA

Joseph L. Ronzio Department of Veterans Affairs, Veterans Health Administration, Washington, DC, USA

Erica Z. Shoemaker Department of Psychiatry, Keck School of Medicine at USC, Los Angeles, CA, USA

Jay Shore University of Colorado Anschutz Medical Campus, Centers for American Indian and Alaska Native Health, Aurora, CO, USA

Peter Shore Department of Psychiatry, Oregon Health & Science University; VA Northwest Health Network (VISN 20), Department of Veterans Affairs, Portland, OR, USA

Peter W. Tuerk Department of Psychiatry and Behavioral Sciences, Medical University of South Carolina; Ralph H. Johnson VA Medical Center, Department of Veterans Affairs, Charleston, SC, USA

Kristen H. Walter Mental Health Service, VA San Diego Health Care System, La Jolla, California, USA

Stephanie Y. Wells University of California, San Diego/San Diego State University Joint Doctoral Program in Clinical Psychology, San Diego, California, USA

Joah L. Williams Medical University of South Carolina, Charleston, SC, USA

Kathryn Williams Mental Health Service, VA San Diego Health Care System, La Jolla, California, USA

Peter M. Yellowlees UC Davis Department of Psychiatry, Health Informatics Fellowship Program UC Davis, Sacramento, CA, USA

Part I
For Clinic Managers and Administrators:
A Sequential Guide to Establishing
Sustainable Programming

Chapter 1
Technologies and Clinical Videoconferencing Infrastructures: A Guide to Selecting Appropriate Systems

Peter W. Tuerk, Joseph L. Ronzio and Peter Shore

Chapter Summary

Purpose   This chapter provides basic and intermediate-level key concepts related to clinical videoconferencing (CV) technologies for the purposes of assisting clinical administrators in choosing a CV system. It defines the common types of CV systems and considers the strengths and limitations of hardware-based vs. software-based platforms, as well as web-based vs. cellular-based signal transmission. The chapter also highlights the importance of defining the specific needs of a clinical ecology on a hierarchy to help achieve a balance between optimizing clinical utility and available budget when choosing CV systems.

Context   The information is helpful to clinical managers or administrators who are in charge of choosing/purchasing a CV solution for their facility or practice. The field of telehealth, and the availability of accompanying commercial technology options, is expanding rapidly with no end in sight. Both the development of new technologies and the daily identification of novel clinical demands for technologies are fueling continued growth in the field. Accordingly, administrators new to CV purchasing and decision making need a concise starting place to get a handle

P. W. Tuerk (✉)
Department of Psychiatry and Behavioral Sciences, Medical University of South Carolina; Mental Health Service, Ralph H. Johnson VA Medical Center, Veterans Health Administration , Charleston, SC, USA
e-mail: Tuerk@musc.edu

J. L. Ronzio
Department of Veterans Affairs, Veterans Health Administration, Washington, DC, USA
e-mail: joe@ronzio.org

P. Shore
Department of Psychiatry, Oregon Health & Science University; VA Northwest Health Network (VISN 20), Department of Veterans Affairs, Portland, OR, USA
e-mail: shore@ohsu.edu

© Springer International Publishing Switzerland 2015
P. W. Tuerk, P. Shore (eds.), *Clinical Videoconferencing in Telehealth,*
Behavioral Telehealth, DOI 10.1007/978-3-319-08765-8_1

on relevant issues. The chapter is also helpful to clinicians, as they are ultimately the driving force in the identification of new ways to use technology in the service of public health needs.

Tools   The chapter provides the following tools: a summary overview of CV system options, including hardware-based, software-based and mixed strategies; a checklist of issues to research when choosing CV systems, a beginners guide to network capacity issues relevant to purchasing CV systems; three vignettes outlining helpful issues related to choosing specific telehealth hardware; a guide for selecting CV software, including the requirements of existing hardware; information on mobile tablets in the CV environment; a detailed discussion regarding health insurance portability and accountability (HIPPA) and FIPS 140-2 encoding; considerations regarding the integration of supporting technologies for CV systems; and a checklist of questions to address basic system needs before consulting with vendors.

1.1   Introduction

Clinical videoconferencing (CV) technology allows for real-time, interactive communication between patient and provider through a television, computer monitor, or tablet screen. Traditionally, CV is clinic based, with therapists located at a larger medical facility and patients located at more remote satellite clinics. However, community-based CV, where patients are treated in potentially unsupervised settings, such as community resource centers and home-based CV, are becoming common practices.

The technology options for any CV service can only be selected after the clinical need is identified. This tenant follows standard project management philosophy because one needs to know the goal before allocating time, money, and resources for implementation. Distinguishing needs from wants, and taking the time to formally operationalize your exact needs are crucial. Rushing ahead with a technology solution before understanding the need, scale of the need, and the clinical, personnel, and institutional capacity to address the need has led to purchases of hundreds (perhaps thousands) of fancy telehealth machines gathering dust, unplugged in the corner of break rooms and closets. As you talk to your local clinicians and stakeholders about, "what would be great," and to potential vendors about all the technology that is out there, you might find your thinking changing (especially if you are excited about the future and solving problems). But we must be careful not to "put the cart before the horse." Every healthcare environment has many unmet needs and limited resources; available technology should not prioritize those needs.

Chapters 1 and 6 contain much information about methods to identify specific clinical needs. This chapter will provide information and resources regarding different technologies which can be used to address those needs. Moreover, this chapter presents a guiding framework for collecting detailed information that matches your needs to the complex technologies available. Ultimately, this chapter aims to aid in the decision-making process surrounding the selection of CV systems.

1.2 Clinical Videoconferencing Technology Options

There are multiple standard and proprietary technologies involved in video tele-communications, and the application of these technologies to clinical settings has increased the ability of the industry to market and sell all manners of related hardware, software, and support services. In 2011, telehealth device and software markets (not including related service packages) registered $ 736 million in sales and are projected to reach $ 2.5 billion by 2018 [8, 18]. In the USA, there are over 400 businesses selling telehealth devices and services [9].

The clinical video technology packages being sold today use a wide variety of provider- and patient-end interfaces with different methods of signal transmission and reception. However, they all have common aspects or patterns that can be boiled down to just a few major decision points that are related. First, a medical provider or practice can opt to purchase specialized hardware, software, or use a mix of hardware and software for CV. Second, systems can be purchased to work with traditional computers or with mobile computing platforms (i.e., Android and Apple phones/tablets). Third, you can decide to operate your CV system with ethernet and wireless networks (for transmission over the internet or available intranet), or with cellular networks (e.g., Verizon, AT&T, Sprint, etc.) if there is adequate bandwidth, or both. Table 1.1 provides a summary list of the common CV system options. A resource directory to search for or investigate vendors of CV equipment and services can be found at: http://atatelemedicinedirectory.com/ [1].

1.2.1 Hardware-Based Clinical Videoconferencing Systems: Overview

Prepackaged hardware-based CV units are meant for use by clinicians and patients when one or both parties are located in an institutional clinic-based setting. Once initially configured, prepackaged CV systems are easy to operate and provide high-quality video and audio output. Some units might only require a staff member to turn them on at the start of the day, rather than requiring user configurations for each individual session. A strict hardware-based solution can involve provider and patient videophones (an all-in-one device that looks like a phone but typically with a small screen and a handset), or more commonly, video endpoints (an all-in-one device typically with a large screen used without a handset). Both of these options are represented by point 1 in Table 1.1. The video camera on hardware systems often can be manually pointed for an upper torso view or it may have a Pan-Tilt-Zoom camera, which is useful to optimize communication. A benefit of hardware-based systems is that most come with fairly self-evident functionality and remote

Table 1.1 A summary overview of the common clinical videoconferencing system options

1. Prepackaged hardware installed at both patient- and provider-end locations, devoted only to clinical videoconferencing, often a "turn-key" solution. These systems can be "proprietary," meaning they only communicate with other same-brand hardware systems, or "standards based," meaning they adhere to standard protocols for conveying information and can communicate with a wide variety of other hardware- and software-based systems
2. Software-based clinical videoconferencing, using existing personal computers and webcams over the internet
3. Mobile device-based clinical videoconferencing using either the internet or cellular signal, facilitated by mobile applications
4. Any combination of specific hardware systems, personal computers, and/or mobile device solutions for providers and patients in different contexts

controls for easy operation. Even the more complex-looking remote controls are easy to operate once providers familiarize themselves with the buttons and options. If providers can switch between the DVD and cable inputs on their home-TV remote control, they have more than the necessary aptitude to master these kinds of CV remote controls.

Some hardware-based systems are proprietary, meaning only like brand items can communicate with like brand items. Others utilize video telecommunications standards and can communicate with any hardware that uses the same standards for encoding and decoding an audio/video stream. Many companies that offer hardware solutions also offer accompanying software solutions. This type of integrated system could be considered "turn key." In other words, you pay the company and they take care of installing easy to use and operable video endpoints, requiring some, but little training for providers. Working with such a company can help to maximize solutions across contexts of care or patient characteristics. For example, it may be ideal to have just *one* hardware interface that providers can learn and use with patients receiving services at satellite clinics, and with patients receiving home-based care over the web with software on their own computers.

Hardware-based CV systems have a number of limitations as well. They are typically the most expensive option for CV programming which can be a significant barrier. Additionally, designing CV programming that is tied to discrete physical hardware units can limit utilization and complicate programming logistics (which is always the most difficult aspect of CV programming). For example, in many programs, it is often the case that a patient presents for care at a satellite clinic, the satellite clinic has an available room with CV hardware, and there is also a provider available at the main hospital who just had a cancelation, but there are no rooms currently available at the main hospital with CV hardware. To add tragedy (or comedy) to the situation, there are available rooms but they do not have CV hardware; moreover, some of the occupied rooms at the main hospital with CV hardware are being used (up) by clinicians conducting in-person services. If every treatment room and standard computer had the same CV software package installed, and a $ 20 webcam, this situation would be not be a problem, and increasing productivity, covering for sick clinicians, or addressing the needs of unscheduled walk-in patients via CV would be easier. Another limitation of hardware systems is that troubleshooting technical or network difficulties often requires specialized product-specific expertise and technicians to be immediately on hand or readily available.

1.2.2 Software-Based Clinical Videoconferencing Systems: Overview

Software-based systems utilize software and existing computers with built-in web-cams and microphones or plug-in USB webcams and microphones. Even if built-in webcams are available, many opt to upgrade to a plug-in camera that is capable of Pan-Tilt-Zoom movement. Software-based systems are useful in a variety of situations involving space or cost limitations, as they are the least expensive option, can produce a high quality CV experience with appropriate bandwidth, and can utilize appropriate encoding for Protected health information (PHI). Software-based systems are often *slightly more streamlined* for allowing patients to receive services on their home computers or on tablets (though "standards-based" hardware systems at the provider-end also have that functionality). Because software CV systems are operated from a provider's computer, it is often relatively easy to share relevant views (i.e., lab results, notes, and diagrams) over the video connection (this option is also available through most hardware systems with some additional configuration, as will be discussed in Sect. 4.6). Additionally, given basic technical abilities and perhaps administration privileges over the computers being used, many troubleshooting techniques can be taught to clinicians to reduce the frequency of calling in specialized technicians to address problems during or directly before CV sessions.

There are limitations to software-based CV systems that are worth noting. Although it may be easier to address problems as they arise, software-based systems tend to be more complex to learn and operate, in general, compared to turn-key hardware systems (where an on button and self-explanatory remote control is all that is necessary). In some cases, separate settings may need to be configured for every person who logs on. Software-based systems also require computers to meet certain requirements (i.e., memory), and for computers to be running a specific operating system. There are known CV software systems where "backwards compatibility" is an issue. As new versions of the software come to market, there is expectation that the consumers will upgrade their operating system to accommodate the new version. In some cases where the operating system is not upgraded, technical issues can have a cascade effect of "unexplained" issues; e.g., random pixilation, audio freeze, etc. When operating these systems within the context of healthcare institutions, forced system upgrades and security issues can affect how the computer software works. In institutional settings, providers typically do not have administrative privileges over their computers, so involving facility IT administrators and technicians is necessary. Getting the buy-in from your facility information security officer (ISO) will be necessary and may require some gentle education and advocacy. It would be important to identify what security requirements your facility, agency, or clinic requires. One hardware-related problem common with software-based systems is that many built-in or plug-in webcams often do not have the ability to pan or sufficiently zoom, which can limit utility. Section 4.5.1 will address the specific benefits of purchasing a sufficient camera for software-based CV systems.

Some companies exclusively deal in software only solutions. Software solutions can also be proprietary or standards based, similar to hardware solutions. It is important to note that some companies' software must be *installed* while other solutions can work through any available web browser, as long as the computer has the proper video encoder and decoder installed (see following paragraph regarding encoding). The distinction between installed software vs. web-based protocols can be important in many CV contexts and in different institutional IT ecologies. It is also important to note that any software solution that works for your institution will also have to work for your patients. This is an especially relevant consideration for home-based care where the patient will need to be able to install and maintain CV software, as well as participate in troubleshooting when technology disruptions occur during an appointment.

The encoders and decoders that are required for CV software to work on home computers are pieces of software that compress a video signal for easier transmission and then uncompress it once it arrives. They are typically the same that are installed for an individual to play DVDs and other media on their computer. Note that encoding can be easily confused with encryption; they sound the same and both processes take a data stream, change it, and then change it back. However, the primary purpose of encryption is to make it harder, hopefully impossible, to openly share data with third parties, whereas the primary purpose of encoding is to facilitate quick and easy sharing of information among many users interfacing with different types of hardware. You may also hear people making reference to a "CODEC," this is just a jargon term for "coder/decoder," but often CODEC is used to refer to a piece of hardware (little box) that does the same thing as the software version installed on home computers.

1.3   Network Capacity for Clinical Video Conferencing

Before beginning your search for appropriate CV hardware or software, it is a good idea to consider bandwidth capacity. You may be in a position where the proposed CV solutions have to match available bandwidth, or you may be able to design your desired CV solution and obtain the necessary bandwidth to match your decision. The bottom line is that the network needs to be capable of supporting the desired audio and video quality. Utilization of audio and video compression changes quite frequently. Table 1.2 provides guidelines for bandwidth by call quality per connection. In order to visually understand the consequences to CV quality of the information presented in Table 1.2, please refer to online resources that display video qualities related to various frames per second (for example: https://www.youtube.com/watch?v=XRaDV8YADiQ, or: http://frames-per-second.appspot.com/). To use these tools, you also need to know your current bandwidth. There are also many

Table 1.2 Required bandwidth for audiovisual quality per connection

Video resolution	Frames per second	Bandwidth
320 × 240	3–6	12–128 kbps
640 × 480	6–12	26–256 kbps
640 × 480	30	256–512 kbps
720p	6–12	256 kbps–1 Mbps
720p	30	384 kbps–3 Mbps
1080i	30	764 kbps–2 Mbps
1080p	30	768 kbps–4 Mbps

instant tools available for you to discover your current bandwidth, just simply type "bandwidth test" in any available web search engine for instant testing of available internet speeds at your workstation. A good example of these tests is provided by OOKLA (http://www.speedtest.net/). Likewise, in order to test cellular speeds, you can quickly download Speedtest mobile application for Andriod and iOS markets. Of course, work with your network administrator, but also test what he or she says at different time of the day at your workstation and share your findings.

The above table is just a guideline, you should check with the hardware or software vendor for the direct capabilities and compatibilities of the systems you are evaluating. Planning for desired call quality is complicated by the fact that you need to multiply the bandwidth needed by the number of endpoints/videophones and computers that will be connected. (That is why, it is a good idea to use tools to check out individual workstations, in addition to using the global information provided by your network administrator). If there is one patient and one provider, you will need the appropriate bandwidth multiplied by 2 (for information being sent and received). Cisco provides an online resource similar to Table 1.2 but also considers the number of connections needed [5]. Keep in mind that the optimum capability of the selected system may be reduced based on the capabilities of the oldest or least capable system participating in the call. So, if someone has an older system or software version that has less capability and requires more bandwidth, your system will automatically negotiate to maintain a call, if possible, and will adjust the audio and video connection speeds and quality to compensate. Basically, one weak link can cause everyone on the call to use more bandwidth, and possibly have scratchy audio or grainy video. You may not be able to control, or even know or plan for, the bandwidth available for patients at home or in other facilities, but at the very least, the provider system should be able to handle proposed volume.

Networks are not as simple as many Internet service providers advertise to consumers. Service provider packages for high bandwidth offerings are currently available for cable modem and cellular data services. These services are typically advertised for an optimum or ideal situation. What is not advertised is that most of these services are using locally shared resources. This means that a neighborhood, cellular tower, or street has a total capability and everyone who has contracted for the service gets a share of the usage. However similar to sharing a cake, if someone takes a gargantuan piece, or if too many people take a piece (at the same time), everyone might only get a small slice. Running tests is important, especially for busy clinics. In some cases, there is a limitation to the number of concurrent CV sessions that can operate due to the network capacity. In the worst case, data at times can get lost or dropped until a device retransmits the information. This affects home users as well as businesses that have telecommunication contracts that specify dedicated or burstable bandwidth capacity. It is critical that systems are monitored to ensure you get what you are paying for. There have been experiences where telecommunication companies have not provided contracted services that were detected by system monitors. Accordingly, make your providers aware of speed test tools, and, in turn, they can make patients aware of them, in case advocacy is needed. It is also important to note that if the patients are on their tablet for a CV session, the signal might be compromised if their mobile phone and laptop computer are also drawing on the bandwidth resources.

1.4 Clinical Videoconferencing Hardware: Specific Examples

This section considers a few specific examples to flush out potentially relevant and helpful details. Let us consider a specific case where a hospital administrator conducted a moderately adequate needs assessment. The results of the assessment suggested that the most prescient areas to address with new CV programming would be in providing support services from the main hospital to a small satellite clinic in a moderately rural area with a rapidly growing population base. Psychiatric medication consults, specialized PTSD treatment, and behavioral pain management were the three services that made the cut as having a broad need and adequate buy-in from the clinical managers and staff. You are tasked with selecting the CV systems. You are given a budget range for initial purchasing and installation, which could be increased if initial programming is successful (special funds were earmarked and designated for this 2-year pilot expansion). You guess that the majority of the cost will be associated with ongoing fees, and were told to keep that in mind, but to primarily focus on finding the right technology for the job with the pilot funding (ongoing fees, if programming was successful and permanent would be coming out of the general operating budget and weighed against revenue). You also were encouraged to pilot different solutions before committing to testing a longer term technology strategy.

You first consider going for quality. Conducting CV with proprietary or standards-based hardware between clinical facilities can give the best CV call quality, but this comes at the highest price. The reason is that the provider/clinic/hospital needs to purchase all of the hardware, software, licenses, and network bandwidth to implement a service that delivers a top quality video presence. The highest quality videoconferencing systems aim for an "immersive experience," like the Polycom Immersive Studio [15] or Cisco equivalent [4]. It includes hardware, software, room furnishings, three 84-inch screens (making an 18-ft "media wall"), and requires a minimum bandwidth expectation of 10 MBps or higher, with dedicated network connections to minimize delay. These systems are designed to give participants an immersive experience with life size, whole body or near-whole body viewing (sample videos are available on YouTube). This may be the ideal "experience" for video teleconferencing, but it costs more than most operating budgets can afford, and allows for only extremely limited use, since each instance requires dedicated rooms and bandwidth that can only be used for communication with known locations at specified times. Also, it is unclear what added health benefits can be expected from an immersive CV experience as compared to an experience that is good enough. In this example, you suggest purchasing the Polycom Immersive Studio, believing that it will create patient demand and "really put the clinic on the map." You are demoted immediately.

On the other end of the spectrum is the Tandberg Centric 1000 MXP; it is affordable (< $ 300, to purchase and install, not including ongoing service fees), fairly mobile, provides adequate picture quality, and does not put undue strain on bandwidth (max 768 kbps; i.e., even when maxed out, only 8 % of the bandwidth is needed by the immersive studio). However the monitor is only 12 in. Certainly, the monitor and audio functioning are adequate to convey health related information, and even to conduct effective psychotherapy with willing patients. However, depending on the CV context, the "experience" for patients might be a little too suboptimal, and you are worried that referral streams for the proposed CV programming might dry up due to low user satisfaction. Even so, in this example, you purchase a few of them as a test to see how far they can go in meeting your identified CV needs.

You put the lead psychologist at the satellite clinic in charge of testing them. He reports that the portability of the products is extremely helpful because staff can move them to whatever empty room is available with active internet ports. Further he reports that he has been telling patients about the new telehealth capabilities and has been able to recruit enough patients to confirm that the units can effectively support medication consults to the main hospital. However, he notes that it can be difficult to arrange comfortable seating for patients on the fly because the viewing area is small and requires fairly precise seating. Since proper desks/chairs have not been placed in the exam rooms, some patients have to hunch over, which is uncomfortable for longer consults. Additionally, some of the patient's grumble that, "THIS is your version of telehealth?! I heard so many good things about telehealth on the news." But the psychologist found if he introduced the consult as a phone call, as in "Let's call the psychiatrist and see what she says," then patients were pleasantly surprised and reported liking the exchange. He doubts that these small monitors would be very comfortable for conducting longer psychotherapy visits though, which was an identified need to treat PTSD. The psychologist also "heard" that, in addition to connecting to the similar machine at the main hospital, that these devices could also work with videoconferencing software, called Jabber, to connect patient's to his clinic using their smart phones. He thinks it might be a great way to "check in" with his chronic pain patients without them having to leave the house. Chronic pain was identified as a target need area on your program assessment and charter. You are excited and feeling like an innovation aficionado. The next day you call the vendor representative to get help with figuring out how to use Jabber to connect to mobile devices. He informs you that the 1000 MXP's are phased out and are no longer supported. Even if you could get the older version of Jabber (called MOVI) to work, it will likely not work for patients with the newer operating systems on their mobile devices (iOS 7 for Apple and KitKat for Android). He teases you for purchasing a product that was obsolete before it even shipped and promises that, "As your new sales rep., I would never let you do that."

Somewhere in between the 12-in video-phone screen and the 18-ft screen is the Cisco EX-90. It has a 24-in screen, is a "standards-based" hardware system (i.e., compatible with the market), and like the video phone, it is able to adapt to low and high bandwidth situations. It also has a built in "document camera," and USB inputs for Bluetooth. The initial cost of the unit and installation is about $ 5000. You are fairly certain that this system can meet all the core needs identified, and now that your clinical staff had a successful test run with the video phone, they are eager to get going. You are not sure if the price can be supported at-scale, and considered the 21-in EX60, but the initial price difference was not impressive and ongoing cost of running the two systems was negligible.

The clinical staff and patients are impressed with the picture and functioning, many noted that a slightly smaller screen would also have been adequate, though, some preferred the wider view for group/family consults. Given the investment, you also made sure that the patient-end rooms were equipped with adequate furniture. The consulting psychiatrists used the equipment for 20–40 min patient consultations scheduled every 2–6 months, and the PTSD psychologists used it for 90-min psychotherapy on a weekly basis. Both groups reported high levels of satisfaction and rare instances of technical difficulty. The psychologists specifically commented on the efficiency of the built-in document camera for the frequent exchange of assessment materials with the patient, and the administrative support staff also appreciated that function because it saved them from having to relay multiple faxes, such as patient self-report questionnaires, on a weekly basis. The pain psychologist, who held clinic at both sites, was able to establish a protocol for conducting and relaying biofeedback relaxation training information in real-time between the sites using the system's USB bluetooth functionality. Although he had to employ the help of an onsite staff member to fit the sensors on the patients, the biofeedback CV sessions helped with improving access to that specialty service. The biggest problem was that the CV machines were in high demand and scheduling the various services on them is logistically complex and labor intensive. Dealing with those logistics is now your problem because your good work was rewarded with a promotion to clinic director.

1.5   Considering Software-Based Clinical Videoconferencing Solution

Section 1.2.2 discussed an overview of software-based CV solutions, the following section explores specific issues related to feasibility and functioning. Most health professionals have access to computers at their workstations and most US households (80%) have access to a home computer [17], while 60% of Americans have a smartphone, and 40% have a tablet [14]. Accordingly, the strategy of improving access to care by having patients load software onto the devices they already own is a logical and attractive one, but it may not be the best fit for your CV programming needs. Or it may be a good fit for the needs, but a bad fit for the institutional ecology or capacity.

1.5.1 Hardware Necessities for Software Solutions

The ability to choose a software-based CV solution is at least partly dependent upon hardware-based factors. More specifically, the capacity to functionalize an existing computer as a CV station involves addressing at least three hardware-related questions: (1) Is there enough computing power in the hardware to encode and decode the CV session? (2) Can a second monitor be connected to the existing computer if needed for clinical context? (3) What webcam should be chosen and used? As technology has evolved, desktops, laptops, and mobile devices have developed adequate capability to serve as video telecommunication endpoints. Most of these devices have built-in processors of adequate capability to conduct video teleconferences. Accordingly, for most modern computers, it is easy and inexpensive to add video teleconferencing as an option. However, many home computers do not have a modem, or are not running the most up to date operating systems, or simply do not exist (i.e., 20% of households do not have a computer), especially in highly rural or economically stressed areas (i.e., areas likely to be targeted for CV programming). Accordingly, care must be taken to ensure that a software-based solution will not exclude a significant portion of your target patients, or that alternative plans are made for those patients, or that the lack of services is at least known and accepted. Not being able to provide services to everyone, does not necessarily mean that you should not provide services to some, and there are creative, affordable stop-gap solutions to cover patients who might fall through the cracks. For example, we maintain a modest supply of tablets with active cellular contracts, to mail off to patients who are in need of home-based CV services for PTSD, but who do not have a computer, internet service, or their own smart device. We also mail them a preposted box, so they can send the tablet back after completing a course of evidence-based treatment. The total cost of this "stop gap" program is under $ 2000/year.

For some healthcare sites, the challenges related to existing hardware capacities are not limited to the patient end. Large healthcare settings often have heavily networked computers, shared drives, central control, and many programs running in the background, all of which can slow down processing speeds. The ability to add additional monitors is also not always a given. Even so, the current technological capability of plug-in webcams has evolved over the past 2 years and most can provide a 1080P HD quality image for a high quality video teleconference session quite easily. Higher end webcams can accomplish the video capture and video compression functions internally, leaving the computer available for other processing tasks.

Table 1.3 Issues to consider or research when choosing clinical videoconferencing (CV) software

1. Ease of use for clinicians and patients
a. Installation
b. Steps required to log on
c. User interface
d. Stability/dropped calls
e. Difficulty connecting
2. Availability
a. Microsoft Windows
b. Mac
c. iOS
d. Android
3. Security/encryption
a. FIPS 140-2 certified
b. Point-to-Point Encryption (P2PE)
c. HIPAA
4. Cost/license structure
a. One-time
b. Ongoing fee
c. Can provider pay for unlimited connections
d. Charge per minute of use
e. Is vendor approved for your facility
5. Functions and interoperability
a. How will software interact with computer (share interactive desktop?)
b. Can screen captures be used and shared? (better control of what patient sees)
c. Can encounter be tracked and logged?
d. Show presence of provider on-line or restrict visibility
e. Is there a virtual waiting room or other health care-related functions?

A basic webcam costs approximately $ 20–50, while a high-quality HD webcam costs between $ 90 and 400 from Microsoft Corporation [11], Cisco [3], or Logitech [10] (see references for links to photographs). The prices here are for one-person to one-person webcam options. Nefsis also provides an online resource to choose cameras based on your specific bandwidth [13].

1.5.2 Selecting Software for Clinical Videoconferencing

After determining that provider-end and patient-end computers are adequately positioned for CV software, a software package can be chosen. There are many options for video teleconferencing software packages that are appropriate for CV, several options and their benefits or drawbacks are documented at http://www.zurinstitute. com/telehealthresources.html. Note that you are not limited to choosing only one; it may be helpful to chose 2 or 3 and test them out for your specific needs. Table 1.3 identifies some basic Issues to consider when choosing CV software packages. Remember that patients will also have to install and operate the software.

1.5.2 Tablets

Given the variability in home computers and steps to install/operate software at the patient end, simple is usually better. This tenant makes utilization of tablets with mobile applications for CV an attractive option. Mobile applications are easy to download, there are no system settings on the hardware that need to be modified, and the functional operation of software in the mobile application environment is often streamlined, as compared with software designed for desk or laptops. Additionally, mobile devices are mobile. Typically in CV services, we think about using hardware-based solutions for care between facilities, and mobile solutions are reserved for home-based care. However, the fact that tablets are mobile makes them well suited for medical center environments, to maximize room use and time, for facility-to-facility care, or for facility-within-facility care. They can be attached to medical carts, placed in exam rooms where patients are waiting, or used by patients in cancer wards to interface with the myriad of necessary providers more efficiently with fewer interruptions. Most importantly, 40 % of individuals in the USA already own a tablet [14], which has large implications for health care access, equipment-based cost avoidance in CV programming, and space-related limitations of health-care. There are several drawbacks of mobile solutions for CV such as small screens, patient use in less secure environments, and limited interoperability with computer-based functions and information. However, the role of tablets for CV is on the cusp of burgeoning (indeed by the time this book is published, it may already have done so), which may lead to better, more targeted products and solutions. Accordingly, it is worthwhile to consider how a mobile-based CV approach might help you meet some of your defined goals.

1.5.3 HIPAA and FIPS 140-2

When selecting software, it is important to keep in state or federal regulations and also who is paying for the service, since there could be relevant considerations or contractual issues which need to be considered. For example, if you are working with the federal government, agencies will most likely require that software encryption meet NIST FIPS 140-2 requirements and certification [12]. This federal requirement for federal healthcare networks is often confused as a de facto HIPAA regulation. But in actuality, the HIPAA standard for data security is a bit more vague.

The HIPAA Security Rule basically says that health care providers are responsible for the technological security of transmitted data (see Chap. 7, Sect. 7.5.4 for more information regarding the HIPAA security rule). Taken to its logical conclusion, many people interpret this to mean that the CV signal must be encrypted, or encrypted up to a certain specified level of security. But HIPAA defines encryption in nontechnical terms. Accordingly, if you have chosen an industry standard CV software package, then the chances are good that the software has adequate levels of encryption to meet HIPAA's nontechnical definition of encryption. The software may even be on par with FIPS 140-2 standards (at least technologically). However, companies can have software products on par with FIPS 140-2 level encryption, but have not gone through the process of becoming NIST FIPS 140-2 certified, including creating avenues for government access for confirmatory validation of the cryptographic standards, and reporting where/how they store the ability to decrypt transmissions.

The ability of software companies to decrypt transmissions (if they wanted to) and to provide the government with information about where they store decryption keys is a significant aspect of this national conversation and also has ramifications for HIPAA compliance. Even if you have chosen a software company with high technological standards for encryption, you still need a HIPAA-required Business Associate Agreement (BAA) with the company for CV services to be HIPAA compliant. However, there is an exception to this requirement if the software company is providing the service strictly as a conduit of information. This exception, referred to as the "conduit rule," can be applied to video telecommunications. This means so long as the signal is encrypted, and cannot be unencrypted by the software company, and not recorded or stored at any location, it should be fine to use [16].

Software/mobile application vendors are invested in efforts to be or appear HIPAA friendly, but many do not enter into BAAs or even make it easy to find information about that possibility. Companies may report not being able to unencrypt their own transmissions, but might leave out information regarding the storage of (for example) instant text messages sent during a videoconferencing session. Competitors of Skype have been quick to point this out in the past. Apple has recently put out a white paper on iOS security [2] indicating that that they cannot decrypt Facetime transmissions. Likewise, Citrix, in support of its GoToMeeting videoconferencing platform, has recently published a GoToMeeting HIPAA Compliance Guide [7]. Like many similar information products, the guide lists HIPAA rules and provides bullet points about related functions in the software, it is suggestive that the product can be used for HIPAA compliant services, but it does not put too fine a point on it. What this means for Facetime's or GoToMeeting's current or future status as widely accepted viable options for CV depends on who you ask. There seems to be a bit more consensuses that Skype, in its current form, is not an attractive solution for HIPAA compliant CV programming, the company does not claim to qualify for the conduit rule and it does not offer BAAs. The Zur Institute has quite a few documents discussing the use of Skype for CV [19, 20] and the information is good supplemental reading for anyone who is going to go through the software selection process. It is important to note that software or hardware systems cannot be "HIPAA compliant;" meeting the regulations set out in HIPAA depends on services, how the software is used, and many other aspects of healthcare programming.

Obliviously, considering HIPAA compliance as it relates to CV software is a complicated issue and vague language in the laws, conflicting interpretations, vagaries in vendor information, and difficulties in getting information about BAA's make clear interpretation difficult for healthcare managers and even experts. We believe that it is easier to meet HIPAA requirements using CV software than all the confusion suggests. In response to this situation, some software companies are building their market strategy around HIPAA, rather than trying to fit or slant existing services into the model.

For example, Doxy.me (https://telemedicine.doxy.me/) and VSee (https://vsee.com/) advertise not being able to decrypt their own signals, and not storing any information exchanged during videoconferencing. The companies go an important step further in making it easy and affordable to enter into a HIPAA friendly BAA. You can start the process easily online. Note that Doxy.me and Vsee, like other companies, also makes the case that their software qualifies for the HIPAA conduit rule exemption (and hence would not necessarily need a BAA), but their promotional materials make it easy for providers to choose their level of comfort, i.e., a free version, without a BAA, and a version with a BAA for a fee. The potential importance of obtaining a BAA was made more relevant by the HITECH Act of 2011, aspects of which are beyond the scope of this discussion, but the conduit rule still applies.

Like Doxy.me and Vsee, Cisco has built services around health-related standards for videoconferencing. As noted, it is common for software promotional materials to quote various snippets of HIPAA regulations and then provide facts about their software, leaving it up to the reader to decide if the case has been made or not (and wondering what relevant information has been left out). By contrast, Cisco, in support of its videoconferencing software, Jabber XCP, uses some of the clearest HIPAA-related language we have seen, "Jabber XCP is secure enough to support compliance regulations such as the Securities Exchange Commission (SEC) and HIPAA. Jabber XCP security is used and trusted by the US federal government" [6]. This is still a highly word-smithed statement, but it is useful for those shopping for CV platforms, and is accurate—the Jabber platform is approved for CV use in many VA Medical Centers and other federal settings. However, it is important to note that these claims apply to Jabber XCP (not the free version of Jabber) and licensing for the product may come at premium (or be affordable) depending on your specific situation.

For managers who are working with a federal health network, and want that option in the future, or who have to respond to State or local facility requirements of FIPS 140-2 certification for videoconferencing software, a very helpful resource is the regularly updated list of validated FIPS 140-2 cryptographic modules, available at http://csrc.nist.gov/groups/STM/cmvp/documents/140-1/140val-all.htm. The list provides company/vendor names and validation certificate numbers. Note that not all vendors with videoconferencing products create their own cryptographic modules, so you will not necessarily see every compliant company or product on the list. Because of this, and because it is difficult to know how the listed modules are used in larger products (i.e., to determine how and if company X's FIPS 140-2 certified module is used in their videoconferencing software product), the government webpage also contains very clear directions on how to obtain that relevant information from vendors. Basically, it suggests that when you are selecting a product you should: (1) verify from the vendor that the certified module is either the product itself or that the certified module is embedded in the product; and (2) ask the vendor to provide a signed letter or statement: (a) affirming that the unmodified validated cryptographic module is integrated in the product; (b) affirming that the module in the product provides all the certified cryptographic services; and (c) providing references to the module's validation certificate number from the listing.

This seems like a lot of work, but from our perspective it is not just worth it to make sure your solution is a safe one for your practice or institution, but it is worth it because it is actually faster to talk to vendor sales representatives than it is to sift through hours of web pages searching for hidden meanings and vague language regarding FIPS 140-2 certification. Also, from our perspective, in a rapidly changing market, we must resist the temptation to just go with the known solution that others are using. Many new products compete because they offer something valuable or innovative not otherwise addressed by established solutions. Often the innovation is in the form of compatibility with other software products, for example Vidyo CV software (http://www.vidyo.com/solutions/healthcare/) is compatible with a number of specialty products to functionalize the CV environment (e.g., to handle emergency room flow, provide specific tools for treating stroke, or to facilitate critical care patient monitoring). Other recent innovations include customizable functions that are native to the CV platform, for example, a HIPAA-friendly virtual waiting room (https://telemedicine.doxy.me/), which providers can tailor, post assessment forms on, or use to manage their time more efficiently. Though often what new products or vendors offer is affordability.

1.6 Integrating Clinical Videoconferencing with Supporting Technologies

Every CV system has strengths and limitations, but managers and providers do not necessarily have to accept those limitations when constructing a communication context. Additional technologies, infrastructure, and equipment can be used during CV treatment to supplement communication, share materials, and gather information.

The most obvious resource not to overlook is the web. Gathering information by means other than CV might be a nice way of streamlining services and saving time, but there will be other security questions that need answering. Even so many web-based products have already been developed that address security concerns. Patients can be asked to enter information into secure web survey forms, some information can be sent via email, videos can be created and downloaded for review by the patient or provider. These technologies can all be classified as "store and forward telehealth." In most cases, they are simpler to accomplish but lack the real-time interaction, which can be achieved via CV. See Chap. 10 (Sect. 10.6) for more information about methods of collecting information in CV contexts.

Regarding workstation hardware and software, clinicians should know how to switch between CV input sources for various devices. If planning to share electronic medical records or simply the screen of the desktop computer, make sure your vendor is aware of the preferred system output (i.e., RCA, S-Video, VGA, DVI, HDMI, etc.). If you are unable to tell a VGA from an HDMI output by sight, then it is a good idea to familiarize yourself, especially if you are in charge of telehealth purchasing. Multiple online resources exist (with helpful photographs) to educate consumers about common video connecters (see http://www.hardwaresecrets.com/printpage/Video-Connectors-Tutorial/157). Once a desktop is connected to a CV system, then many other devices can be configured to be shared via CV with the right connections. For example, blood pressure monitors and many other medical devices can be connected to desktops via bluetooth wireless transmission.

Smartphones and tablets can be used to record session exercises, communicate, or provide clear close-up photographs. Mobile applications can also provide additional CV functionality, outside of the primary CV system. Mobile applications used with auxiliary plug-in sensors can assist with physiological measurements (i.e., EKG, EEG, and GSR) and can send the information in a non-PHI format to providers instantly. Applications can also be used to track and display information handwritten by the provider during session (e.g., Bamboo Paper), a simple screen capture can then be used to send session notes, directions, or reminders to the patient instantly. Older technologies, such as fax machines, scanners, email, and document cameras also continue to play a large role in modern CV.

When considering how to optimize any videoconferencing system, it is worthwhile to become educated regarding potential supporting technologies that you may already not know about or are off your radar. As an example, let us consider a much underutilized piece of common technology, the Apple TV. The product is a small black box, about 4-in wide; it plugs into TV monitors via an HDMI cord and costs $ 99. In addition to allowing users to watch their favorite shows and movies, it allows for screen mirroring of devices on the same wireless network. In other words, if you have an operating wireless network, you can enable whatever images and sounds are being displayed on an iPhone (5-in screen) to be pushed to a TV monitor (42-in screen). Accordingly, in nonclinical videoconferencing environments, two facilities could use Facetime, Skype, GoToMeeting, etc. to connect with each other on phones, but then push or "mirror" the incoming audio and video onto larger monitors. In this way, facilities could use two existing TVs, two existing phones, two existing cellular plans, and for the cost of two $ 99 products, they could "rig" a very satisfactory administrative videoconferencing system. Most videoconferencing applications support a high quality image so there is some, but minimal, degrading of the image as it is enlarged. We do not suggest using this method for CV because even though the two TVs are not communicating with each other, the signal is going from a local phone through a local wireless network to a TV, so there are clear security problems involved, i.e., it does not matter how secure the local network is if the signal being pushed to it is not encrypted. Regardless, the point we are interested in with this example, is that technology is always evolving and there may already be existing products off you radar that could facilitate improved programming when used along with CV systems. Accordingly, before designing and purchasing a CV system, it is important to at least become familiar with the developed technologies already being used for the specific patient populations or diagnoses that the programming is intended to address. Talk to your providers and

Table 1.4 Questions to address basic system needs before consulting with vendors

1. Will all the provider and patient connections both be taking place in a clinical setting? Yes/No
a) If Yes, it is assumed that the clinical setting has adequate controls of surroundings and network for privacy?
b) If No, will you be connecting to a patient in their home? Yes/No
I) If Yes, it is assumed the patient has adequate control of their home surroundings and network for privacy?
II) If No, what is an acceptable risk to patient privacy given need for services?
2. Will you be using video telecommunications hardware? Yes/No
3. Will you be using video telecommunications software with webcams and computers? Yes/No
4. Will you be using tablets and mobile phones? Yes/No
5. Will you be using a mix of hardware, software? Yes/No
6. Will patients need to establish a call over broadband (Cable Modem, DSL)? Yes/No
7. Will patients need to establish a call over cellular data?
8. Will you be contracting with a service provider? Yes/No
9. What is an acceptable audio delay and frames per second for this clinical service?
10. How much bandwidth do you currently have, and how much will you need for the scale of services?

get them to list out all the technologies used to treat the target population identified in your needs assessment.

1.7 Organizing Information Regarding Clinical Videoconferencing Needs to Choose the "Right" System

It is helpful to have a basic outline of the system you want before speaking with vendors. Vendor representatives can be good resources for helping to educate and shape thinking about what is possible, given a budget. But it is a good idea to gather information from clinicians, administrators, and colleagues, identify a basic strategy or two and then start interacting with vendors. There will be time to match the scale of your plan to the budget, after basic information is collected and stakeholders are on the same page. Additionally, clinicians tasked with using the technology will likely be more bought in if they were consulted in the selection of the technology platforms. The following outlines a standard list of questions that can be used to create a very basic outline of technology needs for implementing CV services.

Conclusion

The answers to the questions on Table 1.4 will provide a broad outline for discussions with your administration and vendors. Those discussions will bring you closer to a solution for your CV infrastructure, as well as establishing the cost for the services and hardware. The costs may be relatively inexpensive but they could be extreme, depending on the expectations, requirements, and scale of the system. At the same time, even very well-prepared clinical ecologies with clear plans and broad support for CV expansion struggle early on with creating consistent referral streams and with navigating the logistical coordination of multisite services. Acquiring the technology to conduct secure clinical services is the easy part of telehealth implementation. You do not want to get ahead of your clinical capacity by overpurchasing at the beginning. Doing so also may limit your ability for course correction if a certain technology is not working out. If you take nothing else from this chapter, you will do well if you start small, try out different technologies, and build up from false starts and success.

References

1. American Telemedicine Association. American Telemedicine Association. n.d.. http://www.americantelemed.org. Accessed 9 March 2014
2. Apple Inc. White paper on iOS security. http://images.apple.com/nz/ipad/business/docs/iOS_Security_EN_Feb14.pdf. Accessed 5 May 2014.
3. Cisco. Cisco telepresence precisionHD USB cameras. n.d. http://www.cisco.com/c/en/us/products/collaboration-endpoints/telepresence-precisionhd-usb-cameras/index.html. Accessed 9 March 2014.
4. Cisco. Immersive telepresence. http://www.cisco.com/c/en/us/products/collaboration-endpoints/immersive-telePresence/index.html. Accessed 9 March 2013.
5. Cisco. Installing and upgrading desktop components of the Cisco Unified videoconferencing Solution. 2009. http://www.cisco.com/c/en/us/td/docs/video/cuvc/design/guides/desktop/7_0/cuvc70dg/buildnetwk.html#wp1750046. Accessed 17 March 2014.
6. Cisco. Jabber XCP frequently asked questions. n.d. http://www.cisco.com/c/en/us/products/unified-communications/jabber-extensible-communications-platform-xcp/jabber_faq.html. Accessed 15 May 2014.
7. Citrix Systems, Inc. GoToMeeting HIPPA compliance guide. http://news.citrixonline.com/wpcontent/uploads/2013/07/GoToMeeting_HIPAA_Compliance_Guide.pdf. Accessed 20 May 2014.
8. Curtiss ET, Eustis S. Telemedicine monitoring: market shares, strategies, and forecasts, worldwide, 2013 to 2019. 2013 Sept 11. Retrieved March 17, 2014, From Wintergreen Research, Inc. http://wintergreenresearch.com/reports/telemedicine.html. Accessed 17 March 2014.
9. IBIS World. Telehealth Services Market Research Report. 2014. http://www.ibisworld.com/industry/telehealth-services.html. Accessed 5 May 2014.
10. Logitech. Webcams. n.d. http://www.logitech.com/en-us/webcam-communications/webcams. Accessed 9 March 2014.
11. Microsoft Corporation. Webcams. n.d. http://www.microsoft.com/hardware/en-us/webcams. Accessed 9 March 2014.
12. National Institute of Standards and Technology. Federal information processing standards 140-2. 2002 Dec 3. http://csrc.nist.gov/publications/fips/fips140-2/fips1402.pdf. Accessed 9 March 2014.
13. Nefsis. Nefsis high definition HD cameras bandwidth. n.d. https://www.nefsis.com/pdf/nefsis-high-definition-HD-cameras-bandwidth.pdf. Accessed 17 March 2014.
14. Pew Research Center. Pew research internet project, mobile technology fact sheet. 2014. http://www.pewinternet.org/fact-sheets/mobile-technology-fact-sheet/.

15. Polycom, Inc. Polycom realpresence immersive: video conferencing & telepresence solutions. n.d. http://www.polycom.com/products-services/hd-telepresence-video-conferencing/realpresence-immersive.html. Accessed 9 March 2014.
16. Reinhardt R. (2013, February 20). Hipaa final rule and the conduit exception. From tame your practice. http://www.tameyourpractice.com/blog/hipaa-final-rule-and-conduit-exception. Accessed 9 March 2014.
17. U.S. Census Bureau. Current population survey, computer and internet access in the United States: 2012. 2014. https://www.census.gov/hhes/computer/publications/2012.html.
18. Winter Green Research Report. Telemedicine monitoring: market shares, strategies, and forecasts, worldwide, 2012 to 2018. 2012. http://www.reportlinker.com/p0847924summary/Telemedicine-Monitoring-Market-Shares-Strategies-and-Forecasts-Worldwide-to.html.
19. Zur Institute, LLC. Telehealth & telemental health: the new standard. n.d. http://www.zurinstitute.com/telehealthresources.html. Accessed 9 March 2014.
20. Zur Institute, LLC. Utilizing Skype and VSee to provide telemental health, e-counseling, or e-therapy. 2014. http://www.zurinstitute.com/skype_telehealth.html.

Chapter 2
Conducting a Telehealth Needs Assessment

Noah DeGaetano and Jay Shore

Chapter Summary

Purpose This chapter is organized in a step-by-step manner that will lead readers through the process of conducting an initial assessment of needs to inform telehealth program development. As the name suggests, a needs assessment defines the specific needs of a target population and program, while identifying potentially inaccurate assumptions regarding the value, purpose, or intent of establishing new services. We start by discussing why this process is essential to developing successful telehealth programming regardless of scale. We then review a streamlined approach based on an example of a psychologist who is the mental health manager of a small rural clinic interested in establishing limited clinical videoconferencing (CV) services. This example is included to keep the first pass of material as simple and accessible as possible. The chapter then covers another scenario with greater scope and complexity by focusing on the perspective of a director of telehealth who is tasked with implementing telehealth programs across a large hospital system.

Context The information is helpful to clinical managers, administrators, and clinicians because it is easy to assume that the gaps in services to be addressed by proposed CV programming are self-evident or face-valid. However, experienced program managers know that carefully considering, defining, and confirming clinical, programmatic, and regulatory needs before program planning and implementation prevents wasted time and resources. More specifically, we denote how critical gaps in program-

N. DeGaetano (✉)
VA Palo Alto Healthcare System, Palo Alto, CA, USA; Stanford School of Medicine, Stanford, CA, USA
e-mail: noah.degaetano@va.gov

J. Shore
University of Colorado Anschutz Medical Campus, Centers for American Indian and Alaska Native Health, Aurora, CO, USA

© Springer International Publishing Switzerland 2015
P. W. Tuerk, P. Shore (eds.), *Clinical Videoconferencing in Telehealth,*
Behavioral Telehealth, DOI 10.1007/978-3-319-08765-8_2

ming and barriers to change can be identified through data collection and analysis, before jumping to solutions or implementation strategies built on impressions rather than facts.

Tools   The chapter provides a number of data collection and decision-making tools for novices and experts in telehealth program development. It includes guided questions to appropriately scale an initial assessment, a list of patient,- provider,- and organization-related questions to identify and prioritize clinical needs, a checklist for identifying common useful sources of data that may already exist, a list of data sources commonly developed for needs assessments and accompanying major factors included in final reports, a table identifying and defining common types of cross-state licensure agreements for telehealth, a list of exceptions to state licensure requirements, and a list of telehealth recourse centers by geographical location with links to their websites. For investigating needs associated with larger programs, the chapter provides comprehensive checklists for conducting a needs assessment in three multifaceted phases, and tables that identify the pros and cons of employing different types of needs assessment data gathering methods.

2.1 Defining a Needs Assessment

A needs assessment is the first critical step towards building an effective and sustainable telehealth program. Ryan Watkins and colleagues define a needs assessment as "an approach that helps people make informed and justifiable decisions that accomplish desired results" [1]. It is a systematic process for identifying and addressing needs or the gaps between current conditions and desired results. The discrepancy between current and desired results must be measured to appropriately describe the current "need." Simply put, a needs assessment is a tool for making better decisions.

2.2 Why Perform a Needs Assessment?

Telehealth programs are often started because there is some obvious unmet healthcare need that might be addressed through CV services. Perhaps the need is primarily patient-oriented, such as patients at a particular rural clinic requiring better access to medical center specialty services. Perhaps the need is more program-orientated, such as a program wanting to expand the relevant catchment area. Or perhaps there is a more targeted and specific goal, such as implementing CV home monitoring of chronic disease patients in order to reduce hospital and emergency department admissions. Whatever the reason, your first task is to determine what the most pressing needs are for your patients and community and to figure out if telehealth can really address those needs.

You may ask why you should perform a needs assessment if you already have made up your mind to incorporate telehealth or have been given a directive or grant to start a telehealth program? After all, you are already familiar with your clinic or hospital and the needs of patients, right? Why not just start buying equipment and begin implementing so that you can get services to patients and help staff as quickly as possible? Getting it right (or close to right) the first time around saves time and money, which is important when dealing with something as costly, labor intensive, and complex as CV program implementation. The most successful CV programs take the time to carefully identify and define program needs before beginning. If you make decisions without necessary information, many of your decisions will have to be revised [2, 3].

Too many managers make the mistake of equating efficiency with decisiveness in quickly selecting a solution and plowing ahead. Ultimately, because of the costs of changing course after resources are allocated, it can be difficult to adjust to new realities, leaving many projects to falter until they ultimately fail [1]. Research shows that the tendency to implement the first plausible solution, dubbed by Paul Nutt, "an emergent opportunity," leads to less-successful results from your decisions than if you follow through with a complete needs assessment, which he refers to as "discovery decision making" [4].

2.3   The Scope of Your Needs Assessment

A needs assessment can exist anywhere on a continuum from short and simple to ongoing and complex. Needs assessments can be scaled for any size project, time frame, or budget. So what kind of needs assessment is right for you?

A good rule of thumb for determining the size and scope of your needs assessment is to let the decisions to be made be your guide. In other words, clearly establish what decisions have to be made, and reverse engineer your needs assessment on the basis of the information needed. If you are a solo practitioner then you may be able to determine this independently. If you are part of a larger organization go to your supervisor, collaborators, or other leaders in your organization to help clarify how they would like to use the results of an initial needs assessment. Figuring out where you are going can help you know where to start. For a bigger project in a large organization it may be necessary for you to gather a team that will do the work of developing a needs assessment. The point is this—you can spend more or less time on any of the steps in a needs assessment depending on your situation, just don't skip any of the steps.

This chapter is organized in a step-by-step manner that will lead the reader through the process of conducting a needs assessment. We start by reviewing a streamlined approach based on the fictional narrative of a psychologist who is the mental health manager of a small rural clinic. This is done to keep the first pass of this material as simple and accessible as possible. The chapter then covers another fictional scenario with greater scope and complexity by focusing on the perspective of a director of telehealth who is tasked with implementing telehealth programs across a large hospital system. Outlines and specific steps to guide this second, more comprehensive approach, are presented. If you are already familiar with CV and needs assessments or are in the position of managing a telehealth program across a large healthcare system feel free to skip ahead to Sect. 1.9 for a more comprehensive and complex discussion of telehealth program development.

2.4   Starting Your Needs Assessment: Identify, Analyze, and Decide

Although we have laid out the approach to starting a telehealth program in a stepwise manner please keep in mind that in reality these tasks may not proceed in a chronological stepwise manner. The following example illustrates this point. Suppose that you have identified a patient population with a huge need that can be well served through a CV program offering evidence-based specialty mental health services. However, when you try to get "buy in" or assess the "readiness" of this service you find that either the leadership does not support it or no "clinical champions" within the staff of that service emerge to help get the program going. Even though you may have determined that this is a great need with a perfect CV solution you still need to get "buy in" to make it work [2]. It would be prudent of you to recognize and address this issue so your telehealth initiative and its expensive equipment don't end up collecting dust. The issue of "buy in" and organizational "readiness" is discussed in more detail in Sect 1.10.1.

The following sections present a fictional scenario that will illustrate the steps of a basic needs assessment. Imagine a mental health manager of a small rural clinic that has been asked by the director of a regional medical center to decide if she wants her clinic to be included in a grant that has been awarded to start CV programs in the hospital system. They want to provide specialty care and expertise from a large tertiary care medical center to her small rural clinic. So what is the next step? Any needs assessment can be compartmentalized into three basic steps: (1) *identify* needs by collecting information, (2) *analyze* the information collected, and (3) *decide* what to do next.

2.5   Identifying the Need

This seemingly simple approach (identify, analyze, decide) is specifically designed to help focus managers on understanding a situation before generating solutions. Of course, no one would argue against the proposition that one must understand and define needs before making decisions on how to implement or address those needs. We all agree that healthcare decisions should be well informed and justified [1]. Even so, as experts in healthcare, we all also are tempted from time to time to believe that we already know what is going on. We all often, knowingly or un-knowingly, jump to conclusions based on our experiences or beliefs. Accordingly, this 3-step mantra (identify, analyze, decide) is less a comprehensive road map for successful needs assessment implementation than it is a reminder to catch ourselves when we have decided something about future programming without due diligence. If you are a manger contemplating CV program development, then you might al-ready be surprised by how much planning or pre-planning you are doing in your mind without adequate information. Creative contemplation regarding the future is important and having a vision is key to effective leadership, yet the nitty-gritty of CV program development should be informed by data not fantasy, no matter how experienced the dreamer is.

2.5.1   Identifying the Need: Determining Necessary Data

The first step in identifying needs is to determine what data are required. Clinical situations and ecologies vary too much for there to be only one or a few relevant questions. The manager in our current scenario is asked: Given the resources, would you like to participate in developing limited CV programming for specialty men-tal health care? From the manager's perspective, she considers two overarching questions that need to be addressed before providing her answer or recommenda-tions. The first is: what disorder or population should be targeted in my clinic for specialty CV mental health services? The manager is aware that she is being asked to develop referral streams and programming for a limited resource, and so she is appropriately invested in identifying a high-priority population in her clinic. The second most relevant question for the manager is: will specialty CV care for the identified population in my clinic be feasible? Of course, questions of feasibility are paramount for any CV program development, but in the current circumstance, feasibility is a special concern because the manager would not want under-informed recommendations to contribute to the director or program being unsuccessful. In other words, there may be other clinics in the ecology where success might be more likely; accordingly, the manager places a high value on an accurate assessment of needs and feasibility in her clinic so that the director can make an informed decision about including her clinic.

The scope and focus of needs assessments will vary depending on the top infor-mation priorities. Moreover, appropriately scaled data collection should only target the top priorities. Although we may want to take on all of the unmet needs of the patients we serve, part of the needs assessment process is limiting and precisely defining the scope of what to recommend. One way to start is to target a specific illness or a particular geographic location. Using our scenario, and given that the manager already serves a relatively small population spread out over a large area, she decides that targeting a specific illness would probably be the best route to fol-low, rather than a geographical location.

Table 2.1 Patient, provider, and organizational questions to identify and prioritize needs

Relevant realms	Questions to address
Patient considerations:	What unmet healthcare needs do your patients have?
	Which of those needs could be met using telehealth?
	Among those diagnoses which ones are the most prevalent?
	Are your patients ready and willing to accept telehealth care?
	What additional services are your patients most likely to want/use?
	Is there demand for services as well as need?
	Which services are your patients most often traveling to the tertiary care facilities for? Could any of these services be delivered via CV to save the trip?
	If your patients have to travel to other sites to get consultations and services are they making the trip when referred or are they missing their appointments?
	If they are missing their appointments why are they missing them?
Provider considerations:	What diagnosis do your patients have that your clinic does not have the time/expertise to deal with effectively?
	What additional patient services do the other providers in the clinic most want?
	Are your providers ready and willing to provide telehealth care?
	What level of training for your providers will be available?
	What provider needs or opportunities might be met with telehealth? (e.g., training opportunities, frequent/timely collaboration with specialist providers)
Organizational considerations:	Are there resources allocated by organization to perform a needs assessment?
	What specialty services are best suited to telehealth?
	What are the range of technologies available to provide telehealth?
	What legal and reimbursement rules governing telehealth practice exist locally and regionally?
	Will your telehealth initiative be in line with your organization's mission or strategic plan?
	Does the tertiary care facility that we will be connected to via telehealth have the capacity to treat those diagnoses more effectively than we can?
	What telehealth services would be the most complementary to the services you are already providing?
	Are there any major organizational or technology barriers in the clinic or organization that should be addressed before starting development of this program?

Note that while it is important to value patient-centered factors, a needs assessment should also consider how telehealth can serve providers' needs as well. They will be the people facilitating and providing CV care, as well as shouldering the burden of starting something new [2, 3, 5,]. While CV programs are often embraced once they are working smoothly, initially they can provoke anxiety, disrupt workflow, and threaten the status quo [6]. Table 2.1 provides a list of sample questions you can ask at the outset of your needs assessment to identify top patient, provider, and organizational priorities. If this list looks dizzyingly, keep in mind that you can pick and choose questions that suit your particular needs. Also, if you

Table 2.2 Identifying data that may already exist

1. Does your clinic collect metrics regarding patient demographics or clinical outcomes, are they available in an electronic medical records system (EMR)?
2. Are consults tracked in your system?
3. Does your larger hospital system track metrics and can you access those data?
4. Is there a way for you to review the number of patients with a specific diagnosis in your clinic through your EMR?
5. Does your hospital system have a strategic plan that contains data about areas for improvement that you could review?
6. Has your clinic or hospital system compiled any information that was used for internal or external regulatory reviews or grants that might be useful?
7. Does your billing department have information about the diagnoses, procedures, or payer mix through claims data that would be useful?
8. Is there any public health data for your clinic's catchment area (local or state) that you could review?
9. Are there any U.S. government statistics that exist? Note, your clinic may operate in a federally designated specialty shortage area and so relevant data might be available (Mental Health HPSA Designation Criteria: http://bhpr.hrsa.gov/shortage/hpsas/designationcriteria/mentalhealthhpsacriteria.html provides all of the criteria used to determine a health professional shortage area)

are performing a large-scale needs assessment there are online toolkits with even more comprehensive question lists, see: http://www.caltrc.org/knowledge-center/program-development/your-path-to-telehealth-success/ [2].

2.5.2 Identifying the Need: Collection From Existing Data Sources

The second step in identifying needs is to determine what to access from already available sources of data. Knowing what questions you want to answer will inform what data you need, but also the availability or feasibility of obtaining data will necessarily limit what questions you can answer. Data can be dived into two groupings: Data that already exist and data you need to collect. Table 2.2 presents questions that are helpful in identifying data that may already exist. Considering these questions can assist managers to think creatively about potentially relevant information and can protect against missed opportunities. Note that Chap. 6 contains a thorough discussion regarding gathering data to support ongoing program evaluation; necessarily the information overlaps with the content of the present chapter and should be reviewed as an ancillary resource for data gathering strategies.

The advantage of obtaining data that already exists is that you may not have to expend very much time or energy to obtain it. The downside is that they may have been collected with a different purpose in mind and not be relevant to your question. It may be difficult or time consuming to analyze. It may also be difficult to verify the quality or accuracy of the information collected [1].

2.5.3   Identifying the Need: Determining What Data Need to be Collected

The third step in identifying needs is to specify what information is needed that is not already available. After you have surveyed what data already exist, you can start to think about what additional data should be collected from primary sources. A good way of identifying the sources of primary data is to review all of the stakeholders who will be affected by or take part in the telehealth program. In the present example of a small rural mental health clinic, this might be patients, other staff at the clinic (psychologists, physicians, nurses, physician assistants, medical technicians, clerks), and the administrator(s) who originally designated CV as an area of interest [7].

Knowing what questions should be answered in this scenario, the manager reviews the hospital system's strategic plan and notes that there has been a pledge by the hospital's chief of staff and director to significantly increase the provision of mental health services especially in federally designated physician shortage and rural areas. Following this cue, the manager asks the service chief if she can send some data from the electronic medical records system on the prevalence of different diagnoses among patients treated in the clinic.

The list provided by the service chief documents high levels of depression, substance abuse, and diabetes among the rural patient population accessing the clinic. The manager is aware that providing referrals for specialty mental health providers located at the medical center is a common practice in the rural health clinic, but that many of the patients never follow up with their mental health specialist appointments. Practitioners have heard from a number of patients that they do not want to travel all the way to the hospital for these services. Moreover, the manager remembers a number of articles citing the negative impact that untreated mental health issues have on patients' medical comorbidities. Accordingly, it *appears* as if the present system in place to provide mental health specially care to the rurally-based patrons of the clinic is inadequate, may be contributing to an exacerbation of medical conditions, and might be solvable via CV. *At this point the manager has a decision to make; she can formally or semi-formally gather quantitative, qualitative, and literature-based data to support her assumptions, or she could become very interested in the scale of the problem and potential scale of the CV-based solution. The former decision would provide evidence to support CV program development; the later decision would provide additional and specific information to help her craft a goal-driven and successful program.*

There are several options open to her for gathering additional information. She could follow-up her initial request for medical center-level data with another request to discover the no-show rate of patients referred to mental health specialty care. She could task her local clinical staff to do a record review for the past month to ascertain how many referrals were made. She could schedule interviews with her staff, the director of telehealth, the chief of the medicine service, the director of the medical center outpatient mental health clinic, mental health specially clinicians, clinical staff that work in a clinic similar to hers in another rural country, and current or past patients. In addition to individual interviews, she could also host focus groups as described in a recent article [7]. Although she would have liked to survey the local patients, she was discouraged by the low response rate in the past and by the approval process needed to go through to send out surveys to patients. However, she decided that she could push out a simple survey to her staff through email, and could address remaining questions in a focus group with them. She also was able to buy her staff into conducting brief chart reviews to ascertain the number of referrals made and outcomes over the past month. Her staff were motivated by the prospect of having clinical help locally for chronic or high-needs patients.

2.5.4 Identifying the Need: Data Collection

The fourth step of identifying need is actually collecting the information that was previously unavailable. The manager educates herself on basic focus group techniques and conducts the group during an extended lunch break in the clinic. She makes her best effort to stay on topic while starting with open-ended questions and narrowing questions to get more specific answers as different themes emerge. She encourages colleagues not to provide solutions, but rather to focus on what needs have not been met, to outline the scope and character of the problems. She shares the outcomes of the local chart review and assesses the staff's reaction to the needs that are identified. This includes the demographic and diagnostic information describing the need for specialty consultations for depression, substance abuse, and complications of diabetes (nephrology, podiatry, ophthalmology, vascular surgery, etc.). She discusses possible reasons for the low adherence to and availability of those consultation appointments. Her discussion reveals several themes, one of which is that other providers share her feelings of being ill equipped to help patients with depression and/or substance abuse especially when they are co-occurring with complicated medical diagnoses that need to be addressed in brief visits.

Armed with this information she schedules interviews with her administrator, the head of outpatient mental health, and a peer mental health manager in another clinic who has been given the same task by the service chief. During these conversations she finds out that proposed services will include hiring mental health providers with specialized training in treating depression and substance abuse. Given the difficulty of reaching patients in rural clinics, the mental health outpatient director is eager to collaborate with her on the project. She is also able to convince this director to lend her a psychologist who is adept at getting clearance for patient interviews and who can conduct a focus group with patients. This seems like a good opportunity given this psychologist's experience in running groups with patients and given that she does not have funds to hire an outside consultant.

From the patient focus group she determines that there is indeed interest among this group of patients in receiving CV specialty services. Very few of them report being willing to travel the distances required to receive those services and some allow that they might have been able to prevent worsening of their health if they had followed up with specialty services earlier. They also complain that although there are some specialists who travel to your clinic one day every other week, these hours are so limited that your patients often get frustrated with trying to schedule an appointment and often give up on trying to do so. You find that this focus group is helpful in illustrating the gap between current and desired results and demonstrating that if telehealth services were available, patients would be willing to try these services, especially for mental health.

2.6   Analyzing the Information

Now that all the information is collected, it is time to make sense of it. Some of the data are quantitative in nature and so can be analyzed with simple statistics and displayed with charts. Some of the data are qualitative and so require a different medium of presentation (e.g., patient and provider direct quotes illustrating certain perspectives), and some are qualitative that can be quantified (e.g., "68% of the focus group demonstrated an openness to CV services"). After some interviews with the representatives of several specialty services, the manager realizes that many of them are not yet willing, prepared, or adequately staffed to offer telehealth services to her clinic. These data need to be analyzed and reported on in a sensitive manner so as to not have the effect of pointing fingers or burning bridges. Even so, it is important information that underlies a previously unidentified and incorrect assumption regarding the readiness of the system to innovate. Analysis also revealed a common concern among specialty SUDs and depression providers that some of the services require the performance of procedures that are either not available locally or would require more expensive and complicated redesign than using just clinical videoconferencing for mental health services (e.g., urine capture and analysis). This finding is noted in a running list entitled, "unforeseen potential barriers to effective CV programming."

   As noted, a needs assessment should be designed to identify the gap between a current level of need being met and a proposed level of need to be met. That is to say, it is not enough to demonstrate needs; good needs assessments will also fill in the gaps regarding how much additional need could/should be met with the proposed programming. We cannot expect CV programming to solve all patient needs and so specific benchmarks for success are required to inform program development. Chapter 6 addresses program goal setting within the context of data analysis (Sects. 6.2, 6.4, and 6.9 are especially relevant).

   Analysis of data in the context of a needs assessment is more than just reporting a list of outcomes. The information should be organized and, as much as possible, that organization should be designed to answer the specific key questions at hand. Perhaps findings illustrate a number of positive and negative themes regarding the proposed change, staff ambivalence, or strong advocacy. Perhaps findings illustrate that some of the proposed goals can likely be met, but others are not feasible without a more integrative plan or additional resources. Whatever the case, analysis of the data require an organized approach to identify themes (or the absence of expected themes). For example, analyses could be organized by the key questions identified. Alternatively, the analytical report could be organized by *specific* findings grouped under broader points of *general* outcomes. Organizing the analytical report promotes a cohesive product to share with stakeholders, but more importantly, it challenges the person conducting the needs assessment to think critically and prospectively about the data and meaning. Decisions regarding programming development usually flow out of the analytical report writing process.

2.7 Decide

The needs assessment process cued the manager to realize that successful CV programming necessitated more buy-in from key stakeholders involved. She noted that not only was there resistance from specialty care providers, but also, all of the members of her clinical staff did not think that treating depression and substance abuse through CV should be the highest priority. She decided to use the report process to begin to build buy-in and create ownership. Accordingly, she invited her staff to define specific criteria to be used to decide which patients should be referred for CV specialty services and which patients should remain in standard care. Additionally, she allowed for the small scale "piloting" of referrals for other disorders, if the interested clinicians felt compelled to develop and problem solve referral stream throughput.

The manager compiles all the information she collected into a brief needs assessment report that clearly outlines her recommendations. The report addresses the manager's previously identified two most important questions: (1) Which clinic patient group represents the highest priority to receive specialty mental healthcare via CV; and (2) are the proposed CV services feasible? The report highlights her findings organized into seven major factors, which are, in turn, supported by specific data points and sources (Table 2.3) [2]. She is pleased to see that emails back from staff and leadership indicate that everyone is impressed by her thoughtfulness in making these recommendations and is eager to help make the well-reasoned initiative work.

When assessing needs assessment data and making decisions, it is particularly important to be aware of unidentified assumptions. Just as the hospital director in our example assumed (knowingly or unknowingly) that outpatient specialty clinics would be eager to service CV-based referrals, your own perspective and assumptions will shade what and how questions are analyzed. A creative method for guarding against this concern is to consider the proposed programming from the perspective of all stakeholders involved, especially those for whom the programming will create more work. Note, the exercise is of little worth unless you are prepared to value those perspectives as valid. A more concrete method of addressing this concern is to share findings with key stakeholders involved for a brief period of comment before finalizing findings or conclusions.

Table 2.3 Chapter scenario: Major factors in needs assessment report and data sources

Major points included in needs assessment	Specific data sources
Prevalence of co-occurring SUDs/depression diagnoses in the clinic	Supported by centralized data obtained from director's office
Current and proposed availability of specialty services	Supported by chart review data from local clinical staff and projections obtained from interviews with specialty clinic managers and staff
Number of consults that are discontinued due to lack of patient follow through and probable reasons for lack of follow-through	Supported by chart review data and current patient focus-group data
Alignment with strategic plan priorities	Obtained through requested documentation provided by director's office
Potential hidden costs to the healthcare system for untreated illness	Supported by the clinical literature
Ease of integrating services: Logistical fit and willingness of support, clinical, and leadership staff	Supported by staff e-mail survey outcomes, interviews, and focus group outcomes
Barriers to integrating services: Logistical fit, buy-in, and previously un-identified specific issues	Supported by staff e-mail survey outcomes, interviews, and focus group outcomes

It is entirely possible that limitations in resources will restrict the ability of a needs assessment to provide definitive data in all relevant areas. Yet decisions still have to be made. Acknowledging the limits of your data and basing decisions on other factors, such as the facility's strategic goals, the particular zeal of a clinical champion on your staff, or your own values, is a viable strategy, as long as you and stakeholders are aware of the reasons. Expectations regarding those particular goals or decisions can be judged accordingly. Additionally, since you designed the needs assessment with limited resources in mind to specifically address the most salient question/s, the majority of decisions and goals should be well informed and data-driven.

2.8   Needs Assessment vs. Program Evaluation

Needs assessment uses tools and techniques that may overlap with evaluation and implementation efforts. The difference is the intention with which these tools are used. The intention in a needs assessment is always to start with a blank slate that does not include solutions and to most broadly explore what the current needs are, how to define and measure those needs, and then how to compare alternative solutions to those needs. It is important to emphasize that this occurs before any decisions are made about what to do, which vendors to use, or what a program will look like. In contrast, an evaluation approach is often (though not always) applied after initial decisions about what to do have already been made with the goal of improving performance or determining the value added by the current processes

[1]. Note, Chap. 6 provides a progressive model of program evaluation that also includes consideration of initial program development steps and measuring feasibility prospectively. Accordingly, we recommend considering the materials presented here in tandem with the initial steps addressed in Chap. 6.

Although the implementation of CV programming and future program evaluation are outside the scope of a needs assessment, the initial needs assessment lays the foundation for those steps. Accordingly, the manager from the scenario above concludes her report with a series of questions that should be addressed before implementing her recommendations. She also identifies future metrics that would be most ideal to gauge the impact of the CV intervention. One of them is tracking how many referrals for depression and substance abuse treatment are made and how many are completed by referred patients, as compared to before CV services were available. She also notes that it would be useful to look at how patients who start receiving specialty mental health services through CV do on primary care measures that are already being tracked before and after they engage in CV-related services.

2.9 Larger Scale Programming Needs Assessments

Previously, you were asked to imagine organizing a needs assessment from the perspective of a clinical mental health manager in a small rural clinic. The director in that scenario gave the manager little guidance or direction. The manager in the rural clinic was largely left on her own to perform a needs assessment and get a program going. However, now we will ask you to reimagine the same scenario, but this time imagine that you are the chief of medicine who has been designated as the medical director of telehealth for a large hospital system. While there is considerable overlap between these two scenarios as director of telehealth you will have a wider scope and far more complexity to take into account. On the positive side, as director you may have considerably more resources at your disposal and easy access to hospital leadership. Given that you are now already familiar with the basic process of a needs assessment, we will present a more comprehensive overview that operationalizes this process and discusses certain aspects in greater detail.

One of the things that can make heading up a telehealth program for a large hospital system difficult is knowing where to start. Given the size, geography and diversity of your healthcare system, it may be difficult to know which projects to recommend. Remember, when you are building a program across a hospital system it is important to start small and then expand only after your initial pilot programs prove successful. You will likely learn valuable lessons from focusing on the successes and failures of those initial programs.

Making well informed choices can be achieved through your needs assessment by developing a hierarchy of needs similar to the one that was illustrated in the first example where the mental health manager in the rural clinic decided what diagnosis she was going to focus on. As director of telehealth you have many added layers of decision making that you may be responsible for including financial, legal, geographic, cultural, political, and technological considerations, not to mention the clinical ones. Therefore, in this scenario a more extensive needs assessment is warranted. It is important to note that in addition to the doing all of the necessary data collection and analysis there is one other important consideration that the director of telehealth must remember. The mental health manager in the first scenario had the advantage of being a clinician and embedded in the community that she was trying to provide mental health for. She understood the geography, the local communities, the sentiments and character of her patients and the local health care ecology and day to day specific logistics of care in her setting. As the director of telehealth, located in the tertiary hospital you may be very disconnected from all of that. When setting up telehealth programs to remote areas it can be very valuable to travel to or send others to travel to the areas in which you will be providing care, since some details of a community are difficult to capture on the pages of a report [8].

2.10   Educating Yourself About Your Regulatory and Funding Environment

Telehealth raises a number of legal concerns, especially regarding cross-state practice and reimbursement. Early on in the needs assessment process it is important to educate yourself on the regulatory and funding environment issues around telehealth both regionally and locally. In telehealth, licensure requirements can be complicated. The practitioner and healthcare organization needs to ensure that his/her activity is legally sanctioned and protected. For example, how do these issues impact types of service (e.g. are specific providers required to do in-person visits first by that state's medical board) as well as the business model (e.g. what insurances/payers reimburse which aspects of telehealth). These questions need to be asked early because they will have a large impact on the types of services and the business model that you develop. It is essential for the person leading the needs assessment process to educate themselves before or as early on in the needs assessment process as possible. Chapter 4 provides an overview for navigating regulatory CV-related issues, additionally, the Center for Telehealth and E-Health Law, the Federation of State Medical Boards, and the Federal Office for the Advancement of Telehealth have developed online training modules for telehealth legal and regulatory requirements available at: http://www.telehealthresourcecenter.org/legal-regulatory.

2.10.1   Reimbursement Considerations

It is important that you check with your major payers on a regular basis to see if additional services have been added or will be reimbursed. Some organizations, like the California Telemedicine and & eHealth Center offer a guide to the reimbursement policies of major national payers. The National Conference of State Legislature

(NCSL) provides a listing of whether Medicare or private insurance reimbursement for CV services is required for each state: http://www.ncsl.org/issues-research/health/state-coverage-for-telehealth-services.aspx. If Medicare reimbursement will be a vehicle for your target populations, then just like for in-person settings, it is important to stay on top of changing polices so that claims will not be returned. Fortunately, there are several well-developed resources for CV-related Medicare information. The following link provided by the Centers for Medicare and Medicaid Services provides information on payment policies: http://www.telehealthresource-center.org/reimbursement. Another good resource specifically regarding Medicaid in the telehealth context provides Medicaid-related telehealth definitions, guidelines for providers and facilities, and additional information on reimbursement can be found at the following link: http://medicaid.gov/Medicaid-CHIP-Program-Information/By-Topics/Delivery-Systems/Telemedicine.html.

Given the rapid change in the regulatory environment what is true today may not be true tomorrow. However, in general, most of the change is in the direction of drafting legal requirements and reimbursement plans that facilitate and support greater telehealth delivery. As noted, Chap. 4 provides a more in-depth review of CV regulatory issues; for our purposes it is important to be aware of the issues in needs assessment planning and for planning/feasibility of designating planning staff to research and become familiar with applicable regulations.

A sound business case is also needed to support the services that will be offered. The business case must clearly lay out the advantages and disadvantages of the telehealth service and specifically identify the expected costs of providing the service along with the expected revenues, costs savings, or other value added outcomes. Once this case is formulated, it is important to enlist champions to present this case to management in order to gain their commitment. Marketing your needs assessment and the recommendations it produces requires you to use the findings of your needs assessment to educate others as well as play to the political realities of your healthcare environment. Persistence and the ability to address the interests and concerns of a diverse group of stakeholders are essential. Active recruitment is often needed to find or cultivate a senior management champion who understands telehealth and the benefits for both patients and the organization. A thoughtful needs assessment can help you persuade others that your initiative deserves financial support.

2.10.2 Legal Considerations

A practitioner must be licensed, or follow state reciprocity rules, prior to working in a state. Accordingly, you must check state-specific regulations in each state that you plan to practice telehealth in. Practicing medicine without a license in a state can result in civil and/or criminal penalties. Under certain circumstances, such as emergencies, an exception may be made to the requirements for state licensure. Table 2.4, identifying broad exceptions to state telehealth licensure requirements,

Table 2.4 Exceptions to state licensure requirements for telehealth

1. Physician-to-physician consultations (not between practitioner and patient)
2. Educational purposes
3. Residential training
4. Border states
5. U.S. Military
6. Veterans Health Administration
7. Public health services
8. Medical emergencies (Good Samaritan) or natural disasters
9. Regional/Multi-State Authorities (e.g. National Council of State Boards of Nursing's Nurse Licensure Compact)

Table 2.5 Cross state licensure agreements

Agreement type	Basic description
Licensure by endorsement	Currently used by most state boards to grant licenses to health professionals licensed in other states that have equivalent standards
Mutual recognition	System in which the licensing authorities voluntarily enter into an agreement to legally accept the policies and processes (licensure) of a licensee's home state
Reciprocity	Agreements between two or more states in which each state gives the subjects of the other certain privileges, on the condition that its own subjects shall enjoy similar privileges at the hands of the latter state
Special purpose or limited licenses	These licenses allow health professionals to have the option of obtaining a limited license for the delivery of specific health services under particular circumstances in addition to holding a full license in the state where they primarily practice

and Table 2.5, defining examples of cross state licensure agreements, provide summary information adapted from a congressional report and the Telehealth Resource Center, more information is available at: http://www.telehealthresourcecenter.org/toolbox-module/licensure-and-scope-practice [9, 10].

Of course, programs with catchment areas in or near state boundaries must pay particular attention to developing and changing state licensure agreements. However, such agreements are also relevant when designing programs with the intention of providing continuous services for more mobile populations, e.g., patients who travel for work, go on extended vacation, or who are interested in relocation adjustment/hand off services. Table 2.5 identifies the methods by which one state can recognize the license of another.

The prescribing of controlled substances via telehealth is regulated by the Ryan Haight Online Pharmacy Consumer Protection Act [11]. It requires that the prescribing provider must see a patient in person before subsequently prescribing a controlled substance by telehealth. Some organizations, like the Veterans Health Administration and the Indian Health Service are exempted from this requirement and a clinical videoconferencing visit satisfies the requirements of an in person visit [11]. See http://www.telehealthresourcecenter.org/toolbox-module/online-prescribing-and-telepharmacy for more information.

2.10.3 Obtaining Outside Assistance

It is usually wise to seek assistance outside your organization for help in planning and setting up a new program when telehealth is a new undertaking for your organization or when the telehealth initiative being considered is significantly different from those currently offered. For example, if an organization decides to offer a telestroke service when it has previously developed a telepsychiatry service, it would be good to seek outside assistance given the great difference between the two types of services. Outside assistance may also be necessary when there is no internal expertise with the technologies that are being considered for use. Finally, when starting with a new service, external advice regarding legal and regulatory issues, reimbursement and billing can be helpful [2].

Regional telemedicine assistance centers are located across the country and can provide a number of resources specifically relevant to conducting needs assessments. These are federally funded programs for the purpose of providing assistance and consultation on developing a variety of telemedicine programs. Their websites contain program development toolkits and other helpful information including telehealth implementation workgroups [2]. For an example, see: http://www.cal-trc.org/knowledge-center/program-development/implementation-workgroups/. Table 2.6 provides a list of the telehealth recourse centers and links to their websites.

There are a number of other sources available to help managers plan for CV program implementation. Independent consultants and consulting firms have a variety of specialty expertise in telemedicine (e.g. http://telehealth.org/) [12]. A number of equipment vendors are willing to provide consulting services in the design and implementation of telemedicine services that make use of their equipment. These services are typically available through the vendor representatives. Professional organizations concerned with different aspects of telehealth, such as the American Telemedicine Association, have professional meetings that are a good way to find specific guidance of colleagues who may be able to provide assistance. Non-telehealth specialty organizations also have become increasingly interested in telehealth and often have dedicated subcommittees (e.g., the American Academy of Dermatology Telemedicine Task Force). Accordingly, managers may wish to consult with any professional organizations that they are currently members of to inquire about consultation services. Local universities with telehealth programs also may be able to offer assistance or collaboration on telehealth program development. As an example, if you were in the Santa Fe, New Mexico area doing a needs assessment you could probably get a lot of free information and support from the Southwest

Table 2.6 Telehealth resources centers

Telehealth resources centers	States covered	Link to website
Great Plains Telehealth Resource and Assistance Center	North Dakota, South Dakota, Minnesota, Iowa, Wisconsin, and Nebraska	http://www.gptrac.org/
Northeast Telehealth Resource Center	Maine, Rhode Island, Vermont, Massachusetts, New Hampshire and Connecticut, and New York	http://netrc.org/
Northwest Telehealth Resource Center	Washington, Oregon, Idaho, Montana, Utah, Wyoming, and Alaska	http://www.nrtrc.org/
Southeast Telehealth Resource Center	Alabama, Georgia, South Carolina, and Florida	http://www.setrc.us/
Southwest Telehealth Resource Center	Arizona, Colorado, New Mexico, Nevada, and Utah	http://www.southwesttrc.org/
Mid-Atlantic Telehealth Resource Center	Virginia, West Virginia, Kentucky, Maryland, Delaware, North Carolina, Pennsylvania & DC	http://www.matrc.org/
Upper Midwest Telehealth Resource Center	Indiana, Illinois, Michigan, and Ohio	http://www.umtrc.org/
Heartland Telehealth Resource Center	Kansas, Missouri, Oklahoma	http://heartlandtrc.org/
California Telehealth Resource Center	California	http://www.caltrc.org/
Pacific Basin Telehealth Resource Center	Hawaii and Pacific Basin	http://www.pbtrc.org/
National Telehealth Policy Resource Center	All states	http://cchpca.org/
Center for Telehealth and E-Health Law	All states	http://ctel.org/
Office for Advancement of Telemedicine—Health Resources Services Administration (HRSA)	All/most states	http://www.hrsa.gov/rural-health/about/telehealth/tele-health.html

Telehealth Resource Center, The Four Corners Telehealth Consortium, and the University of New Mexico Telehealth Program.

2.11 Choosing Which Specialties Services to Make Available via CV

The decision concerning what types of specialty CV programming to offer obviously should be based on a match between the types of specialty services needed and the availability and willingness of specialists to provide them. An important difference exists between perceived needs, as represented by opinions or intuitions, and actual demand. Demand is determined by the number of patients who have problems requiring specialist care, the willingness of clinicians to refer those patients to a telehealth program, and whether or not insurance will pay for a service delivered by telehealth [9]. One can begin by focusing on the perceived needs, and then sort out the actual demands for services, and then recruit specialists who will provide those services. Alternatively, one can first create an inventory of available specialties that can offer telehealth and then determine the demand for those services. Either approach will identify the one or more specialty consultation services that are in sufficient demand to justify offering telehealth.

The American Telemedicine Association has a webpage with a link to a number of case studies about telehealth interventions. Once you have decided what specialty programs you are going to offer it can be informative to review the literature describing similar initiatives to the one you are planning to undertake. See: http://www.americantelemed.org/about-telemedicine/telemedicine-case-studies#. U1iQX8fF_QQ for more information. Also searching a reference database like Pub-Med (http://www.ncbi.nlm.nih.gov/pubmed) or even Google Scholar can help you to identify published descriptions and outcomes of similar programs. You can save time and money by learning from others, but at the same time remember that you are performing a needs assessment to understand the specific needs of your population [8]. This should help you to recognize if a successful telehealth program described by a colleague, highlighted in the literature, or sold by a vendor, may or may not be a good fit for your organization [5, 13, 14, 15].

Conducting a needs assessment is different from a research study where a hypothesis is generated and then a study is designed to test that hypothesis. Instead, information uncovered in the needs assessment process will frequently transform or expand on the initial information requirements, which will send you back to collect more data to inform decisions. Rigid frameworks for determining what data should be collected restrict the usefulness of needs assessments. With a needs assessment you are not trying to produce a study that is generalizable or reproducible as is the case with most research. Instead you are conducting an assessment that is specific to the particular context and details of your clinic or institution [7]. While papers describing what approaches may have worked to build a successful telehealth program at one institution may offer useful insights, they should not be used as a blueprint to build a program at another institution. Instead a needs assessment should be performed that incorporates those insights to inform the needs assessment process; published findings cannot be treated as ready-made solutions. Keep in mind that during the course of your needs assessment you may also find that a non-CV solution to existing needs emerges. Try to be open to and willing to recommend this alternative solution.

2.11.1   The Importance of Local Referral Patterns

It is also important to distinguish between *actual* demand and *potential* demand, and to make that distinction apparent to various stakeholders. Population-based data regarding diagnoses and the availability of willing specialty providers do not easily translate into successful referral stream development. It is often the case that logical ideas regarding CV service development fail in the early stages or take months to ramp up to adequately productive levels as referring providers, clinical support staff for those providers, patients, medical center PR offices, and the many levels of management between facilities become aware of the availability of new CV-based services. Active advocacy, relationship building, internal advertisement, and adeptness at navigating institutional politics are often necessary to help logical data-based programming come to fruition. Chapter 6 and especially Table 6.1 outline the importance of aligning stakeholder goals for successful CV programming. For our purposes regarding needs assessment, it is important to be cognizant of these factors when identifying future demand for a particular service and appropriate goals in the early stages.

As noted, while there may be a number of patients in need in a remote site's catchment area, the demand for a clinical videoconferencing service is dependent on the willingness of clinicians who care for those patients to refer them. Most clinicians already have well established referral patterns. If local clinicians already refer patients to your specialists for care, then it is likely that the demand for your CV consults will be robust. If those local clinicians refer to other groups of specialists, it is possible that the need is large while the demand for your service may be small. One way to address this is by piloting a small program before committing resources to a larger one to assess demand. Alverson and colleagues [16] found that although they received many requests for telehealth services especially in rural areas (i.e., perceived need), in most instances there was not enough activity to hold monthly clinics on an ongoing basis (i.e., actual demand). In response they stipulated that baseline referral data be gathered prior to instituting a telehealth program for any given specialty. They developed associated assessment tools to determine the likelihood of a successful program [16].

2.11.2   Teleconsultation Models—Do You Need to Build Your Own Program?

If you have been tasked with organizing telehealth services for your institution, you may assume that you need to build a telehealth program "in house" from the ground up. However, given that telehealth providers can be in different locations than their patients there are several different models for organizing telehealth services. These include those offered within a single health-care organization, those offered between healthcare organizations, and those that offer telehealth services that are not part of a healthcare organization. Building a program "in house" has certain advantages like a single electronic health record, established referral patterns, no need to establish a business agreement with an outside organization, and an established legal framework for providing care. However, it may be less expensive, more efficient, and require less commitment to partner with an outside organization for some or all of your telehealth services. For more details see: http://www.telehealthresourcecenter.org/toolbox-module/organization-telemedicine-services.

2.12 Understanding Telehealth Technology

At the outset of your needs assessment it is important to familiarize yourself with the different types of telehealth technology that exist. Chapter 1 provides an overview of clinical videoconferencing technologies and infrastructures. However, there are a host of other existing and emerging technologies that constitute telehealth that can be used in tandem with clinical videoconferencing. Understanding the pros and cons of the wide spectrum of technologies that are available for telehealth is a prerequisite for starting or expanding telehealth programs across a large hospital system. It is important to understand the range of technology because finding the right technology will facilitate the clinical service you are trying to provide [17].

There are also legal and financial considerations that interact with technology choices. For example, clinical videoconferencing that is happening in real time may be treated differently than "store and forward telehealth," where some data is collected from the patient and then reviewed by a provider at a later time. Please keep in mind that as technology continues to advance rapidly, the range of technological solutions and the cost of those solutions are likely to change. A basic familiarity with the range of options is likely to increase the chance that, as the telehealth medical director, you will choose the right technology, at the right time, for the right application, patient population and business model. Chapter 1 provides information and links to a variety of resources regarding telehealth technology.

2.13 Operationalizing the Needs Assessment Process in Three Phases

Given the need for programming on a larger or more complex scale, the "Identify, Analyze, Decide" model we introduced in the beginning of the chapter should be operationalized in a more specific manner. The "Identify, Analyze, Decide" framework may have been adequate to help guide the needs assessment process for one small rural clinic interfacing with its networked medical center, but for larger systems-level programming, a more thorough rendering of the process is merited.

A general framework for assessing needs to inform a wide-spectrum of programs (e.g., construction projects, educational initiatives, vaccine availability programs) has been developed by Watkins and colleagues [1] in their work with the

World Bank. We have adapted and modified that framework, given the scientific telehealth literature, our experience in telehealth management, and the shared developing knowledge base of best practices in telehealth, to provide a guide to a telehealth needs assessment in three phases: pre-assessment, assessment, and post-assessment. Remember that this framework is not prescriptive and you should feel empowered to modify it based on your particular needs and constraints.

2.13.1   Needs Assessment Phase I: Pre-assessment

The pre-assessment phase defines participants and rules for the assessment, identifies specific targets for assessment, and defines what information will be necessary for a successful assessment. Table 2.7 provides the model and steps for the pre-assessment phase.

2.13.2   Needs Assessment Phase II(a)—Assessment and Data Collection

The assessment phase includes gathering already available information, planning for and collecting new information, monitoring the process, and organizing the data. Table 2.8 provides the model and steps for the assessment phase.

Only after a need is identified should possible telehealth initiatives (or non-telehealth initiatives) be generated and compared to close the gap. It is important to emphasize that needs do not equal "wants." More specifically, needs should not imply "wants" like more equipment, more funding, more training, or any other techniques used to achieve desired results. The suggestions of managers to get these things may end up being sound decisions to improve performance, but they are not needs as defined in this process [18]. Ryan Watkins and colleagues aptly note "For every performance problem there is a solution that is simple, straightforward, acceptable, understandable—and WRONG" [1]. Focus must be maintained on generating answers to the specific questions at hand, which will identify the need for and guide the development of specific CV programming.

A needs assessment is often an iterative process. The information that you generate and analyze from your first method of collecting data may help inform your prioritization of needs and offer clues about what other data collection tool(s) would help to fill in the gaps in information. Providing for course correction during the needs assessment process and multiple data collection methods can reduce bias by allowing the needs assessment team to triangulate the most accurate data and conclusions. A needs assessment, which relies on a strategic plan to define desired results, cannot afford to be rigid. Complex and ever changing realities demand flexibility. Flexibility is achieved by gathering information from multiple perspectives, considering a range of alternative solutions, and using techniques that give all partners input in the decision making process. It is better to make use of information to properly understand the true demand for services, than it is to rely on perceived need estimates.

Table 2.7 Clinical videoconferencing (CV) needs assessment phase I: pre-assessment (Synthesized and adapted from: Watkins et al. [1] and Martin [2])

1. Establish the overall process and scope of the needs assessment
a. Determine who should be the main collaborators in designing the needs assessment
b. Schedule a meeting and invite collaborators. Be sure to involve hospital leadership early in the process. Include members who will give the telehealth needs assessment team clinical credibility
c. Determine if you want to hire an outside expert or consultant to be part of the needs assessment team. This can be especially helpful if you are starting a new program or if you can find someone outside your organization who has already done what you are trying to do
d. Create an agenda and designate someone to facilitate the meeting
e. Sketch out the main goals, tasks and design of the needs assessment
f. Decide how decisions will be made about the implementation of the assessment; for larger needs assessments, create a steering committee to guide the process. Note that broad inclusion might invite perspectives far afield from your initial vision, at this point that is a strength
g. Decide what resources need to be allocated for the initial planning
2. Educate yourself and assessment team about non-clinical aspects of telehealth
a. Understand the range of telehealth technology options, their applications, pros, cons, and costs
b. Understand the legal and financial resources and requirements for telehealth initiatives in your state/region
3. Identify the primary clinical problems and opportunities that could be addressed through telehealth
a. Invite clinical staff to identify patient and provider service needs at both host and remote sites. Make sure invited staff represent both patient and provider sites
b. Identify and create a list of which needs may be met using telehealth in a brainstorming session
c. It is okay to be broad with your approach here initially as you will narrow down and assign priority based on data as you progress in your needs assessment
d. Determine how much of the community's unmet needs your team can handle. Are you going to limit your analysis to some specific telehealth application area or some targeted illness or staff need or a particular geographic location?
e. Keep in mind, during the assessment, more or different items may emerge later in the needs assessment process that were not part of your original brainstorming session
f. Prioritize items from this list that the needs assessment should cover
g. Identify which services you will target, which geographical regions you will serve, what modality of telehealth you are thinking of implementing
h. Go visit! There is no substitute for taking the time to visit your remote sites, meet with clinicians, and learn firsthand about their lives, patients, local opportunities, challenges, and concerns
4. Define the data requirements
a. Define the type of data required and sources of that information
b. Establish what data are not readily available, what you might want to collect, and what sources you plan to use
c. Consider what analysis methods may be used
d. Gather any preliminary data that is easily accessible
5. Create a management plan
a. Define objectives for the assessment
b. Prepare a time line and deadlines for tasks
c. Identify the assessment team members, roles, and responsibilities

Table 2.7 (continued)

6. Validate your needs assessment plan
a. Collaborators and steering committee members should review and critique the needs assessment plan
b. Gather feedback from others who will have a stake in the success of the assessment: other providers, patients, patients' families, administrators, community members, funding agencies, etc

One of the first tasks in a needs assessment is to identify those stakeholders both within and outside of your organization who will be useful partners in making a quality decisions, providing information, and participating in focus groups. In Siden's 1998 [7] paper he assesses the need for a telehealth link between several local community clinics and a tertiary-care medical center. The authors defined the "users" as "health care professionals, patients and families." They also noted that "community businesses, schools, provincial ambulance services, and health care administrators" were "stakeholders," but they determined that given the scope of the decisions to be made, or possibly the lack of resources to conduct a broader needs assessment, they would focus only on clinicians, patients and families [7]. In your role as medical director of telehealth you will want to include at least these three groups in your focus groups, but you may want to include others, especially health care administrators. Given the scope of your project you want to be sure that you have enough buy-in from all of the hospital leadership since you will need to enlist leadership across all the specialties that will be providing and referring to clinical videoconferencing services.

There are many different tools and techniques that can be used to gather data. It is beyond the scope of this chapter to discuss them all. However, Tables 2.9, 2.10, 2.11, 2.12, and 2.13 list some pros and cons of the most commonly used data collection techniques that are mentioned in the telehealth needs assessment literature [6, 7, 17, 19, 20, 21 and 22]. A detailed and useful discussion of these tools and several others are available through "A Guide to Assessing Needs" by Watkins et al. 2012 [1].

The purpose of conducting a document or data review is to review a variety of existing sources (for example, documents, reports, utilization data, and electronic medical records data) with the intention of collecting independently verifiable information. Table 2.9 outlines the potential benefits and drawbacks of data, document, or chart review.

The purpose of conducting interviews is to collect information from a single person. The formats of interviews can range from structured, to semi-structured, to unstructured. Table 2.10 outlines the potential benefits and drawbacks of conducting interviews.

The purpose of conducting focus groups is to collect information from a small group (for instance, 5–12 participants) in a systematic and structured format. An effective focus group is designed around a clear and specific goal. Note that in focus groups participants are not selected randomly, but instead are selected because

Table 2.8 CV Needs assessment phase II—assessment/data collection (Synthesized and adapted from: Watkins et al. [1] and Martin [2])

1. Plan the data collection effort
a. Collect existing data to be reviewed. A good guide to categories of existing data for review is provided by CTEC [2]: http://www.caltrc.org/knowledge-center/program-development/your-path-to-telehealth-success/
b. Decide on data collection methods to be used
c. Create data collection instruments: surveys, interview protocols, focus group questions, etc
d. Train data collectors (for example, facilitators of focus groups)
e. Schedule interviews, focus groups, performance observations, or other techniques to be used
2. Verify that the data collection instruments will identify information about gaps
a. Ensure that the information will be collected on both the current and desired results so you can identify gaps
b. Review the data collection techniques with team members so that everyone is aware of the critical information required
c. Obtain clearance from individuals or committees (for example, hospital institutional review board) for data collection instruments and plans if approval is necessary
3. Collect data
a. Manage the collection of data to ensure that all critical perspectives are represented
b. Check that the instruments, techniques, and sources represent varying perspectives about the primary performance issues
c. Review the functioning of assessment instruments and procedures early on to check for necessary adjustments, e.g., ceiling effects on Likert-type scales
d. Determine when assessment has enough information to move to the next task
e. Enter the collected data into a secure database or central location

they are most likely to represent the group being studied (i.e., patients, providers, administrative staff) [7]. Table 2.11 outlines the potential benefits and drawbacks of conducting focus groups.

The purpose of conducting dual-response surveys is to collect information from a large number of people—typically in multiple locations—regarding their perspectives on (1) current, and (2) desired performance. Question items typically allow for answers to be provided from both perspectives. Too often needs assessments assume that the desired performance is known and agreed upon by everyone in the organization when in reality this assumption is rarely the case. Table 2.12 outlines the potential benefits and drawbacks of using dual response surveys.

The purpose of conducting guided expert reviews is to gain informed perspectives from experts or consultants who are outside the system on which the needs assessment is focused. Table 2.13 outlines the potential benefits and drawbacks of conducting guided expert reviews.

2.13.3 Needs Assessment phase II(b)—Assessment/Data Analysis

A well thought out data analysis plan is crucial to getting the most out of the information collected. Needs assessment data come from varied sources and

Table 2.9 Pros and cons of data, document, or chart review (Synthesized and adapted from: Watkins et al. [2] and Martin [1])

Advantages	Disadvantages
The information contained in existing data or documents is often independently verifiable	Information in the documents or data may represent a perspective that is not aligned with your needs assessment project
The document or data review process can be done independently without having to solicit extensive input from other sources	You may want epidemiology records by township, but they are only available by county or state
Obtaining existing data is typically less expensive than collecting the data on your own	Obtaining and analyzing necessary documents can be time consuming
Existing data can establish a current level or scale of services to judge the gap between needs and the availability of healthcare	You can't control the quality of data collected and must rely on the information provided in the documents to assess quality and usability of the sources

Table 2.10 Pros and cons of interviews as a source of data (Synthesized and adapted from: Watkins et al. [2] and Martin [1])

Advantages	Disadvantages
Allows for focused discussions, immediate clarification, and follow-up questions	Time required can be significant
Individuals may share information they wouldn't in a group	Difficult to interview many sources, limits scope/sample for data collection
Can be excellent source of rich information, stories, and context	Interviews may contradict each other or be difficult to analyze
Can observe the nonverbal behavior of an interviewee	Interviewees may be biased or narrow minded

Table 2.11 Pros and cons of focus groups as a source of data (Synthesized and adapted from: Watkins et al. [2] and Martin [1])

Advantages	Disadvantages
Multiple people can be interviewed at once	Group members may not contribute equally; biased by dominant voices
Members can build on each other's comments and reactions	Risk of "groupthink" that can divert conversation away from productive topics
Can develop consensus about difficult decisions like prioritizing needs	Discussions may take too long to highlight all relevant topics/viewpoints
Can help to identify different perspectives and highlight pros and cons of a position	Participants may not feel comfortable sharing sensitive information or views
	If facilitator is not experienced group can easily get "off task"

perspectives, and in different formats; identifying patterns and converging trends, and doing so accurately without bias can be difficult. Table 2.14 outlines analysis methods.

Table 2.12 Pros and cons of duel response surveys as a source of data (Synthesized and adapted from: Watkins et al. [2] and Martin [1])

Advantages	Disadvantages
Captures perspectives of multiple groups	Relies on perceptions so not objective like performance data
Captures data regarding both current and desired levels of performance, i.e., needs	Typically low response rate
Easy, inexpensive to deploy, can collect via web-based methods or over email	No follow up question opportunity
Measures size and direction of needs	Good survey development and analysis often requires skill and experience
Can measure perspective of participants associate with needs	
Flexible format allows for open-ended and close ended questions	

Table 2.13 Pros and cons of expert reviews as a source of data (Synthesized and adapted from: Watkins et al. [2] and Martin [1])

Advantages	Disadvantages
Provides new ideas and fresh insights	Difficult to determine criteria for selecting experts
Increases credibility which can increase buy-in	Experts views may not be relevant
Can inspire confidence for unconventional approach	Expert can be biased. Multiple experts may mitigate this
Can benchmark against other similar systems	Can be expensive
Can save time by outsourcing work	

2.13.4 Closing Out Needs Assessment Phase II; Knowing When You Have Enough Data

Determining when you have enough information to make informed and justifiable decisions depends on the complexity and consequences of those decisions. An indicator that you have collected enough data is when your findings repeat themselves and you don't feel like you are getting new information. For researchers, guidelines about applying statistical standards for sample sizes or confidence intervals are generally clear. However, in a needs assessment, data from one knowledgeable and experienced staff member may be worth more than survey results from 50 randomly selected staff members. The goal of your needs assessment is to inform a decision, which gives you leeway in determining when enough data have been collected. However, as decisions increase in importance, you may want to examine the statistical standards for sample size and related confidence intervals in the analysis of quantitative data. For example, if your needs assessment seeks to identify the needs of the diabetic population across your region, and if you determine that a survey is among the data-collection tools that you will use gather necessary information, then it would be important to work with a statistician to determine the appropriate sampling procedures, sample size, and related confidence intervals before conducting the survey.

Table 2.14 Phase II(b)—assessment and data analysis (Synthesized and adapted from: Watkins et al. [2] and Martin [1])

1. Determine gaps (needs) by analyzing current and desired results
   a. Define the difference between what you currently do and what you envision doing
   b. Describe the current patient, health care services, and provider environment (i.e. what your organization does now) and identify the new or augmented patient healthcare services, and provider environment that will be supported by telemedicine programs (i.e. what you want to do) in the future
   c. Explain what is needed to bridge the "gap" by describing all new or expanded clinical services, the anticipated telemedicine delivery model and high-level technology, provider and other requirements
   d. Verify that the information collected from qualitative techniques (for example, interviews and focus groups) is included in the analysis
   e. Ensure that comparisons between current and desired results use equivalent information (for example, comparing apples to apples)
2. Prioritize gaps (needs)
   a. Use information collected to prioritize gaps
   b. Prioritize gaps according to size, scope, distinguishing characteristics, relative importance and other criteria
   c. Review the prioritized list with the assessment team members and the steering committe
   d. Collect additional information, if required, to refine the prioritization
3. Identify how telehealth can help to address priority gaps (needs)
   a. Identify two or more potential telehealth initiatives that can be used to improve the results identified with each high priority gap
4. Evaluate the potential telehealth initiatives using agreed-upon criteria so you can determine which are most likely to lead to desired improvements
   a. Establish criteria to be used for judging the potential value of each telehealth initiative
   b. Some things to consider as possible items for criteria include:
      i.   Which initiative addresses the greatest need?
      ii. Which initiative will have the biggest impact?
      iii. Which initiative is the most feasible?
      iv. Which initiative has the greatest institutional support?
      v.   Which initiative is most in line with organization's strategic plan?
      vi. Which initiative is the most sustainable?
   c. Be aware that there may be important business and legal considerations to take into account when providing medical services over distance. This is especially true if a telehealth network is being planned that aims to provide service across state lines, or on a national basis
   d. Have the assessment team review the assessment criteria
   e. Judge each potential telehealth initiative using the agreed-upon criteria
5. Recommend telehealth initiatives that will best achieve the desired results
   a. Review all of the information collected and the results of the analyses
   b. Summarize the findings
   c. Recommend telehealth initiatives that are likely to achieve success

Although not collecting enough information is one risk in conducting a needs assessment, another risk is the temptation to continue collecting data in lieu of making a decision. Do not settle for the first one or two possible solutions that arise. Press on and listen to what people are telling you during the needs assessment. At the same time, be discerning about the practical constraints that limit your range of possible solutions.

Table 2.15 Needs assessment phase III—post-assessment (Synthesized and adapted from: Watkins et al. [1] and Martin [2])

1. Summarize your recommendations in a report or presentation
a. Summarize the assessment of potential telehealth initiatives to address each high priority gap (need)
b. Take into account the social, political, technological, cultural, legal, financial and ethical factors that influence recommendations and decisions
c. Review and revise the summary on the basis of feedback from the assessment steering committee
2. Communicate your draft findings to your stakeholders
a. Before releasing the final copy of your needs assessment report, share the findings with stakeholders for review and comment
b. If you relied significantly on data from a few individuals, make sure to have them review the draft report as well
3. Perform a "readiness assessment" to verify that you have "buy in" for the recommendations in your needs assessment
4. Integrate information and document the needs assessment effort
a. Write a summary or full report to communicate the needs assessment steps, decisions, and recommendations
b. Integrate information from your readiness assessment into the recommendations in your report
c. Be mindful of the size and scale of the program you plan on creating. Stay focused on making an initial few sites successful. Starting small can help guarantee success
d. Remember that the needs assessment should be able to be integrated with a program model, business plan, implementation plan, and evaluation monitoring that will follow
e. Create a presentation to communicate the needs assessment recommendations or decisions
f. Send copies to all stakeholders as well as others who provided assistance during the needs assessment

2.14 Needs Assessment Phase III—Post-Assessment

The post-assessment phase is characterized by reported writing and revision based on stakeholder and data source feedback, attaining buy-in from relevant parties, assessing institutional readiness for the solutions the needs assessment process synthesized, and effectively presenting findings to all involved. A needs assessment of the scale presented here is a major undertaking and will likely be informing significant resource commitment. Accordingly, taking the time to thoughtfully complete the suggested work in phase III is a wise investment of time. Table 2.15 outlines the model and steps for the post assessment phase.

2.14.1 Assessing Your Organization's Readiness to Adopt Clinical Videoconferencing

As you finish your needs assessment you will begin to anticipate implementing your recommendations for a telehealth program. Knowing if your organization is ready for the challenges of implementation is essential in a large telehealth program launch. The best time to assess the readiness of your organization is *before* you implement the program. This is your opportunity to identify any serious barriers to implementation. Implementing a telehealth program means an organizational restructuring that will require people to change their behavior. The right technology will not, by itself, ensure that clinical videoconferencing will be fully adopted and utilized. The willingness of an organization and its employees to change and embrace new ways of working is an important thing to assess, or at least not to ignore. When change efforts fail it is often the result of leaders who have not sufficiently assessed an organization's readiness to change. As is the case with a needs assessment, a readiness assessment can be as simple or as comprehensive as needed. Early involvement in the needs assessment design process can generate political good will that might help in the adoption of these programs [2, 7].

In your role as director of telehealth for your large hospital system, you wonder if the clinicians and patients in your organization will be ready and willing to accept, adopt, integrate, and sustain a large telehealth program. A review of the literature reveals that there are a number of readiness assessment techniques [19, 20] and some have been developed with preformatted forms that can be filled out [2, 23, 24]. For an example see: http://www.caltrc.org/knowledge-center/program-development/your-path-to-telehealth-success/. Chapter 6, Sect. 6.4, *Assessing Alignment of Goals,* provides another resource to consult regarding considering an organization's readiness for specific new programming.

Conclusion

While the field of telehealth continues to change rapidly through new developments in technology, regulation and reimbursement, the value of a well planned and executed needs assessment will most likely persist. Despite the changing landscape of telehealth, the basic process of identifying the needs of a population and developing services to respond to those needs is foundational for implementation. We are moving into a future with new and emerging technologies for extending the reach of clinicians and connecting them with patients. Doing a proper needs assessment to select the optimal telehealth solution may become even more relevant in this future. In addition, more data is being collected through electronic medical records, email and text, social networking forums and mobile applications. Given this increased scope and quantity of data, perhaps some of the tools we use to collect and analyze data may change or become more automated. As clinical videoconferencing becomes more ubiquitous, there may be less legal and reimbursement issues to navigate, and less effort expended on convincing providers and patients to be early adopters. Even so, given the ever increasing cost and myriad of choices in healthcare, assessing the most pressing needs of patients and providers by using a strategy to prioritize needs and possible solutions will continue to be an essential function for telehealth in the coming years.

References

1. Watkins R, Meiers M, Visser Y. A guide to assessing needs: essential tools for collecting information, making decisions, and achieving development results. Washington, DC: The World Bank; 2012.

2. Martin C. The CTEC telehealth program developer kit: a roadmap for successful telehealth program development. 2012. https://www.nrtrc.org/content/article-files/Business%20 Plans/2012%20Program%20Developer%20Kit%20-%20Part%201.pdf. Accessed 12 June 2014.

3. Murray E, May C, Mair F. Development and formative evaluation of the E-Health Implementation Toolkit (e-HIT). BMC Med Inform Decis Mak. 2010;10(1):61. doi:10.1186/1472-6947-10-61.

4. Nutt PC. Investigating the success of decision making processes. J Manag Stud. 2008;45(2):425–55. doi:10.1111/j.1467-6486.2007.00756.x.

5. Effective Interventions Unit. Needs assessment: a practical guide to assessing local needs for services for drug users. Edinburgh: Scottish Executive; 2004. http://www.scotland.gov.uk/ Publications/2004/01/18783/32014.

6. Moeckli J, Cram P, Cunningham C, Reisinger HS. Staff acceptance of a telemedicine intensive care unit program: a qualitative study. J Crit Care. 2013;28(6):890–901. doi:10.1016/j. jcrc.2013.05.008.

7. Siden HB. Community and provider needs assessment in a telehealth project to. Telemed J. 1998;4(3):225–35.

8. Shore JH. Stage 1: needs identification. Telemental Health Guide. http://www.tmhguide.org/ site/epage/93817_871.htm. Accessed 10 April 2014.

9. Licensure and Scope of Practice. Telehealth Resour Cent. http://www.telehealthresourcecenter.org/toolbox-module/licensure-and-scope-practice. Accessed 6 May 2014.

10. Telemedicine Report to Congress. 1997:37–39. http://www.ntia.doc.gov/legacy/reports/ telemed/cover.htm. Accessed 3 May 2014.

11. Ryan Haight Online Pharmacy Consumer Protection Act of 2008. 110th Congress. 2008. https://www.govtrack.us/congress/bills/110/hr6353/text. Accessed 14 June 2014.

12. Telemental Health Institute. 2014. http://telemental.org/. Accessed 8 April 2014.

13. Alverson DC, Holtz B, D'Iorio J, DeVany M, Simmons S, Poropatich RK. One size doesn't fit all: bringing telehealth services to special populations. Telemed E-Health. 2008;14(9):-957–64. doi:10.1089/tmj.2008.0115.

14. Jackson GL, Krein SL, Alverson DC, et al. Defining core issues in utilizing information technology to improve access: evaluation and research agenda. J Gen Intern Med. 2011;26(Suppl 2):623–7. doi:10.1007/s11606-011-1789-3.

15. Scott RE, Mars M. Principles and framework for eHealth strategy development. J Med Internet Res. 2013;15(7):e155.

16. Alverson DC, Shannon S, Sullivan E, et al. Telehealth in the trenches: reporting back from the frontlines in rural America. Telemed J E Health. 2004;10(Suppl 2):S-95–109.

17. Clark G, Yarborough BJ. Evaluating the promise of health IT to enhance/expand the reach of mental health services. Gen Hosp Psychiatry. 2013;35(4):339–44. doi:10.1016/j.genhosppsych.2013.03.013.

18. Kaufman R, Guerra-Lopez I. Needs assessment for organizational success. Alexandria: ASTD Press; 2013.

19. Khoja S, Durani H, Schoot R, Sajwani A, Piryani U. Conceptual framework for development of a comprehensive e-health evaluation tool. Telemed J E Health. 2013;19(1):48–53.

20. Légaré É, Vincent, Lehoux P, et al. Telehealth readiness assessment tools. J Telemed Telecare. 2010;16:107–9. doi:10.1258/jtt.2009.009004.

21. Levy S, Bradley DA, Swanston MT. The technology prescription: linking telecare and informatics by using a need-led paradigm. Health Informatics J. 2002;8(2):88–94. doi:10.1177/146045820200800206.
22. Oliver DR, Demiris G, Fleming DA, Edison K. A needs assessment study for the Missouri Tele-hospice Project. AMIA 2003 Annual Symposium Proceedings; 2003:959.
23. Telehealth Readiness Assessment for Mandated First Nations Health Organization's in BC. http://www.google.com/url?sa=t&rct=j&q=&esrc=s&source=web&cd=1&ved=0CCsQFj AA&url=http%3A%2F%2Fwww.phsa.ca%2FNR%2Frdonlyres%2F93E2CE88-13DA47 BC91A91F3D95D8FB9A%2F0%2FMFNHO_Readiness_Assessment_Protocol_FINAL_ Nov051.pdf&ei=U1eU4jsJXwyAH4pYGoDQ&usg=AFQjCNEcNfSus4a106oSbhS5nZW6 wsoASg&sig2=jFXAc74Jqnedlsbym4M-EA&bvm=bv.65397613,d.aWc. Accessed 10 April 2014.
24. Waters P, Schwalbe L, Hartje J. Telehealth capacity assessment tool TCAT (1–22). 2013. http://www.nfarattc.org. Accessed 2 May 2014.

Chapter 3
Common Elements of the Expert Consensus Guidelines for Clinical Videoconferencing

Joah L. Williams, Peter W. Tuerk and Ron Acierno

Chapter Summary

Purpose   This chapter identifies common elements of various expert consensus guidelines for clinical videoconferencing (CV) services. We broadly conceptualize common elements as shared recommendations or themes addressed in the majority of published organizational guidelines (in this case, as identified in at least five of the nine major sets of national-level guidelines). Practice recommendations are discussed in the context of these common elements, specific guidelines are highlighted that represent the shared intention of common themes, and basic core requirements of CV programming are synthesized. We close the chapter by discussing notable variability among the guidelines pertaining to specific issues.

Context   Several professional organizations and agencies have published guides addressing the clinical, technical, and administrative standards applicable to CV-based health services. This information is useful for clinic managers and clinicians attempting to integrate CV into their practice in that these guidelines offer practical strategies for developing safe, patient-centered programs. Yet, a large amount of content related to expert consensus guidelines is available and not all guidelines are

J. L. Williams (✉)
Medical University of South Carolina, Charleston, SC, USA
e-mail: wiljoah@musc.edu

P. W. Tuerk
Department of Psychiatry and Behavioral Sciences, Medical University of South Carolina;
Mental Health Service, Ralph H. Johnson VA Medical Center, Veterans Health Administration, Charleston, SC, USA
e-mail: Tuerk@musc.edu

R. Acierno
College of Nursing, Medical University of South Carolina, Charleston, SC, USA

© Springer International Publishing Switzerland 2015   55
P. W. Tuerk, P. Shore (eds.), *Clinical Videoconferencing in Telehealth,*
Behavioral Telehealth, DOI 10.1007/978-3-319-08765-8_3

agreed on or pertinent to specific contexts. Accordingly, care is taken to represent commonalities of the various guidelines in order to provide a brief synopsis of the core recommendations considered to be essential across a majority of contexts. It is expected that managers and clinicians developing CV programming might use this information as a quick-reference base to begin considering CV procedures and policies, and then judge the merits of additional components from individual guidelines based on local programming needs and circumstances.

Tools   The chapter identifies and provides links to the expert consensus guidelines relevant to CV practice. Summary checklists of core similarities in the guidelines are provided related to CV technical considerations, physical set-up at the provider- and patient-end, clinical and administrative responsibilities, and specific provider behaviors that facilitate successful CV programming. Differences between the guidelines are also highlighted. While efforts have been taken in this volume to minimize the repetition of similar information presented across chapters, the current chapter represents somewhat of a departure from that rule given the overarching content matter. Accordingly, please note that most of the information summarized here is surveyed in much greater detail by the individually themed chapters.

3.1 Clinical Guidelines

Several national organizations have created expert consensus guidelines outlining best practices for CV services. Major guidelines and URLs for specific websites are provided by Table 3.1. Although some state associations have created telemental health and CV guidelines (e.g., Ohio Psychological Association; See: http://www.ohpsych.org/psychologists/files/2011/06/OPATelepsychologyGuidelines41710.pdf), in this section, we discuss common elements of the major expert guidelines published by national organizations. Common elements can be discerned across several categorical areas summarized in the following chapter subsections. However, the importance of individual recommendations should remain the primary focus here, rather than the accuracy of our taxonomy, which was defined merely for convenience and summary purposes. Table 3.2 provides a summary of the elements common to expert consensus guidelines for the provision of CV services.

3.1.1 Informed Consent

Clinicians providing CV services should maintain professional standards and follow ethical guidelines consistent with those that apply to clinical services received in-person. To that end, all existing guidelines stress the value of properly obtaining informed consent for engaging in CV health services.

Table 3.1 Major expert consensus guidelines for clinical videoconferencing and information links

American Academy of Child and Adolescent Psychiatry [1]	http://download.journals.elsevier-health.com/pdfs/journals/0890-8567/PIIS0890856708601549.pdf
American Psychological Association [2]	http://apacustomout.apa.org/commentcentral/commentcentralPDF/Site26_Telepsychology%20Guidelines%20Draft_July2012_posted.pdf
American Telemedicine Association—*practice guidelines for videoconferencing-based telemental health and practice guidelines for video-based online mental health services*[4]	http://www.americantelemed.org/resources/standards/ata-standards-guidelines/practice-guidelines-for-video-based-online-mental-health-services#.Ux9t4j9dXjU
American Telemedicine Association—*evidence based practice for telemental health* [3]	http://www.americantelemed.org/docs/default-source/standards/evidence-based-practice-for-telemental-health.pdf
APA/ASPPB/APA Insurance Trust Joint task force [7]	http://c.ymcdn.com/sites/www.asppb.net/resource/resmgr/guidelines/telepsychology_guidelines_ap.pdf
Australian Psychological Society [5]	http://aaswsocialmedia.wikispaces.com/file/view/EG-Internet.pdf
National Association of Social Workers [8]	www.socialworkers.org/practice/standards/naswtechnologystandards.pdf
New Zealand Psychologists Board (NZPB) [9]	http://psychologistsboard.org.nz/cms_show_download.php?id=141
U.S. Department of Defense [11]	http://t2health.org/sites/default/files/cth/guide-book/tmh-guidebook_06-11.pdf

Clinicians are responsible for obtaining written (i.e., via electronic format) informed consent from patients at the start of services and clinical managers are responsible for supporting those efforts with appropriate staffing or allocation of time-related resources. In some cases, an electronic signature from a patient or legal representative may be acceptable depending on the laws and regulations in the relevant jurisdictions. The American Telehealth Association (ATA) [4] practice guidelines specify that, along with information specific to CV contexts, informed consent should also include a discussion about the services to be provided, record keeping, potential risks, billing, billing documentation, privacy, confidentiality, and the limits of confidentiality. Accordingly, consent procedures for CV services are often performed along with, but in addition to standard consent processes. For example, a program offering CV-based cognitive behavioral treatment (CBT) will likely have one consent form regarding the nature of CBT, that is, discussion re-garding homework, treatment attendance, termination, etc., and another informed consent form related to the CV context of treatment.

Relevant to issues of privacy and confidentiality, the New Zealand Psychology Board [9] recommends that clinicians further discuss clear expectations or prohibi-tions with regard to recording CV sessions. In terms of videoconferencing-specific information to be reviewed during the consent process, both the American Psycho-logical Association (APA) [2] and the ATA [4] guidelines note that patients should be informed about the limits of confidentiality in electronic communications, es-pecially online communications, that may accompany CV services. Similarly,

Table 3.2 Common elements of the expert consensus guidelines

Technical considerations	Choose computers or mobile devices that support professional grade cameras or microphones or have built-in audio/video equipment
	Make sure that video software platforms have appropriate data security parameters
	Ensure that audio/video transmissions are secure using recognized encryption standards (see FIPS 140-2, the Federal Information Processing Standard)
Provider and patient locations	Select a room that is large enough to comfortably accommodate the provider/patient and videoconferencing equipment, including a large monitor, video camera, microphone, telephone, fax machine or scanner, desk, and chair(s)
	Minimize distractions by making sure that the videoconferencing room is not located near noisy office equipment, clinic waiting areas, closets, and/or construction sites
	Camera should be secure and stable to prevent shaking
	Camera should be at eye-level
	Room should be evenly lit with overhead lighting or lighting behind the camera
	Reduce extraneous light from windows or other sources such as lamps
	Place the microphone away from the telecommunication speaker to prevent an echo effect
	Providers and patients should both have access to privacy features, including audio and video muting
Specific to provider location	Consider placing a light blue screen directly behind the provider to help reduce glare
	Keep the room generally free from clutter and other distractions
	Use a stationary chair
Specific to patient location	Ensure enough space between the camera and the patients' chairs to optimize behavioral observations via videoconferencing equipment (especially when treating children who may move around during sessions)
	Ensure adequate privacy
Clinical and administrative responsibilities	Maintain familiarity with relevant laws and regulations regarding the provision of care both in the provider's jurisdiction and the jurisdiction where the patient is receiving services
	Account for sufficient time and resources for ongoing coordination with patient-side support and administrative staff
	Obtain written (i.e., via electronic format), informed consent from patients
	Be familiar with emergency procedures at the patient location/s
	Give patients provider's credential information, office address, and contact numbers
	If possible, collaborate with the patient to identify a Patient Support Person to assist in the event of an emergency
	When conducting psychological testing or assessment arrange for a proctor to verify the patient's identity
	When conducting psychological testing or assessment make sure the patient does not have internet or cell phone access during the testing

Table 3.2 (continued)

Clinician habits	Test the equipment at the provider location prior to each session
	Identify alternate ways of making contact in the event of a technology failure
	Engage in small-talk to enhance rapport with patients
	Maintain eye-contact by alternating gaze between the monitor and the camera
	Wear solid, dark colored clothing
	Avoid large pieces of jewelry that may cause visual distortions
	Verbal and nonverbal (e.g., hand gestures) communication should be more deliberate than in in-person interactions

clinicians should discuss the potential for technical failure and procedures for coordinating services in the event of technical problems. Chapter 7 provides an in-depth summary of the informed consent process in CV contexts and a thorough "turn-key" informed consent from template.

3.1.2   Emergency Service Planning

Most guidelines underscore the importance of planning for patient safety when providing services to patients at distant locations. ATA [4] guidelines offer some practical recommendations to providers in terms of emergency service planning for patients receiving services in both traditional institutional settings and nontraditional settings (e.g., home-based services). For example, if the patient is receiving telemental health services in a traditional institutional setting, other professionals may be readily available and the institution may have established emergency procedures. Providers should be familiar with the emergency procedures in place at such locations, including telephone numbers for clinical personnel at the remote site, room numbers where patients are being seen, and direct-line telephone numbers of remote site security personnel. If patients are receiving services in settings where trained professionals are not readily available, such as in home-based CV contexts, ATA follows recommendations developed by Shore [10] wherein providers collaborate with patients to identify a "Patient Support Person" who can be contacted in the event of an emergency and asked to dispatch local first responders. That is, they are not asked to attend to the emergency themselves, but rather to dial 911 and direct first responders to the emergency location. This accounts for the fact that remote providers cannot simply dial 911 and expect response capability in their client's location. In addition to the Patient Support Person, providers of nonclinic based services should also obtain and test call local first responder resource numbers to verify access to these services. In cases where a patient experiences recurrent emergencies, the APA/Association of State and Provincial Psychology Boards (ASPPB)/ APA Insurance Trust Joint Task Force guidelines [7] suggest that providers refer these patients to in-person services.

3.2   Physical Environment

Most existing guidelines offer recommendations for arranging the physical environment in such a way as to optimize the quality of the clinical encounter. Chapter 10 provides resources and discussion regarding methods to optimize CV settings and several helpful videos clearly illustrating key room and equipment configurations are also available online (e.g., "Telemedicine Room Design and Set-Up" produced by the California Telehealth Resource Center available at: http://www.youtube.com/CaliforniaTRC). Here, we summarize the relevant consensus recommendations, focusing on key noted elements of both the provider and patient environments).

3.2.1   Provider Location

Just as in-person clinical services should be provided in a quiet location to maximize patient confidentiality and attention, clinical services provided via videoconferencing technologies should be provided in a quiet room that minimizes the likelihood of other patients or staff overhearing the session. This is especially important considering that telecommunication speakers may enhance the voices of patients and therapists beyond what might occur in face-to-face contexts. Clinic managers should strive to minimize any extraneous sources of noise at the provider location, perhaps choosing CV rooms away from street noise or noise due to office equipment, which could interfere with the audio quality. Placing rooms near closets, storage areas, or construction sites are likely to amplify distractions through CV modalities. Room size and quality should also be considered, along with location. Repurposed rooms that used to serve a non-clinical function (such as storage closets often converted for CV use because only one person is required to fit in the space) must be carefully scrutinized along parameters such as comfort, design, and decoration.

In terms of the CV equipment, the camera should be on a secure platform, ideally at the same elevation as the eyes so that more natural interaction is possible. It is important that the camera is secure and stable so as to prevent vibration or shaking, which may interfere with the video quality and patient comfort during the session. Moreover, microphones should not be placed near speakers as this may result in an echo effect. While the videoconferencing equipment may be placed on a desk or table, current guidelines generally suggest that no other furniture or tables be placed between the provider and the camera as this may make the provider appear distant and adversely affect rapport. It may also make engaging in facial and other nonverbal communication more difficult. Clinicians and clinic managers should also be mindful of seating arrangements in front of the camera. Seating should be comfortable enough for providers to engage in videoconferencing services, but chairs that move or swivel may create distractions for the patient given that such movement can create video blurring. Therefore, clinicians and clinic managers are advised to use stationary chairs in the CV room.

It is also vitally important for CV environments to be lit evenly and sufficiently. Department of Defense [11] guidelines recommend nondirectional fluorescent lighting in order to avoid casting shadows on the provider's face. Some guidelines also recommend placing a light blue screen or backdrop behind the provider in order to minimize glare, although guidelines seem to differ somewhat as to whether using a backdrop is advisable. For example, AACAP [1] guidelines note that using a blue screen blocks the patient's view of the provider's office, which may make the encounter seem "sterile" for patients (p. 1477). If providers do not use a backdrop, however, the videoconferencing room should generally be free of clutter that may be distracting to patients. Items with patterns such as parallel black and white lines (including provider clothing or dress ties) should also be out of view of the camera since some patterns can impair picture quality.

3.2.2 Patient Location

Creating comfortable, private clinical environments at the patient location can be challenging given that many patients receive CV services outside of institutional settings. Indeed, this is an advantage of the technology. For example, many patients who live at a considerable distance from institutional locations may elect to receive these services at their home using personal computers, tablets, or other devices with CV capabilities. Therefore, clinicians should be prepared to adapt to different challenges that may arise in diverse patient locations.

Accordingly, most of the recommendations regarding physical environment at the provider location should also be used to optimize clinical environments at the patient location. For example, cameras should be placed on a secure, stable platform at eye-level with the patient, and the room should be evenly lit to ensure the best quality visual image for the provider. Providers should work with patients to reduce light from windows or other sources, especially when the source of the light is behind the patient and especially when working with patients who are receiving CV services in noninstitutional settings. However, providers should also work with patients to make sure that light sources are not directly in front of them—lighting directly in front of the patient may make her appear pale and similarly obscure important nonverbal information. AACAP [1] guidelines suggest that a light source placed directly behind the camera is preferable in terms of preserving the visual quality of the video. Again, we point out that many of these recommendations do not apply exclusively to the patient location and should also be considered when creating CV environments at the provider location as well. Thus, overhead lighting that does not cast shadows across the face of either patient or provider is best. For convenience, Table 3.2 organizes room set-up suggestions by items relevant for provider-side rooms, patient-side rooms, and shared items relevant to both provider- and patient-side rooms.

Rather than these preliminary guideline suggestions representing obstacles to care, providers are encouraged to conceptualize the establishment of optimal

CV settings as a collaborative team-building exercise that might jumpstart patient/provider alliance and set the stage for a successful course of intervention. The same is true for teams of providers working in different facilities.

Many potential issues involving CV in the home are related to other household members and the purpose of room. All the guidelines emphasize the importance of good communication, the identification of concerns and logistics up-front, and joint problem solving. Clinicians should make sure that patients inform the provider if another person is present in the room, and both providers and patients should agree to the presence of other people. Patients electing to receive home-based telehealth services should plan for sessions accordingly, making any necessary arrangements with family, friends, or other occupants in the home to have access to a private location for the duration of the session. For example, patients with small children at home may need to arrange for childcare during sessions so that children are not walking into the room during session time. In addition to making arrangements with other occupants in the patient's home, ATA's Evidence-Based Practice guidelines [3] recommend that patients using either home or clinic-based CV services have access to CV features such as audio and video muting in the spirit of maximizing patient privacy.

In some circumstances, several people may need to be present at the patient location, as when providers are working with children and their families. In such cases, providers need to make sure that the room at the patient location is large enough to comfortably accommodate all persons present and ensure that there is sufficient space between patients' chairs and the camera so that providers can still observe children who may move around the room during the session. Of course, creativity and flexibility are helpful in this process and the inability to meet all the parameters of physical room guidelines should not constitute a barrier to care, as perfection is often the enemy of good enough.

Special issues relevant to patient-end locations may also arise when performing psychological testing or ongoing assessments associated with the provision of services via CV. For example, if patients undergoing testing or assessment have access to cell phones or the internet, or are subjected to land lines ringing or knocks on the front door, then the validity of test results may be compromised. APA's [2] proposed guidelines recommend that clinicians performing CV-based assessments coordinate with staff at the patient location to help ensure the security of any testing materials and verify the identity of the patient. APA/ASPPB/APA Insurance Trust Joint Task Force guidelines [7] add that clinicians should be mindful of any sensory distractions in terms of sight, sound, or smell at the patient location that could affect assessment performance. Again, coordinating with staff or family members at the patient location may help minimize any such distractions that could compromise the validity of assessment procedures.

In cases where psychological treatment is being provided, clinicians may wish to have patient's complete self-report symptom measures to monitor patient outcomes. To this end, providers need to make sure that patients have access to computers with printers or fax machines to allow for easy transfer of assessment measures

[6]. Alternatively, providers can read assessment measures aloud to patients, and/or patients can read aloud their responses to providers in real-time. See Chap. 10 for more in-depth discussion of material exchange.

3.3   Provider Habits

Provider habits play a critical role in building rapport with patients, especially at the initiation of CV services. Thus, many existing guidelines provide specific recommendations regarding provider habits that may be helpful in CV contexts. These recommendations include tips for preparing for sessions. For example, providers may wish to test their equipment at both the provider and patient locations prior to sessions to ensure that the audio and video are functioning properly. As mentioned previously, providers and clinic managers should reduce any extraneous sources of noise that may interfere with the audio quality of the session, and providers may be able to partially achieve this goal by placing a sign on the outside of the door prior to the session to remind others to avoid creating excess noise.

At the beginning of each session, and especially during introductory sessions with patients who may be unaccustomed to using CV technologies, providers may wish to first discuss relatively basic topics. These topics might cover how the sessions will work, what to do in the event of a signal loss, or what to do in the event of overwhelming feelings or emotions. Moreover, providers should invite and address any questions about the medium patients may have as a way of letting patients gradually feel more comfortable with videoconferencing, prior to broaching topics of significant emotional intensity. ATA's Evidence-Based Practice guidelines [3] suggest that a "more casual clinical style" may initially help clinicians build rapport with patients, but, even within the context of a casual clinical style, guidelines [5] remind clinicians to use professional language to maintain appropriate boundaries. Providers should also maintain appropriate eye contact with patients but need to be aware that, in order to appear to be looking at the patient, they must be looking at the camera. It should go without saying that checking email or frequently looking away will be disruptive to therapeutic rapport. If cameras are not at eye level, or are not positioned near monitors so that looking at the patient is akin to looking at the camera, providers should alternate their gaze between the monitor and the camera, and even state that they are doing this during the first session to assure patients that they are, in fact, focused on what they are saying. Furthermore, it is important for providers to be mindful of not just what the patient can see during the session but what the patient cannot see. That is, providers may take notes or refer to notes during the session, but, if the patient cannot see this, the provider may appear distracted to the patient. In other words, what may be patently obvious in face-to-face sessions should sometimes be explained in CV sessions. Patients may benefit, then, from being able to see what the provider is doing, or from frank disclosures such as "I may seem to look away from you but I want you to know I am taking notes on what you are saying." These general suggestions are summaries of the consensus guidelines but providers are also encouraged to see Chap. 10 for more comprehensive checklists regarding provider preparation before and during initial CV sessions.

In terms of communication, AACAP [1] guidelines in particular highlight that communication during CV should be "more deliberate and animated to overcome impediments to perception" (p. 1478). Therefore, providers should be sure that speech production is slower and more deliberate than usual. As part of an informal survey of telehealth experts regarding issues pertinent to clinical practice and research, experts generally commented that providers and patients may need to alter their conversational style as well, so as to intentionally increase back and forth dialog [6]. Likewise, motor gestures should be slower than usual in order to prevent pixilation that may occur when movement is too rapid. Hand gestures should also be at or above chest-level, again to ensure that patients are able to see the gestures.

A final issue to consider regarding provider habits is attire. Clothing with complex patterns, such as stripes or plaids, or large, dangling jewelry should generally be avoided as they may cause visual distortions. Department of Defense (DOD)[11] guidelines state that the best way for providers to preserve the quality of the video image is to wear dark, solid colored clothing during sessions.

3.4   Technical and Administrative Guidelines

Many practice guidelines are weighted toward providing information regarding the actual practices of service providers rather than technical and administrative issues. However, existing guidelines also provide a range of recommendations addressing a broad array of technical and administrative issues. Even so, diversity in focus, adapting healthcare climates, and changing technology makes it challenging to collate specific helpful common elements in the non-provider oriented realms. We review a few frequently mentioned practice recommendations here in an effort to draw attention to these important general suggestions and encourage providers to be knowledgeable about issues pertinent to each domain. For more in-depth discussions, readers are referred to Chap. 1 for technological issues, and Chaps. 4 and 5 for comprehensive administrative guidelines in-line with scientific findings and current practice norms.

3.4.1   Technical Guidelines

Because the success of CV depends on the technology being used, clinic managers and clinicians should be careful to choose devices (e.g., computers, mobile devices) that can either support high quality equipment, such as professional grade cameras or microphones, or have adequate built-in audio/video equipment. Of course, high resolution cameras will require higher bandwidth, and available bandwidth will determine hardware selections. ATA [4] notes that any video software platforms used for CV should also have appropriate data security parameters, and necessary steps should be taken to ensure that audio/video transmissions are secure using recognized encryption standards, for example "FIPS 140-2," which is the common moniker referring to encryption standards as laid out in the Federal Information Processing Standard Publication. It is not important for clinical managers or providers to understand the nuances of encoding, but vendors of CV equipment and software should be asked if their systems are FIPS 140-2 compliant, especially, if the system is intended for use in federal healthcare domains. Moreover, both providers and patients should have reliable internet access, and, when possible, wired connections should be used instead of wireless connections to prevent problems with connectivity and to enhance security [4]. When possible, have technical support staff available at both the provider and patient locations.

3.4.2 Administrative Guidelines

As with in-person services, clinicians providing CV services should be licensed and credentialed (or otherwise qualified) to provide services within their specialty area. However, a unique challenge with CV is that these services are often provided to patients that may be outside of the jurisdiction where the provider is licensed. Some states have adopted or are adopting specific telemedicine-related laws, and providers should make efforts to be aware of relevant laws and regulations in their jurisdiction and the jurisdiction where their patient is receiving services [2]. For state-specific information see APA's Practice—Legal & Regulatory Affairs Telepsychology 50-State Review, available at: http://www.apapracticecentral.org/update/2013/10-24/telepsychology-review.aspx, and Chap. 4 for discussion and links related to specific state regulations.

In addition to considerations for practicing outside one's jurisdiction, clinicians who intend to provide prescriptions for controlled substances via internet-based psychiatric services, must adhere to the federal law outlined in the Ryan Haight Online Pharmacy Consumer Protection Act of 2008 (available at: http://www.justice.gov/archive/olp/pdf/hr-6353-enrolled-bill.pdf). The law requires clinicians to conduct a face-to-face visit with the patient prior to commencing any prescription for controlled substances via the internet. One exception is for United States Federal Agencies, whereby clinicians may conduct the first face-to-face visit via clinic-based CV. Readers are strongly encouraged to thoroughly review the Ryan Haight Act to determine which part of the law may or may not pertain to the clinician and/or agency they serve.

3.5   Divergences Among the Expert Consensus Guidelines

Despite common elements across organizational guidelines, there is a great deal of variability among guidelines in terms of specific practice recommendations. For example, some providers in clinical practice prefer to meet with patients in-person prior to beginning CV-based telemental health services, but few organizational guidelines (APA, AACAP, APA/ASPPB/APAIT, NZPB) advise arranging an initial in-person meeting [9, 2, 7, 1]. While none of the guidelines mandate initial, in-person contact, there is consensus that an in-person assessment may be helpful when conducting initial evaluations (especially if there is concern that low-bandwidth or technological problems may undermine clinical assessment or if there is concern about the suitability of CV for a given client). Of course, requiring in-person initial contact recreates the barriers to care that CV technology is supposed to address.

Another area of divergence concerns enlisting a "Patient Support Person" in emergency service planning. ATA [4] guidelines specifically recommend collaborating with a "Patient Support Person" when providing services outside the institutional settings, and, similarly, both the Australian Psychological Society [5] and APA/ASPPB/APAIT Joint Task Force [7] guidelines suggest that, when possible, providers keep in contact with a close family member or another support person to assist with emergency response planning. Other guidelines highlight the importance of working with providers or personnel at clinic-based patient sites in emergency service planning but do not specifically discuss the issue of proactively collaborating with family or community members in planning for potential emergency services.

Current organizational guidelines also differ in the issue of data security. Some guidelines explicitly recommend the use of encryption during any and all CV activities that take place online [4, 1]. Other guidelines, however, only go as far as noting that encryption protocols are necessary when identifiable patient data such as "patient records or forms" are transmitted [11]. Again, many of these divergences likely reflect the challenges in keeping guidelines up-to-date in the context of rapidly changing technological and health care environments.

Conclusion

Telehealth technologies are becoming an increasingly popular and vital part of clinical practice. As more systems of care start to adopt these practices, there is a greater need for clinic managers and clinicians to more easily integrate common elements of existing expert consensus guidelines in an effort to create sustainable telehealth programs. It is hoped that following guidelines will maximize patient care and minimize provider burden without reinventing the wheel. In this chapter, we integrated many of the common elements of guidelines derived from clinical practice and experience. We hope that following these guidelines will help both seasoned and novice CV providers avoid some obvious, albeit common, pitfalls that may be encountered when creating telehealth programs. For example, when establishing our own CV telehealth program, we did not fully communicate that a janitorial supply closet was re-purposed as a telehealth treatment room. While the appearance of cleaning supplies along the walls was a source of humorous discussion each week, between the patient and provider, the significance of our failure to broadly communicate the room's new function to facility staff was made clearly evident when janitorial staff interrupted several exposure therapy sessions in the ensuing days to retrieve cleaning supplies. Hopefully, after reading this chapter, this will be less likely to happen at your practice site.

References

1. American Academy of Child and Adolescent Psychiatry. Practice parameter for telepsychiatry with children and adolescents. J Am Acad Child Adolesc Psychiatry. 2008;47(12):1468–83.
2. American Psychological Association. Guidelines for the practice of telepsychology. American Psychological Association. 2012. http://apacustomout.apa.org/commentcentral/commentcentralPDF/Site26_posted.pdf. Accessed 11 Dec. 2013.
3. American Telemedicine Association. Evidence-based practice for telemental health. American Telemedicine Association. 2009. http://www.americantelemed.org/docs/default-source/standards/evidence-based-practice-for-telemental-health.pdf. Accessed 11 March 2014.
4. American Telemedicine Association. Practice guidelines for video-based online mental health services. American Telemedicine Association. 2013. http://www.americantelemed.org/practice/standards/ata-standards-guidelines/practice-guidelines-for-video-based-online-mental-health-services. Accessed 11 Dec 2013.
5. Australian Psychological Society. Guidelines for providing psychological services and products using the internet and telecommunications technologies. Australian Psychological Society. 2011. http://aaswsocialmedia.wikispaces.com/file/view/EG-Internet.pdf. Accessed 11 March 2014.
6. Gros D, Morland L, Frueh B, et al. Delivery of evidence-based psychotherapy via video telehealth. J Psychopathol Behav Assess. 2013;35(4):506–21.
7. Joint Task Force for the Development of Telepsychiatry Guidelines for Psychologists. Guidelines for the practice of telepsychology. Am Psychol. 2013;68(9):791–800.
8. National Association of Social Workers and Association of Social Work Boards. Standards for technology and social work practice. National Association of Social Workers. 2005. http://www.socialworkers.org/practice/standards/naswtechnologystandards.pdf. Accessed 11 Dec. 2013.
9. New Zealand Psychologists Board. Draft guidelines: psychology services delivered via the internet and other electronic media. New Zealand Psychologists Board. 2011. http://psychologistsboard.org.nz/cms_show_download.php?id=141. Accessed 11 March 2014.
10. Shore P. Home-based telemental health (HBTMH): standard operating procedures manual. VA Psychology Leadership Conference. 2011. http://conference.avapl.org/pubs/2012%20Conference%20Presentations/HBTMH%20SOP_Shore_11-12-11%20copy.pdf. Accessed 11 Dec. 2013.
11. U.S. Department of Defense, National Center for Telehealth & Technology. DOD telementalhealth guidebook. National Center for Telehealth & Technology. 2011. http://t2health.org/sites/default/files/cth/guidebook/tmh-guidebook_06-11.pdf. Accessed 11 Dec. 2013.

Chapter 4
Policy Development, Procedures, and Tools for Navigating Regulations

Elizabeth A. Krupinski

Chapter Summary

Purpose: This chapter addresses policy development, procedures, and tools with respect to behavioral clinical videoconferencing (CV) practice. Particular attention is given to tips and tools that are useful in relation to institutional, regulatory, and legal entities when establishing or promoting a behavioral telehealth practice.

Context: The information is necessary for clinical managers and/or clinicians because navigating regulatory requirements, including the writing of new institutional policies, presents a common barrier for CV program development, especially for frontline clinicians and managers, whose expertise may lie outside the specialized realm of policy development.

Tools: The chapter provides the following tools: References and links to existing relevant resources, a primer on Medicaid reimbursement for CV, a list of relevant CPT codes for CV, a template for constructing telehealth agreements between facilities (Memoranda of Understanding), ethical considerations and provider selection/competence considerations, a list of procedures for impacting policy at your local institution and/or state laws concerning CV, strategies for overcoming resistance to change, and templates for promoting legislative initiatives.

4.1 Introduction

Telemedicine is rapidly becoming a part of mainstream medicine after what is actually a relatively long history of starts and stops leading up to the present level of implementation and successful expansion [1]. There are however a number of

E. A. Krupinski (✉)
Arizona Telemedicine Program & Southwest Telehealth Resource Center,
University of Arizona, Tucson, AZ, USA
e-mail: krupinski@radiology.arizona.edu

© Springer International Publishing Switzerland 2015
P. W. Tuerk, P. Shore (eds.), *Clinical Videoconferencing in Telehealth,*
Behavioral Telehealth, DOI 10.1007/978-3-319-08765-8_4

significant barriers preventing complete and widespread use of telemedicine. One of these barriers (in the USA and internationally) is policy, which encompasses everything from licensure, credentialing, reimbursement, to what types of interactions are allowed via telemedicine and by whom [2–6]. A recent review of the telemedicine policy literature identified 99 policy issues that fell into nine broad themes: (1) networked care, (2) inter-jurisdictional practice, (3) diffusion/digital divide, (4) integration with existing systems, (5) response to new initiatives, (6) goal-setting for policy, (7) evaluation and research, (8) investment, and (9) ethics [7]. In order for e-Health and telemedicine to succeed these issues must be addressed at the global, national, and local levels. It should be noted that these are broad issues and only a few are likely to directly impact a given telehealth program. In fact, many of these issues are being addressed by a number of professional societies and organizations like the American Telemedicine Association that have a presence on Capitol Hill and are lobbying actively for changes and direction in all of these areas.

In recent years in the USA, the Health Information Technology for Economic and Clinical Health Act (HITECH) (part of Title XIII of the American Recovery and Reinvestment Act) of 2009 and the Patient Protection and Affordable Care Act (ACA) of 2011 [8] have provided a significant impetus for modern telemedicine in large part by promoting the "Meaningful Use" of Electronic Health Records (EHR) and other technologies in health care [8, 9]. There is, however, a lot of work that needs to be done at the federal, state, and local levels. The question is, how can those involved in telemedicine effectively and efficiently promote policy changes at the local level?

4.2 Policy-Related Basics for Establishing Clinical Video Conferencing (CV) in Your Institution or Private Practice

Much of this chapter will be devoted to providing readers with the resources and knowledge to challenge or advocate for policy changes to expand CV services. However, many providers and clinical managers may already be empowered to establish or expand CV services in their institutions or private practices, but may lack the experience to know where to begin. Accordingly, before we consider effective methods of advocacy for policy change, we will briefly address the basic realms of formal policy necessary to support CV programming and identify where in this chapter and volume specific relevant information can be found for program development. Whereas, it is not necessary for formal written program policy to reproduce in great detail all the administrative and clinical protocols needed to support CV services; it is helpful for program policy to address the broad issues and identify, by name, the local source documents responsible for guiding implementation, as well as to indicate where the documents are stored, and who is in charge of ensuring that the polices are followed. Having formal written policies in place to consult with when questions arise, or to refer to when being audited by health care accreditation agencies is strongly recommended. To that end, the following section defines common realms of CV-related policy to be addressed.

4.2.1 Memoranda of Understanding

Conducting CV often requires a collaboration or agreement with other external institutions or other internal institutions working under a common umbrella agency. In both cases it is helpful to formally define the agreement, scope of practice, allocation of billed or existing resources, and the responsibilities of each institution. Memoranda of Understanding (MoUs) are a common vehicle used to define these roles and responsibilities in order to guide the collaboration of institutions and make for smooth intrafacility relationships. MoUs can be quite brief, especially when followed or accompanied by an actual contract for services, or service agreement, which specifies fees and scope of services within in a legal context. Appendix 4.A provides a thorough template for establishing an MoU.

4.2.2 Reimbursement

Aside from potential fee sharing arrangements identified in facility service agreements, it is helpful for CV policy to identify the types of services for which reimbursement can be expected from consumers, insurers, and other their-party payers. See the *Current Reimbursement Policy,* and *Current Procedural Terminology (CPT) Codes* sections in this chapter.

4.2.3 Mapping Provider Time

Some large health care institutions, such as the Veteran's Health Administration (VHA), and smaller organizations, such as hierarchical private practices, find it helpful to designate or "map" how provider time is expected to be allocated in order to track productivity. For example, a clinician in a VHA facility might be "mapped" at 60% effort to provide services to the General Mental Health Clinic, 30% effort for services to a Specialty Clinic, and 10% effort for administrative work. Likewise, some private practice partnerships have agreements regarding expectations for the number or percentage of clinical intakes a provider covers in relation to weekly psychotherapy or some other service the practice provides. If the mapping scheme is not changed to address CV-related encounters, and associated administrative coding, clinical managers in large institutions might find themselves having to explain why their clinical productivity look low, in spite of having fully productive therapists. This is a fairly common occurrence.

Likewise, in private practice settings, the addition of a CV site might be associated with nonrandom increases in a particular diagnosis or clinical need, and associated CPT codes, which may impact billable productivity or lead to disparities among clinicians who may have come to expect referral parity among providers in the practice. It should be noted that, while providing CV services might lead to general increases in referral streams; it is almost always associated with extra administrative and technical burdens on providers' time, which should be accounted for in CV policy. Conducting a thorough Needs Assessment prior CV implementation (Chap. 2), and understanding logistical issues in CV implementation (Chap. 5), will assist managers in knowing if and how the new programming will impact clinician productivity and expectations.

4.2.4 Equipment

Chapter 1 addresses aspects of choosing and operating CV systems, related policy should at least briefly denote who is responsible for maintenance of CV equipment, and in large institutions, what procedures are required to get the equipment certified or approved for use. For example, some facilities require all new equipment to be inspected by facility specialists, with predefined rules for regular cleaning. The type/use of the CV system and type of facility will likely determine whether the CV equipment will be considered in the realm of biomedical equipment or information technology (IT) equipment, which in turn will determine the specific rules and polices related to use.

4.2.5 Clinical Space

Space is always at a premium in healthcare facilities and often CV providers have to share patient-side clinical space with on-site providers or other remote CV providers. As CV referral streams wax and wane, and the needs of partner facilities and other new programs are in flux, program managers may find themselves in a constant battle to defend or gain access to clinical space for CV implementation. Additionally, as defined in Chaps. 9–11, implementing CV requires a certain level of control or authority to configure the remote clinical space for CV. Accordingly, overarching program policy should address space-related issues, even if it is just to mention that space issues are covered in the MoU or service agreement.

Limited access to CV equipment on the provider side may also impact space needs. For example, a provider who conducts 50% of her sessions via CV and 50% in-person, may be asked to move offices for her in-person sessions, so that other providers may use the CV equipment. Accordingly, CV policy should address this potential, while keeping within whatever union rules may be in place with regard to moving providers. It is a good idea to consult with union representatives well before trying to implement office sharing. Space-related policy should be written to be as flexible as possible, while also protecting the core goals of the program.

4.2.6 Patient Safety

Chapter 8 provides in-depth procedures and protocols to address patient safety and emergencies in CV contexts. *Overarching policy documents should refer to such procedures and identify where they are stored.* Agreements or MoUs with partner facilities should allow the provider site to withhold clinical services if the patient-site staff and managers cannot follow through on agreed upon protocols for safety. Of course, the individual rights of specific patients to not have services interrupted should come first, but it is prudent to develop policy guiding continued site collaboration prefaced on safety standards. Friction between CV sites can often be assuaged if patient safety remains the focus of discussion, rather than work-load issues. But holding cites to the agreement is essential and it fosters positive relationships in the long run. Even if it creates short term friction, the process of referring to the agreement at disputed junctures, cues parties to be more invested in clear communication and in making sure their needs are accounted for in future agreements. When sites start drifting away from the agreement in the milieu of daily care, or if the agreement becomes de facto irrelevant, it opens up opportunities for ambiguity, mission drift, bad feelings, and most importantly, patient safety issues. This goes for policies related to individuals receiving services in their homes as well. For example, a common clinical policy is that CV services may be withheld or terminated if there is no other way to reach the patient other than the CV link. Whereas, Chap. 8 provides specific clinical protocols to safeguard patients, developing separate and additional program policy to point to in rocky situations may provide a safety net to protect the clinical program or institution. It also gives clinicians an appropriate safeguard to prematurely terminate or deny services in risky situations.

4.3 Using Standards and Guidelines to Promote Policy Changes

Managers and clinicians wishing to implement new CV programming will run into many existing policy-related barriers, including the total absence of local CV policy to rely on. One key factor when approaching health care facility or service directors in an attempt to change or create policy is ammunition. In healthcare, and especially for telehealth, that often means empirical evidence [10, 11] based on solid research (and maybe even a uniform metric for evaluation of services) [12]. Having access to and knowing the relevant the scientific literature can be a powerful tool in justifying change. Research is not only valuable in that it provides evidence that telemedicine is effective, cost-efficient, readily accepted and so on, but it also provides the infrastructure upon which practice guidelines are established. Accordingly, consulting published practice guidelines, in addition to, or instead of performing in-depth scientific literature reviews can be an effective and efficient strategy to support local changes. Chapter 3 (Table 3.1) provides links for a number of national consensus guidelines, which can be used to inform both clinical practice and the development of policy.

When someone questions whether or how CV can or should be adopted, presentation of a set of national guidelines, such as those endorsed by the American Telemedicine Association (ATA) [13–20] is often quite convincing. They were rigorously developed and based on current research, evaluation, and the expertise of the developers. Having practice guidelines in place that are approved by the ATA Board of Directors or endorsed or approved by other professional organizations also provides a solid foundation to develop local policy, defend your programming to accreditation organizations, lobby the government for reducing limitations on the practice of telemedicine, and lobby to payors for increased telemedicine reimbursement.

The ATA logs over 500 standards-related downloads per month, with the Telemental Health Practice Guideline being the most commonly downloaded document (accessed approximately 100 times per month) [15]. In a recent survey about the guidelines [15], the majority of respondents (96.5%) believed telemedicine/telehealth should have standards and guidelines, with the top three common reasons being that guidelines add credibility to practice via telehealth, standardize approaches to practice via telehealth, and decrease liability. These were followed by patient safety, consistency, quality of care, and patient/provider satisfaction. When asked about what impact standards and guidelines have on the way they provide healthcare, responses were: improved provider acceptance and understanding of telehealth (79.8%), improved patient outcomes and quality of care (63.2%), improved access to care (44.8%), provided information to justify reimbursement for payers (37.4%), and reduced costs (26.4%).

With respect to the practice of behavioral CV in particular, there are a number of published guidelines. Most guidelines, such as the ATA's, cover the provision of mental health services provided by a licensed healthcare professional using real-time CV services transmitted via the Internet or closed network. They pertain to services conducted between two parties (i.e., do not address multipoint videoconferencing), and include recommendations for services when initiating, receiving, or when both sites use a personal computer with a webcam or mobile communications device (e.g., "smart phone", laptop, or tablet) with two-way camera capability. They do not address communications using texting, e-mail, chatting, social network sites, online "coaching" or other non-mental health services [19].

4.4 Current Reimbursement Policy

Medicaid is actually the single largest payor of mental health services in the USA. It accounts for 26% of the total national mental health care spending and over half of all Medicaid beneficiaries with disabilities are diagnosed with a mental illness [21]. There are currently 44 states (all but CT, IA, MA, NH, NJ, RI, and DC) that cover some form of reimbursement for telehealth, including CV (CV, $n=44$), "store and forward" ($n=7$; not including teleradiology), remote monitoring ($n=11$), or all three ($n=3$) [22]. For a state-by-state summary of the various Medicaid programs, program administrators and state laws/regulations, refer to the Center for Connected Health Policy website and their recent 2013 summary (available at: http://cchpca. org/about-cchp/publications) [22]. For CV specifically, refer to the ATA State Medicaid Best Practice Telemental and Behavioral Health document released in August 2013 [23]. In this document are summaries of policies from AK, CA, IL and NM that are notable in terms of inclusive definitions of technology with few restrictions on technology that can be used for clinical purposes, geographic area served, applicable health services and conditions, provider eligibility, reimbursement methodology, and level of coverage and affected health care plans. Being able to point to such policies and even adopting the language used in these examples can be quite useful when advocating for change in your own facility or state.

For the most part, telehealth-provided services covered under state Medicaid plans include mental health assessments, individual therapy, and medication management, but generally only allow physicians/psychiatrists and psychologists to conduct the telemedicine encounter. Some states are beginning to allow other providers (i.e., licensed professional counselors in AZ, NM, TX, VA, WY; licensed social worker in MI, NV, NM, NC, VA, WY) to conduct and be reimbursed for behavioral CV health encounters. Overall, as of 2013, 39 states have some type of coverage and reimbursement for CV services (AL, AK, AZ, AR, CA, CO, DE, GA, HI, ID, IL, IN, KS, KY, LA, ME, MD, MI, MN, MO, MT, NE, NV, NM, NY, NC, ND, OK, OR PA, SC, TX, UT, VT, VA, WA, WV, WI, WY). Some evolving reimbursement models include the use of primary care providers to help conduct mental and behavioral health assessments with appropriate specialists connected via CV during routine office visits; and a home health model [24] that the Affordable Care Act (ACA) created to aid Medicaid patients with at least two chronic conditions, one chronic condition with risk for developing a second one, or one serious and persistent mental health condition. There are 11 states that use this model (AL, ID, IA, ME, MO, NY, NC, OH, OR, RI, WI) and 10 have legislation pending (IA, IL, MD, MA, NY, OK, SD, VT, WA, WV). It is important to note that school-based CV services often include behavioral and mental health treatments that Medicaid covers in some states [25].

Although no states reimburse for store-forward telemental health services, there is some evidence that in some circumstances this mode of interaction can be quite useful, potentially providing the needed evidence to eventually promote policy change. For example, in a recent study Yellowlees et al. [26] videotaped mental health interviews of Spanish-speaking patients. The interview video, history, and translated summary were sent to remote psychiatrists for consultation and a diagnostic assessment. Agreement between the expert diagnoses and the diagnoses from the Spanish consultations revealed acceptable levels of agreement for major diagnostic groupings among the Spanish- and English-speaking psychiatrists. They propose that the approach may be useful across national boundaries and in a variety of ethnic groups where real-time consultations are difficult or not feasible due to language barriers.

Recent efforts at the Federal level for Medicare include the "Telehealth Enhancement Act" (H.R. 3306), a bipartisan proposal calling for the adoption of payment innovations to include telehealth and make other incremental improvements to existing telehealth coverage. Basically it would do four things: (1) add incentive for fewer Medicare hospital admissions; (2) create a new Medicaid optional package for high-risk pregnancy and birth networks; (3) cover telehealth under Medicare payment bundles for post-acute care; and (4) allow Medicare Accountable Care Organizations (ACOs) to use telehealth for Medicare managed care plans. Whether or not this specific bill becomes law, it is representative of an advocacy-stance regarding telehealth in congress. Clinical managers should consider staying abreast of developing laws that might support new or existing CV-based services.

4.5   Current Procedural Terminology (CPT) Codes

It is important to know how to use CPT codes for reimbursement of telehealth in general, and for CV services, more specifically. A useful site on how to do this is provided by the University of Colorado Denver "Eliminating Mental Health Disparities" (http://www.tmhguide.org/site/epage/93990_871.htm). The site provides a brief webinar discussing how CPT coding for telehealth (and accompanying qualifications for eligible services) varies by payer and provides links to specific CPT information for Medicare, Medicaid, and large private insurers. For Medicare in particular, the service must be provided to an eligible Medicare beneficiary in an eligible facility (originating site) located outside of a Metropolitan Statistical Area, but there is no limitation on the location of the health professional delivering the medical service (referring site) as long as they are licensed in the state they are practicing in and are credentialed by the organization for which they are providing care. Eligible originating sites include the office of a physician or practitioner, a hospital (including critical access hospitals), rural health clinics, federally qualified health centers, skilled nursing facilities, hospital-based dialysis centers, and community mental health centers. Table 4.1 provides the 2013 list of Medicare telehealth-covered services relevant to CV and accompanying CPT codes.

4.6   Parity Legislation

Telehealth parity legislation may be particularly relevant for clinicians and clinical managers operating in private practice, or within a private hospital system. One key concern that potential users of CV have is that they will not be reimbursed at the same rates as in-person consultations/visits, and thus shy away from engaging in CV. To address this, a number of states have or are proposing parity legislation. Parity laws basically establish that insurers must cover services provided through telehealth programs if the insurers pay for those same services when they are provided in traditional clinic or hospital settings. As of 2013, there are 19 states with laws

Table 4.1 Medicare telehealth-covered services relevant to clinical videoconferencing with CPT codes

Service provided[a]	CPT code
Psychiatric diagnostic interview exam w/out medical services	90791
Psychiatric diagnostic interview exam w/medical services	90792
Individual psychotherapy	90832 (30 min), 90834 (45 min)
Individual psychotherapy, in addition to outpatient E/M code	90836 (45 min), 90838 (60 min)
Neurobehavioral status exam	96116
Individual health & behavior assessment/intervention	96150 (15 min)
Family/group health and behavior assessment/intervention	96154 (15 min)
Smoking cessation services for symptomatic pts	99406 (10 min), 99407 (>10 min)
Smoking cessation services for asymptomatic pts	G0436 (10 min), G0437(>10 min)
Telehealth consultations, emergency dept. or initial inpatient	G0425 (30 min), G0427 (70 min)
Alcohol or substance abuse assessment & intervention	G0396 (30 min), G0397 (>30 min)
Annual alcohol misuse screening	G0442 (15 min)
Brief face-to-face behavioral counseling for alcohol misuse	G0443 (15 min)
Annual depression screening	G0444 (15 min)
High-intensity behavioral counseling to prevent sexually transmitted infection	G0445 (30 min)
Individual annual, face-to-face intensive behavioral therapy for cardiovascular disease	G0446 (15 min)
Face-to-face behavioral counseling for obesity	G0447 (15 min)
Inpatient pharmacologic management	G0459

[a] Eligible providers include physicians, nurse practitioners, physician assistants, nurse midwives, clinical nurse specialists, clinical psychologists, clinical social workers, and registered dietitians or nutrition professionals

mandating private insurance of telemedicine and 9 with pending legislation (http:// atawiki.org.s161633.gridserver.com/wiki/index.php?title=File:Map-States_with_ Telemedicine_Parity_Laws.jpg). The rest of the states have no such legislation, but it is important to note that there are a number of insurers that cover telemedicine services without having to be mandated to do so.

4.7 How to Affect Policy Related to Establishing Telehealth Programming

So—how does one advocate for changes in state policies, such as parity legislation, or in local existing institutional policies that present barriers to CV services? Every instance is of course unique to some extent, but there are some common strategies

Table 4.2 Common communication strategies to impact policy

In the first sentence succinctly define the issue and state your position
State exactly what action you want to be taken and why. In other words, do not present a problem without a solution, or a solution without a problem
Specify how the change will affect you, your organization, and even the state
Clearly demonstrate that you know the issue and have well-informed opinions based in fact
Relate a personal story (or use a testimonial) relating to the issue
Insure all of your information is accurate and up to date as possible, reference this certainty in communication
Bring data with you in a concise form, for example, fact sheets or very basic charts—even though you may not have time to present it, you might be able to leave it for future reference
Make use of information or data sources already developed from states or programs that have the desired target policies in place
Make use of published research findings and expert consensus guidelines
Match your language to your audience. In public settings use terms that everybody will understand. Avoid terms and abbreviations that are not known that well outside your field or institution. The opposite tactic might be useful when communicating on a local level to clinical administrators, who are used to speaking and thinking in specialized jargon and acronyms
Identify your allies: Who else is committed to work on the issue? Identify professional societies, patient advocacy groups, or other like-minded advocates. In state settings these allies demonstrate legitimacy and represent potential constituents. In local settings, allies demonstrate legitimacy and represent institutional readiness for change; they might include other service lines or clinics, potential referring providers, treating providers, and patients
Align your goal with other important existing goals of the target audience, that is, will the change have "value added" components that can address multiple issues?

that can be used to help insure success. Table 4.2 provides communication strategies specifically geared for impacting policy that have been found to be helpful.

Now that you know *what* to communicate, *how* do you communicate it? In general, communication is critical. As you are already aware of avenues to communicate with your boss or clinical administrators, perhaps the most salient tip is to not to spring a discussion on them. Make an appointment for a convenient time when they will be able to focus on what you are saying, even if it is only for 5 min. Another important tip for local advocacy is to begin by using the appropriate chain of command. There are times when mid-level managers are out of step with the needs and values of colleagues below and above them in the institutional hierarchy, when tactfully testing the waters regarding "going above someone's head" might be appropriate. However, that is not the place to start for effective advocacy.

Methods of communicating with state legislators may not be as familiar to you. Fundamentally, you are marketing a new concept to a potentially naïve and maybe even an indifferent or antagonistic audience, so the way you approach them is critical to success. There are four main ways to communicate with those who influence state or federal policy. Table 4.3 presents methods of communication and tips geared for impacting state law.

Appendix 4.B presents an example of a one-page summary of the argument made for parity in Arizona by the Arizona Telemedicine Program in 2013 (it was successfully signed into law). It can be used as a lobbying template for parity legislation

Table 4.3 Methods of communication to impact telehealth legislation and policy

Writing letters	The use of traditional hard copy letters or email is a helpful place to start, especially if the target audience or individual already has designated addresses specifically designed to elicit ideas and feedback. If you start with a letter, you can then reference your prior communication in future encounters, demonstrating that have used the provided and preferred avenues of feedback and that you are committed to the issue. Many lobbying groups will set up a portal specifically for submitting emails and will even provide a template for such letters, making it easier to get higher response rates. When designing such a template or writing your own letter, it is important to address it properly, and have the content be brief, specific, reasonable, and courteous
Making phone calls	This is an effective means of communication although it should be recognized that you will often not speak directly with a legislator (or other policy maker), but are more likely to speak with a staff member. In this case it is important to find out who the right staff person is, as there are often multiple staff members and perhaps only one deals with healthcare issues. Getting the right person is critical as they are often the liaison to and chief source of information for the legislator. As with letters, it is important to keep the content brief, specific, reasonable, and courteous
Personal meetings	These are typically done in-person, but if feasible videoconferencing is a useful alternative to demonstrate the benefits and ease of the modality (but only if you are sure there will be no technical glitches that might be detrimental to your argument that telehealth is viable). Be aware that your time is likely going to be limited—maybe as little as 5 min, so be prepared, polite, prompt, and responsive
Committee hearings	This is perhaps the ultimate opportunity to present your argument to a broad audience with the most influence and power to change policy. The same rules apply again—be prepared, polite, prompt, truthful, and responsive. In this venue, you may have a little more time to present your case so it may be useful to make it more personal. Talk about how this policy will affect you and your family (as well as theirs!). Testimonials from actual users, both patients and providers, whether in-person or by video, are especially effective in this venue. However, be selective in your choice of speakers as you want them to be focused and on point

in other states and easily modified for other telemedicine related issues. Note the style—it uses short sentences and paragraphs with succinct topic headings. This makes the document easy to read, so that it will take someone just a few short minutes to review. Legislators often have many documents handed to them with little time to attend to or read them all. Some other key points include providing a brief background summary, noting other states that already have similar laws passed, and a summary of the benefits.

4.8   Navigating the Politics of Inertia and Policy Change

When dealing with those who resist change in general, or are openly opposed to creating policies in support of telehealth, it is important to discern—as quickly as possible—the motivations for resistance. Of course, it is natural for reasonable people
to disagree on an appropriate course of action in the realm of health care. In these
cases, open discussion can reveal where the divergences in opinions come from and
how they might be bridged. Chapters 2 and 6 provide many useful resources and
strategies for building broad consensus, identifying aligned and nonaligned goals
of stakeholders, and inclusively gathering information/perspectives to support new
programming and policies. However, it is also wise to recognize and be prepared
for overt resistance and less-authentic communication styles from those not exactly
operating on "good faith" principals of communication. This is especially true when
trying to initiate political or institutional change, or change that might be perceived
as creating more work, or threatening professional/political turf. As the saying goes,
"Expect the best, be prepared for the worst." Table 4.4 identifies some common
strategies used to derail communication and efforts to change or innovate. Be prepared to identify them, so as to counter or maneuver around.

All of the strategies in Table 4.4 have been employed before, specifically in
the service of derailing policies to support new CV programming or technology-
assisted mental health care. However, many of them can be successfully navigated,
especially if constituents desiring innovation band together. Techniques to counter
some of these tactics are identified in Table 4.5

4.9   Keeping up with Policy Change and Initiatives

It is not easy to influence policy on your own or even within the greater context of
your organization, but it is a little easier to keep track of what other larger organizations are doing to influence policy. For telemedicine, the key organization to turn to
for information about policy and advocacy is the American Telemedicine Association (http://www.americantelemed.org/). The website has links to policy efforts and
updates   (http://www.americantelemed.org/get-involved/public-policy-advocacy/
policy-issues), legislative summaries and announcements about pending actions, a
blog that often deals with policy topics, webinars and videos that periodically summarize the state of important telemedicine policies (http://www.americantelemed.
org/learn/this-month-in-telemedicine), a policy wiki (http://atawiki.org.s161633.
gridserver.com/wiki/index.php?title=Main_Page), and a State Policy Toolkit for
Improving Access to Covered Services for Telemedicine (http://www.american-
telemed.org/docs/default-source/policy/ata-state-policy-toolkit.pdf?sfvrsn=18) that
contains talking points, rebuttals for common arguments against telehealth coverage, and a template with model. Attending the annual and/or midyear meeting may
be useful (http://www.americantelemed.org/learn/ata-meetings) as policy updates

Table 4.4 Common strategies used to derail authentic communication and change

Deflection (e.g., not my responsibility/jurisdiction)
Delay (e.g., needs more review)
Willful miscommunication (e.g., addressing related but different/off topic questions or concerns)
Discounting/denial (e.g., it's not that bad of a problem; there is no problem)
Exaggerating (e.g., the problem is too big or complex for us to solve)
Straw-man (e.g., presenting an overly simple version of proposed solution and poking holes in it)
Deception (e.g., not mentioning knowledge of data)
Stonewalling (e.g. non-responsive to emails or communication efforts)
Division (e.g., finding weak links in groups)
Appeasement (e.g., offering less effective options)
Discrediting (e.g., negating credentials or expertise of proponents)
Destruction (e.g., harming proponent's reputation, programming, or other valued resource)
Duplication of efforts argument (currently a hot-topic in management, but it can be overly applied)
Dealing (e.g., without truly negotiating)
Intimidation (e.g., outright bullying or notion that change will threaten jobs)
Glad-handing (e.g., outwardly agreeing, secretively sabotaging)
Bad cop above (boss above is blamed for resistance; very effective when there is no access to boss)
Misdirection (e.g., steering conversation to hot-button issues, often done in group settings)

Table 4.5 Techniques to counter inauthentic communication strategies

Understanding others' legitimate perspectives (e.g., genuine concerns causing inauthentic response)
Understanding others' less-valid motivations (e.g., turf issues, fear, laziness, inertia, politics)
Naming it (e.g., publicly identifying and calling out derailment strategies)
Building consensus with other stakeholders
Olive branch (e.g., working on relationship in other off-topic realms)
Inclusion (e.g., creating a sense that rising tide raises all boats)
Grounding conversation in clinical need, access, or patient safety issues
Turning negatives into positives
Getting advice from others' who may know the players better or in a different context
Information blitz (e.g., sending many articles, data, examples of successful programming)
Shaping discussion (e.g., creating agendas before group meetings—can be focused on blitz materials)
Reframing the issues
Keeping opponents off balance
Use existing salient local examples of others' experiences
Compromise
Persistence
Reboot/pass the torch (e.g., knowing when to designate another champion to take the lead)
Timing (waiting it out)

are typically presented in various venues. The ATA also actively lobbies the federal government for policy changes as they relate to and/or impact telemedicine.

The Center for Telehealth and e-Health Law (CTel) is also a very useful resource (http://ctel.org/a-voice-for-telehealth/). In 2006 they created the Telehealth Leadership Initiative (TLI) which is a nonprofit advocacy group dedicated to advancing telehealth initiatives. Since its inception, the TLI has represented the telehealth community before the legislative and administrative branches of numerous local, state, and national governments, dealing with such policy issues as credentialing and privileging of providers, and increased Medicare and Medicaid reimbursement for telehealth services. They regularly host telehealth advocacy seminars and conduct "Telehealth Capitol Hill Advocacy Days" to facilitate meetings between those in the telehealth community and their Congressional representatives.

4.9.1 Getting Help at the Local Level

Finally, there are the Telehealth Resource Centers (http://www.telehealthresource-center.org) including the National Telehealth Policy Resource Center (http://telehealthpolicy.us/). There are 14 Resource Centers, each covering a given section of the US with one dedicated solely to technology and one to policy (see Chap. 2, Table 2.6 for specific links to each center). They are funded by the US Department of Health and Human Services' Health Resources and Services Administration (HRSA) Office for the Advancement of Telehealth (OAT) and their mission is to provide support and advice to programs, individuals and institutions establishing new or looking to expand existing telehealth programs. They offer training and education via on-site workshops, courses, webinars, online modules, and blogs; provide many other useful tools, tips and strategies for advancing telehealth including toolkits, blogs, templates for consent and other aspects of a telemedicine encounter; and provide information on local, regional, state and federal policies, laws, and regulations. As they each cover a distinct region of the country, each one is quite familiar with the policy issues related to the states they cover and thus serve as a great resource for keeping up on local policy changes and initiatives. The resource centers are also potentially useful to contact for help gathering data and arguments if you want to initiate a policy change in your state.

4.9.2 Keep in Touch with Your Legislators

Policy change is difficult or at least challenging for the most part, but it can be somewhat easier if your legislators and/or other local leaders are already aware of local telemedicine activities. In Arizona, the Arizona Telemedicine Program (ATP) has kept the legislature involved and up to date on its progress since inception in 1996. Perhaps related to this involvement, The Joint Legislative Budget Committee (JLBC) of the Arizona State Legislature created the Arizona Telemedicine

Council (ATC; http://www.telemedicine.arizona.edu/app/about-us/atc) which has played an important role in ATP's sustainability, as well as that of other telehealth programs across the state [27, 28]. The ATC meets quarterly, enhancing communication and interoperability between government and various other programs and provides a venue to make attendees aware of what program course changes might be needed related to policy changes at the local and federal levels. The ATC plays a significant role in promoting telemedicine in Arizona and influencing policy at a variety of levels. It serves as a model of how telemedicine programs can potentially communicate better with their legislative representatives to promote success and sustainability of high-quality telehealth programming. Another example of a successful non-US telehealth network that has worked successfully with its government in promoting favorable telehealth policy is the Ontario Telemedicine Network (OTN) [29].

Conclusions

Telemedicine is growing exponentially and utilizing a variety of new venues (e.g., mHealth), but in the end it is not a new clinical specialty but is simply a different way of utilizing telecommunications and other technologies to bridge the gap between patients and providers to improve healthcare. Policy does need to change, but it should reflect this core belief that telemedicine is just another tool in our arsenal to fight disease and attempt to provide equitable healthcare services to everyone everywhere in every circumstance. Telemedicine policy should be founded on evidence (of which there is plenty in the literature), sound practice guidelines established by experts in the field, and to some extent on common sense. There are numerous tools and resources to help those interested in changing policy and/or promoting new policy, just a few of which were provided here. Hopefully, within the near future we will not need special (separate) policies for telehealth or CV, as they will soon be an integral and ubiquitous part of the healthcare system and standard operating procedures.

Appendix 4.A

Template for a Memorandum of Understanding: Regarding the Provision of Clinical Videoconferencing Services

MoUs are often required when establishing business and/or other working relationships between telemedicine organizations/practitioners. MoUs are often followed or accompanied by an actual (legal) contract for services that specifies fees and scope of services. Most MoUs include the following sections and types of information.

1. Background and Basic Information:

   a. PARTIES. This MoU is a non-binding administrative guideline made and entered into on January 1, 2014, by XX, hereinafter referred to as "Telepsych, Inc." and YY, hereafter referred to as "Provider Q".

   b. AUTHORITY. This agreement is authorized = under the provisions of ZZ (local authority if necessary).

   c. PURPOSE. Dr. Q is entering into this agreement with Telepsych, Inc. for the purpose of providing telepsychiatry services.

   d. BACKGROUND. Telepsychiatry can improve access to specialty healthcare services, reduce travel burdens, and enhance provider–patient interactions. Both parties understand the requirement to treat all information generated from, or in conjunction with, a telepsychiatric consult as they would a traditional face-to-face consultation and comply with current HIPAA privacy & security rules.

2. Services and Standards:

   I. WHEREAS, Telepsych, Inc. has as a goal to improve access to psychiatric care for all patients with mental illness in the state of XX; and

   II. WHEREAS, Telepsych, Inc. aims to increase access using video-conferencing-based technologies; and

   III. WHEREAS, Dr. Q wants to provide clinician consulting services for those with mental illness via video-conferencing-based technologies; and

   IV. WHEREAS, the following terms, have the following definitions:

   a. Telepsychiatry services: The use of real time, interactive audio and video to provide and support psychiatric care when providers and patients are geographically separated.

   b. Practice guidelines: The clinical standards that apply to in-person psychiatric encounters will apply to Telepsychiatric encounters, and both parties shall adhere to the American Telemedicine Association's Telemental Health Guidelines to the extent feasible and appropriate.

   c. Practice setting: The location of the patient receiving the telepsychiatry service defines the clinician's license, practice, and privilege requirements.

   d. Scope of practice: Clinical telepsychiatry encompass diagnostic, therapeutic, and forensic modalities across the lifespan. Common applications include prehospitalization assessment and posthospital follow-up care, scheduled and urgent outpatient visits, medication management, psychotherapy and consultation.

   e. Originating/Distant site: The patient location is referred to as "originating" and the provider location as "distant."

3. Obligations

   Telepsych Inc., is responsible for:

   a. Providing, operating, and maintaining all originating site equipment and supplies, as well as necessary technical support and training to establish and maintain telecommunications sessions with Dr Q.

b. Scheduling the telepsychiatry services, schedule confirmations.

c. Providing intake procedures to include, but are not limited to patient orientation, consent forms, guidance on privacy and security.

d. Distributing prescriptions for Schedule II Controlled Substances as appropriate and with provider's original signature as required by law.

e. Providing client case records to provider(s), within 3 days of an encounter, that include chief complaint, medical history, medications, allergies, current diagnoses, and treatment plans.

f. Providing originating site clinicians to assist client as part of treatment team.

g. Compensating Dr Q at agreed upon rates for agreed times.

Dr. Q is responsible for:

a. Cooperating with Telepsych, Inc. to facilitate provision of services.

b. Complying with Telepsych, Inc. rules, operational guidelines and regulations.

c. Providing space, equipment, and telecommunications, unless provided by Telepsych, Inc.

d. Providing timely completion of clinical documentation and pharmacologic management as required by Telepsych and respective oversight entities.

e. Ensuring provision of a current license and/or certification to provide mental health services, is Medicaid and Medicare registered, possesses a National Provider Identification (NPI) number, and holds and maintains medical malpractice liability insurance for the provision of telemedicine services. If providing services across state lines multistate malpractice coverage is required.

f. Ensuring that procedural safeguards are followed in confidentiality requirements according to all federal, state and local requirements.

g. Complying with requirements for provider credentialing and privileging as required by originating (patient) facility and in compliance with CMS and the Joint Commission.

h. Responding to Telepsych, Inc. requests to consult with client's clinical team as necessary.

i. Complying with all Audits, Surveys, Reviews, and Inspections as requested by Telepsych, Inc.

j. Sending a monthly invoice for agreed upon services performed within the previous 30 day period on a standard billing form approved by Telepsych, Inc.

4. Parties' relationship: The relationship created by this MoU is of independent contractors and does not constitute an employee–employer relationship. This MoU is not intended to create nor shall it be deemed or construed to create any relationship between the Parties other than that of independent entities agreeing to the provisions of this MoU. Neither of the parties, nor any of their respective officers, directors, or employees shall be construed to be the agent, employer or representative of the other.

5. Intent: The terms outlined in this MoU are nonbinding and may serve as the basis for a separate Services Agreement between parties. This MoU does not constitute an obligation by either party to enter into a Services Agreement. Telepsych, Inc.:

By:_____ Title:_____Date:_____
YY:
By:_____ Title:_____Date: _____

Appendix 4.B

Summary of Argument Made for Parity in Arizona by the Arizona Telemedicine Program in 2013 (It Was Successfully Signed into Law)

Promote Cost-effective Telemedicine Treatment

AZ Senate Bill for health insurance; telemedicine is targeted to be on the 51st legislation first Regular Session docket. This telemedicine reimbursement parity bill will restrict insurers or healthcare service plans from discriminating against telemedicine service coverage. It will require insurers to cover access to tele-healthcare under equivalent terms and conditions as ordinary coverage.

Background The United States Institute of Medicine defines telemedicine as "the use of electronic information and communications technologies to provide and support healthcare when distance separated the participants."

The proposed bill defines telemedicine as "the use of audio, video, or other electronic media for the purpose of diagnosis, consultation, or treatment. It does not include the use of an audio-only telephone, a facsimile machine or electronic mail."

This definition includes both synchronous and asynchronous (real-time and store-and-forward) use of interactive audio, video, or electronic media for delivering health care. It would not discriminate by a patient's geographic location.

Currently 15 states have passed similar parity reimbursement laws: California (1996), Colorado (2001), Georgia (2006), Hawaii (1999), Kentucky (2000), Louisiana (1995), Maine (2009), Maryland (2012), Michigan (2012), New Hampshire (2009), Oklahoma (1997), Oregon (2009), Texas (1997), Vermont (2012), and Virginia (2010).

At least five states have pending legislative proposals: Arizona (S.B. 705), Florida (S.B., 1842, H.B. 60), New Mexico (H.B. 591), Ohio (S.B. 280), and Pennsylvania (H.B. 2730).

National supporters of parity legislation include the American telemedicine association, the National Organization of Black Elected Legislative Women, and the National Hispanic Caucus of State Legislators.

Benefits of Telemedicine *Consumer choice*—Patients should be able to choose how they receive a covered service, including their urgency, convenience, and satisfaction.

Non-discrimination—Telehealth methods of providing covered services should be on parity with in-person methods. This legislation does not require new coverage.

Reduce disparities in access to care—For many people access to in-person services is very difficult for a wide variety of reasons, notably their mobility limitations, major distance or time barriers, and transportation limitations (don't drive, have a car or have transit available). For existing programs however funded, track metrics of interest to the legislature (miles saved, transfers avoided).

Improves service availability—Many areas of the state already have numerical shortage of needed providers. Another problem is a lack of clinicians providing specific evidence-based care, or willing to treat patients of a particular payor (usually for reimbursement reasons). Telehealth methods can reduce provider's practice costs, improve their productivity, and facilitate triaging for specialty care.

Improve quality of care—Identify key state identified health status indicators that can be improved with improved access (diabetic retinopathy, infant mortality). Wider patient choices will foster provider competition.

Using innovation—Each state, as the regulator of insurance policies offered to its citizens, has a strong and vital interest in taking advantage of health care delivery innovations, especially to improve quality, reduce costs, improve timely access to needed care, and improve citizen satisfaction.

References

1. Bashshur RL, Shannon GW. History of telemedicine: evolution, context, and transformation. New Rochelle: Mary Ann Liebert; 2009.
2. Bashshur RL. Invitational symposium workshop on the sustainability and promise of telemedicine. Telemed J E Health. 2013;19:333–38.
3. Ney JP. Changes to CMS reimbursement rules for intraoperative neurophysiological monitoring: implications for telemedicine. Telemed J E Health. 2013;19:791–3.
4. Bashshur RL. Compelling issues in telemedicine. Telemed J E Health. 2013;19:330–2.
5. Garcia-Lizana F, Giorgo F. The future of e-health, including telemedicine and telecare, in the European Union: from stakeholders' views to evidence based decisions. J Telemed Telecare. 2012;18:365–6.
6. Broens THF, Huis int'l Veld RMHA, Vollenbroek-Hutten MMR, Hermens HJ, van Halteren AT, Nieuwenhuis JM. Determinants of successful telemedicine implementations: a literature study. J Telemed Telecare. 2007;13:303–9.
7. Khoja S, Durrani H, Nayani P, Fahim A. Scope of policy issues in eHealth: results from a structured literature review. J Med Internet Res 2012;14:e34.
8. Affordable Healthcare Act. http://www.healthcare.gov/law/index.html. Accessed 5 Oct 2013.
9. Meaningful use. http://www.cms.gov/Regulations-and-Guidance/Legislation/EHRIncentive-Programs/Meaningful_Use.html. Accessed 5 Oct 2013.
10. Krupinski EA. Current evidence base. In: Lustig TA, editor. The role of telehealth in an evolving health care environment. Washington, DC: The National Academic Press; 2012. pp. 61–6.
11. Saliba V, Legido-Quigley H, Hallik R, Aaviksoo A, Car J, McKee M. Telemedicine across borders: a systematic review of factors that hinder or support implementation. Intl J Med Inform. 2012;81:793–809.

12. Mars M, Scott R. Telemedicine service use: a new metric. J Internet Res. 2012;14:e178.
13. Krupinski EA, Antoniotti N, Burdick A. Standards and guidelines development in the American Telemedicine Association. In: Moumtzoglou A, Kastania A, editors. E-health systems quality and reliability: models and standards. Hershey: Medical Information Science Reference; 2011. pp. 244–52.
14. American Telemedicine Association Standards & Guidelines. http://www.americantelemed.org/practice/standards/ata-standards-guidelines. Accessed: 6 Oct 2013.
15. Krupinski EA, Antoniotti N, Bernard J. Utilization of the American Telemedicine Association's clinical practice guidelines. Telemed eHealth. In Press 2013.
16. American Telemedicine Association's Evidence-based Practice for Telemental Health. http://www.americantelemed.org/practice/standards/ata-standards-guidelines/evidence-based-practice-for-telemental-health. Accessed 24 Sept 2013.
17. American Telemedicine Association's Practice Guidelines for Videoconferencing-based Telemental Health. http://www.americantelemed.org/practice/standards/ata-standards-guidelines/videoconferencing-based-telemental-health. Accessed 24 Sept 2013.
18. American Telemedicine Association's Practice Guidelines for Video-Based Online Mental Health Services. http://www.americantelemed.org/practice/standards/ata-standards-guidelines/practice-guidelines-for-video-based-online-mental-health-services. Accessed 10 Oct 2013.
19. American Telemedicine Association's Core Standards for Telemedicine Operations. http://www.americantelemed.org/practice/standards/ata-standards-guidelines/core-standards-for-telemedicine-operations. Accessed 24 Sept 2013.
20. American Telemedicine Association's Expert Consensus Recommendations for Videoconferencing-Based Telepresenting. http://www.americantelemed.org/practice/standards/ata-standards-guidelines/recommendations-for-videoconferencing-based-telepresenting Accessed 24 Sept 2013.
21. Kronick RG, Bella M, Gilmer TP. The faces of medicaid III: refining the portrait of people with multiple chronic conditions. Hamilton: Center for Health Care Strategies; Oct. 2009.
22. State Telehealth Laws and Reimbursement Policies: a Comprehensive Scan of the 50 States and District of Columbia. Center for Connected Health Policy. July 2013. http://www.cchpca.org. Accessed 5 Oct 2013.
23. American Telemedicine Association State Medicaid Best Practice Telemental and Behavioral Health. August 2013. http://www.americantelemed.org/docs/default-source/policy/ata-best-practice-telemental-and-behavioral-health.pdf?sfvrsn=8. Accessed 22 Oct 2013.
24. Medicaid Health Home State Plan. 2013. http://www.medicaid.gov/State-Resource-Center/Medicaid-State-Technical-Assistance/Health-Homes-Technical-Assistance/Approved-Health-Home-State-Plan-Amendments.html. Accessed 5 Oct 2013.
25. American Telemedicine Association State Medicaid Best Practice School-Based Telemealth. July 2013. https://www.google.com/#q=25%29%09American+Telemedicine+Association+State+Medicaid+Best+Practice+School-Based+Telemealth. Accessed: 22 Oct 2013.
26. Yellowlees PM, Odor A, Iosif AM, Parish MB, Nafiz N, Patrice K, Xiong G, McCaron R, Sanchez R, Ochoa E, Hilty D. Transcultural psychiatry made simple—asynchronous telepsychiatry as an approach to providing culturally relevant care. Telemed J E Health. 2013;19:1–6.
27. Krupinski EA, Weinstein RS. Telemedicine in an academic center—the Arizona Telemedicine Program. Telemed J E Health. 2013;19:349–56.
28. Weinstein RS, Barker G, Beinar S, et al. Policy and the origins of the Arizona Statewide Telemedicine Program. In: Whitten P, Cook D, editors. Understanding health communications technologies. San Francisco: Jossey-Bass; 2004. pp. 299–309.
29. Brown EM. The Ontario Telemedicine Network: a case report. Telemed J E Health. 2013;19:373–37.

Chapter 5
Pulling It All Together: Logistics of Program Implementation

Sara Smucker Barnwell and Thao N. Bui

Chapter Summary

Purpose   This chapter addresses the logistics of establishing clinical videoconferencing (CV) programs and denotes commonly unforeseen barriers to implementation. The authors provide recommendations on central issues related to successful programming: where clients will be served, relationships with partner clinics, identifying program services, reviewing laws and policies, secure communication with patients, transitional programming, and recruiting clinicians.

Context   The information is necessary for clinical managers and/or clinicians because the greatest challenges in initiating a telehealth program are often organizational and logistical. The diversity of common pitfalls inevitably requires one to venture outside of her area of expertise. Awareness of the issues and potential solutions facilitates efficient program implementation.

Tools   The chapter includes a framework to plan for institutional partnerships, a list of basic requirements for partner sites, a list of roles and responsibilities for clinical partner sites, a synopsis of regulatory questions to consider, a template for defining and formalizing partnerships (i.e., memoranda of understanding), a list of specific procedures regarding patient/provider communication, a list of answers to frequently asked questions by providers new to clinical videoconferencing, links to helpful organizations, relevant references to literature, and a chart providing an overview of issues covered in this chapter.

S. S. Barnwell (✉)
Department of Psychiatry and Behavioral Sciences,
University of Washington, Seattle, WA, USA
e-mail: ssmucker@post.harvard.edu

T. N. Bui
The Anxiety Center at EBTCS, Seattle, WA, USA

© Springer International Publishing Switzerland 2015
P. W. Tuerk, P. Shore (eds.), *Clinical Videoconferencing in Telehealth,*
Behavioral Telehealth, DOI 10.1007/978-3-319-08765-8_5

5.1   Introduction

Clinical videoconferencing is a relatively new area of practice with fewer experienced practitioners than other domains of behavioral intervention. Absent formally canonized recommendations for implementation, early program administrators found that the greatest implementation challenges are typically related to the minutia of service delivery. The old adage "the devil is in the details" is salient. New CV program administrators and/or clinical managers may benefit from practical guidance from those who have already established CV programming. To this end we offer fundamental knowledge based in the empirical literature and in practical experiences.

5.2   Where to Provide Services

Determining the contexts in which patients will be recruited, enrolled, and served is among the first and most critical decisions in thoughtful CV program implementation. Many times, a specifically identified and obvious clinical need drives implementation, but often CV expansion or new program development requires mapping out a basic plan to identify the target population, geography, and services. The patient's location significantly impacts many facets of service delivery, including which services are appropriate, program inclusion criteria, and emergency management protocols. Once a needs assessment identifies clinical needs in specific geographic locations (see Chap. 2), CV program administrators must determine the environment in which services will be delivered. Typically, the options include delivering services to clinically supervised clinic-based settings (e.g., partner medical clinics) or to unsupervised non-clinic based settings (e.g., residences). However there is growing program specification of services provided to supervised, but not clinically-supervised, or to partially clinically-supervised settings (e.g., forensic settings, military settings, college resource centers, etc.). Occasionally, options can also include delivering services to clinically-supervised nonclinic settings (e.g., residence in a retirement community) or unsupervised clinic-based settings (e.g., Veteran Center or other facility after typical operating hours).

Different settings provide different programmatic benefits. Clinically unsupervised environments may offer improved care access, especially for patients too medically ill to travel or geographically far from care, who perceive stigma associated with mental health care, or possess other barriers [15]. Clinically supervised environments often offer superior technical, clinical, and emergency management resources for the delivery of specialized services. A patient population in need of a medically monitored controlled substance (e.g., opiate substitution therapy) may be better served in a supervised clinical environment, while patients in a rural area requiring psychotherapy may be better served in their residences. To assist administrators in planning for relationships with partner facilities, we offer a broad 7-point

Table 5.1 Institutional partnerships planning tool

1. Identify the availability of a partner clinic in the geographical area identified by the needs assessment
2. Identify the feasibility of establishing and maintaining a collaboration
3. Identify broad outlines of video-connection plan (Chap. 1) and feasibility of plan
4. Denote types of CV services (e.g., consultation, therapy, and prescription) and context of services (e.g., stand-alone, augment in-person care, or delivered under auspices of a treatment team)
5. Define the collaboration with a formal agreement or MOU; note that review of Table 6.3 might assist reader in identifying the types of under-assessed background issues that might complicate or facilitate partner collaborations
6. Informally identify basic key aspects of plan that are not specified in the MOU. It may be helpful to leave key details out of MOU to facilitate flexibility, or to not overly burden the MOU process. The identification of who will specifically will carry out the responsibilities of supporting personnel on the ground (Table 5.2) may fall into this category, as listing them all might make for a too-detailed and rigid MOU, but not making partner site leadership aware of these needs up front might lead to extra work thrown onto key personnel during implementation, threatening the perceived burden or usefulness of CV partnership with essential players
7. Identify and plan for the unique needs and characteristics of targeted patient population (e.g., rural, high risk, etc.)

outline to guide "big picture" thinking and help organize relevant information (Table 5.1). We suggest that managers fill in as many of the known and unknown specifics they can think of under each point to get a grasp on how they might wish to proceed and what information will still be needed to forge an institutional partnership.

In order to be sustainable, CV collaborations require ongoing coordination, staff education, and commitment. Staff turnover is a consistent threat to established systems and, of course, technology is an ever-evolving variable. Accordingly, once CV services are established, managers can also use this simple 7-point outline as a tool to consider how proposed changes to the services might impact or have unintended consequences on the ecology of the CV system.

5.2.1 Supervised Settings

If CV program administrators elect to serve clients in a clinically supervised environment, they must identify and partner with a site (e.g., clinic, correctional facility) that will serve as the patient location of care [21]. Relationship management with partner sites is often the most difficult aspect of CV program administration. Adequate time-related resources or personnel should be identified beforehand to manage these dynamic relationships. If administrative resources are not available for ongoing communication and logistical course correction, then managers should be aware that coordination and relationship maintenance work will fall on the clinical providers, and will impact clinical productivity. Ongoing needs assessment and collaborative communication with clinic leadership, other clinicians, and patients

Table 5.2 Key stakeholder roles at supervised or clinic-based partner sites

1. Program champions: point of contact for the partner site; maintains regular communication with CV administrators, support staff, and clinicians (often the program champions are clinicians)
2. Referral sources: educates patients about CV options, refers them for services
3. Technical champion: maintains and supports CV equipment at the patient site
4. Telehealth clinical support representative: greets CV patients, verifies identities, and checks the patients in; establishes the CV connection for patients; assists CV providers with hands-on help to collect documentation or react to emergencies [5]. Typically, this staff person has both technical and clinical skills that permit her to both operate/maintain CV equipment, capture helpful biometric data (e.g., blood pressure, assessment of involuntary movements), and relay pertinent clinical observations about patients not readily apparent to providers (e.g., gait, wheelchair, odor, etc.)
5. Scheduling staff: manages the equipment calendar and schedules telehealth appointments
6. Onsite security staff: responds to potential emergencies and provides facility security for after-hours appointments if indicated

will help ensure that CV services remain valuable to the partner site. While CV services provide needed resources to a partner site, they simultaneously introduce demands on space, staff, and other resources (e.g., internet bandwidth). Despite the logistical inconvenience of travel, the authors recommend visiting partner sites and forging these relationships in person, as well as planning for periodic site visits as patient-end administrative, clinical, and managerial staff turnover [26]. In-person visits help CV providers to foster strong bonds with staff at the partner site, and observe the resources, needs, strengths, and limitations of the site firsthand.

Identifying and assigning key stakeholder roles at the supervised partner site is critical. One staff member may serve all roles, or the duties may be divided among the staff. Selecting staff with appropriate education to perform these tasks [5] and providing telehealth training will help them succeed in their roles. Some partner sites may have limited staffing, and the introduction of stakeholder roles may prove burdensome. CV programs with greater resources may place a dedicated staff member at the partner site to serve these functions. Important partner site stakeholder roles are included in Table 5.2. Though all of the identified roles in the list are critical, the list is not intended to necessarily denote mutually exclusive roles. In practice, it is often the case that one employee assumes responsibility for two or more roles.

A template is provided in Appendix 5.B for collecting and organizing the contact information of important stakeholders at patient and provider sites. In addition to organizing and maintaining necessary staffing to operate a CV program, partner sites must possess the infrastructure to support CV services. Whereas these individual topics are covered more exhaustively elsewhere in this book, Table 5.3 represents basic requirements for partner sites.

Clearly documenting the above mentioned stakeholder roles and requirements for services in the form of an MOU or telehealth service agreement (TSA) can reduce misunderstandings and conflict between patient and provider sites, and prevent undefined necessities from falling solely on clinicians. Appendix 5.A provides a MOU template. This document must be maintained collaboratively in order to

Table 5.3 Basic requirements for partner sites

1. A private, quiet physical space for telehealth encounters [11] and approved telehealth equipment [24]
2. Adequate bandwidth to support videoconferencing (e.g., 128 kbs) [6]; higher rates will facilitate the detection of more subtly detailed clinical cues [28]
3. Adequate staffing to greet and guide CV patients to the room, and respond to emergencies if necessary
4. A mechanism to share patient records and manage remote prescriptions. Web-based electronic medical records and prescription management tools provide a format conducive to sharing information securely and over a distance
5. A mechanism to share CV equipment among multiple providers (e.g., Outlook/SharePoint calendars)

reflect changing staff/staff roles, partner site resources and needs, and services. Regularly scheduled check-ins help ensure that these agreements remain updated. A brief MOU template is available at the end of this chapter (Appendix 5.A).

5.2.2   Unsupervised Settings

In delivering services into clinically unsupervised environments (e.g., patient residence), administrators consider a diversity of factors, such as patient technical capabilities, privacy, confidentiality issues, emergency management, technical support options, and referral resources. Clinically unsupervised environments must possess adequate telehealth equipment (e.g., computer, web camera), internet bandwidth appropriate for CV [12], and a physical space conducive to patient privacy and confidentiality (e.g., a room that family or community members will not enter during care).

Delivering services into clinically unsupervised environments introduces different risks to patient safety relative to clinically supervised care. Notably, however, a burgeoning empirical literature finds that clinically unsupervised care can be delivered without compromising patient safety [8, 14]. Still, CV administrators must develop an emergency management policy appropriate for the clinicians serving unsupervised environments (e.g., medical, psychiatric, or technical problems) that includes capturing contact information for clinical collaborators (e.g., other providers), technical resources (e.g., a technically savvy family member), and emergency contacts (e.g., police, emergency room) local to the client (see Chap. 8 for in depth emergency planning resources). Appendix 5.B provides a template for gathering pertinent contact information related to the patient-site context.

Attaining and managing new referrals for clinically unsupervised services may be challenging. Partnership with a referral source local to the targeted service area (e.g., primary care provider or mental health clinic) or established in telehealth (e.g., large company offering telehealth services) can improve the appropriateness of incoming referrals. Such partnership can also bolster the service's credibility in the local community and the identification of emergency services.

5.3 What Services and Population

Clearly articulating which services a program offers provides insight into what practical environment is best suited for care. Doing so also prevents program expectations from creeping over time to a scope that is impossible to fulfill. Programs may offer consultative services or direct care [6, 17], and may augment in-person care (e.g., an in-person client who is temporarily traveling) or provide a stand-alone service. Administrators must determine which clinical services staff will provide (e.g., psychotherapy, medication management, etc.). Clear clinical and technical inclusion criteria articulate which patients are appropriate for CV services, and provide a standard of care less vulnerable to complaints or even legal recourse [1]. Typical exclusion criteria for CV may include clinical instability likely to require emergency intervention (e.g., current, active suicidal, or homicidal ideation), ideas of reference regarding cameras/recording and, for home-based services, lack of computer or Internet [23]. Please note that given the hundreds of thousands of safe CV encounters already completed in the USA, we do not believe inclusion criteria need to be overly rigorous or otherwise prohibitive, especially in situations where CV-based intervention represents the only reasonable option for services.

5.4 Laws and Policies

Administrators must be familiar with applicable telehealth laws, policies, and licensing requirements at both the provider and patient locations for the proposed CV services. For example, programs that cross geographic boundaries designated by clinician licensure jurisdiction and/or credentialed and privileged domains must take measures to ensure service legality [12]. Insurance panels and malpractice insurance policies may provide coverage for some CV environments (e.g., rural, medical clinics) but not others (e.g., residences) [22]. Legislation may limit the types of services that may be offered into some environments (e.g., the prescription of controlled substances into the home; implementation of the Ryan Haight Online Pharmacy Consumer Protection Act of 2008, 2009) and/or what levels of security are appropriate (e.g., HIPAA, HITECH compliance) [24]. Forensic and correctional environments possess additional policy and regulatory requirements and considerations [4]. Legal consultation may be merited. See Chap. 4 for a number of pragmatic tools to help navigate these issues.

A thorough review of the laws and policies relevant to the proposed services will help guide decision making regarding where CV may be delivered appropriately. The breadth of information necessary to understand the regulatory issues surrounding CV is great. The American Telemedicine Association (http://www.americantelemed.org/) provides administrators with access to policy briefs and discussion forums relevant to CV. Published guidelines and summary documents [7, 13, 28, 30] provide excellent direction and Chap. 3 reviews the core official guidelines endorsed by relevant professional organizations and entities. Still, the

Table 5.4 Synopsis of regulatory questions to consider

1. Will the services provided cross provider licensure jurisdictions?
2. Which insurance carriers, if any, cover the services proposed in the patient location? How does that impact the program's targeted population (e.g., Medicare recipients)?
3. Where may I seek legal counsel to address if or how HIPAA (http://www.hhs.gov/ocr/privacy/), HITECH (http://www.hhs.gov/ocr/privacy/hipaa/administrative/enforcementrule/hitechenforcementifr.html), the Ryan Haight Online Consumer Pharmacy Act (http://www.deadiversion.usdoj.gov/fed_regs/rules/2009/fr0406.pdf), and similar laws and regulations impact the services proposed?
4. Which professional guidelines are relevant to the program's clinical staff?

lack of uniform standards or an established benchmark for competencies leaves many desiring additional guidance. The authors recommend reviewing one of many comprehensive published works regarding these issues [12] and/or obtaining appropriate consultation from a seasoned CV administrator, legal expert [9] and/or telehealth training provider (identified by the Telemental Health Institute, or clinical literature). A state-by-state review of CV licensing regulations is provided by the APA [2] but the review should not substitute for due diligence and independent verification of state laws. Table 5.4 provides a brief synopsis of points to consider specifically regarding regulatory issues.

5.5 How to Communicate Securely with Patients

Secure communication over a distance poses unique challenges to patient privacy, confidentiality, and information security. Successful programs identify methods for communicating information to patients (e.g., appointment times, handouts) and capturing written materials from the patient (e.g., informed consent documentation, psychoeducational materials, homework forms). Traditional methods of distance communication (e.g., fax, mail service) are often slow and inconvenient. Faster electronic forms of communication (e.g., unencrypted email, text, instant message, etc.) pose threats to patient privacy and confidentiality and may be out of compliance with jurisdictional and federal laws and regulations.

Anticipation of important written materials, selection of an appropriate technology, and a documented policy regarding appropriate communication between providers and clients facilitates secure communication. Requiring clinicians to predict which paper-based materials will be central to CV appointments facilitates providing them in advance. For example, home-based clients can receive a mailed packet of paper-based information relevant to their care in advance of their first appointment. Partner clinics can equip CV clinic rooms with frequently used questionnaires and homework forms. Remote printing, fax, and email attachments offer means of providing materials that are not readily available before or created jointly during the session, but rely on availability of clinic staff and equipment. See Chap. 9 for a more thorough review of current methods of document exchange.

Table 5.5 Specific procedures to discuss with patients regarding out of session communication

1. How to contact the provider/provider clinic (e.g., telephone, email), and what constitutes appropriate information
2. When to contact providers/staff at a clinically supervised setting, regarding scheduling and care
3. Any risks associated with the specific method of contact (e.g., email, text)
4. How the provider/clinic will treat information (e.g., limits of confidentiality, mandated reporting, treatment of ambiguous information, confirming the source of information)
5. Response times for different contact methods (e.g., 24 h/telephone vs. 48 h/email)

CV administrators may also generate policies regarding how patients contact providers and deliver clinically relevant information (e.g., completed questionnaires). Written local policy will help ease transition associated with staff and clinical turnover, and compiling all relevant information in one hard-copy or electronic folder for easy reference is essential. Larger CV programs may possess staff at the patient location who are responsible for collecting information and transmitting it securely and quickly to the provider. Smaller programs will not possess access to extensive resources, but may invest in tools that facilitate collection of patient information, document transfer, and bidirectional communication with clients while complying with jurisdictional and federal laws and regulations (e.g., encrypted email programs, secured file transfer services; [23]). Other programs elect to use the telephone to communicate with clients, and require clients to share sensitive information (e.g., questionnaire responses) verbally during CV sessions. Many CV programs elect to use email, text, or other unencrypted methods of communication with patients. Some limit what information is shared this way (e.g., only administrative information), while others do not. These common practices may come under increasing scrutiny from regulatory entities. The authors recommend that program staff provide patients with a written policy that reviews the items covered in Table 5.5 (see Chap. 7 for tools regarding the informed consent process.)

5.6 Scheduling Clinical Video Sessions/Managing Equipment and Room Sharing

Probably the most commonly underaddressed logistical consideration of CV programming is the real-time coordination of available CV equipment and rooms among multiple providers and patients. This problem is magnified exponentially for programs planning to provide care to two or more sites, or for programs adding a site to be serviced by the same providers already servicing a CV site. When adding a site, you cannot assume that the same procedures will translate. Not only does the additional site place extra burden on your providers, but the ecology, personalities, and willingness of staff to cooperate at that new site will likely not replicate the existing site, for better or worse. Not planning for scheduling protocols that account for moving provider availability, no shows/cancelations, and patient needs: (a) puts the limited resource at risk of being underutilized, (b) places *significant burden and stress* on the staff that it will fall to, and (c) encourages "on-the-fly" solutions by those staff, which typically minimize administrative burden by limiting the scheduling availability and flexibility of CV equipment and rooms for patients and providers. See Chap. 1 (Sect. 1.2.1 *Hardware-based clinical videoconferencing systems*) for a common example of how scheduling difficulties often play out.

There are a number of common solutions to CV scheduling that fall on a continuum from prioritizing ease of administrative scheduling, to providing maximum access to services and clinical productivity. A common solution that prioritizes administrative ease is to designate certain blocks of time for patient-end and provider-end CV rooms to specific therapists. In this model, it is up to the therapist to "fill" her schedule in that block of time. The benefits of this plan are that it is straightforward, administratively simple, and encourages streamlined communication and conditions between providers and patient-end staff. For example, if 2–6 p.m. on Tuesdays is Dr. Smith's time on the equipment, support staff at the provider end can develop a clear sense of Dr. Smiths's preferences (i.e., the need for faxed self-report measures) and clinical context (i.e., this slot serves a mostly geriatric patient base, so extra care might be needed when walking patients back and explaining the CV equipment.) The clear downsides of this model involve system-end sacrifices (e.g., if Dr. Smith gets a cancellation, the room goes unused and productivity is down) and patient sacrifices (e.g., limited flexibility in when patients can see Dr. Smith).

On the other end of the spectrum is a fluid scheduling system where providers share an electronic calendar updated in real time for room availability. In this system, when making an appointment with a patient, the provider or support staff logs onto the shared room calendar and blocks off an available time slot. As soon as a patient cancels a scheduled appointment the provider or support staff logs on and clears off the slot so that it can be used by someone else. In this case, it is also helpful for providers or staff to email or text to make others aware that a slot became available or is needed. The benefits of this system is that it maximally addresses clinical need, provides flexibility to patients, reduces the prospects of wasted resources, and provides a real-time way to arrange partial or complete coverage for providers who have called in sick using an already designed administrative protocol. It also promotes close collaboration among providers, which can increase a sense of team work and a "we're all in this together" attitude. The down sides are that it is a complex system to run and often requires a dedicated support staff to manage, especially if there are more than two CV machines or partner sites. Without specialized software, providers or support staff may have to check multiple shared calendars. It can also confuse the responsibilities of patient-side staff (i.e., logging onto a shared calendar to determine who to contact in a technical emergency), moreover, if the clinical team is not cohesive, it can create conflict rather than encourage team work. Managerially, in this system, it is more difficult to track specific provider productivity or CV use. In most cases, this is a system that sounds good on paper, but is too difficult to implement in practice.

There is no preferred or suggested system of CV scheduling that can meet the needs of every clinical context. However, we recommend a blending of the two extremes presented, with close provider communication so that available slots can be utilized. We also recommend a collaborative, iterative process involving clinicians and support staff to determine the plan, the method of preferred communication, and ways to assess how it is going. For a manager, the most important thing is to not minimize how difficult, complex, and time consuming CV scheduling can be and to devote appropriate thought and resources to it.

5.7   Transitional Programming

As in traditional in-person care, CV requires thoughtfulness regarding the lifecycle of care. Specifically, managers of successful CV programs consider the role of CV in care, instruct referral sources and clinicians on how best to orient new clients to CV, and consider what community options for discharge exist. Educating patients about CV (e.g., how it works, benefits, limitations) can increase their comfort with the modality and rapport with their provider [4]. Providing patients who are unfamiliar with CV, with an orientation to the technology facilitates informed consent and allows them to experience CV in a more general way before committing to services. Chapter 10 offers specific helpful suggestions regarding methods of introducing patients to the CV context.

Identifying treatment options for patients who do not complete care or become clinically inappropriate for CV during an episode of care poses an ethical challenge for administrators and clinicians. While clinically supervised partner sites may possess on-site staff available to assume or augment care for clients no longer meeting CV inclusion criteria, unsupervised settings do not have access to similar resources. Administrators must look to the client's local community for referral options. In rural settings, these may be limited to emergency services.

5.8   Recruiting Telehealth Clinicians

Just as recruiting and maintaining patients and care sites are critical to CV program strength, recruiting and educating CV clinicians is a cornerstone of program success. Clinician attitudes [19, 25] and education [5] regarding technology play critical roles in their adoption of telehealth technologies as well as how patients perceive the program [4]. In the authors' experience, clinicians often have more difficulty conceptualizing the use of CV than patients. The creation of evidence-based educational materials (e.g., a folder containing published articles, easy to reference guidelines) for telehealth clinicians to address their clinical and technical competencies is a worthwhile investment [18]. Opportunities to see examples of successful CV sessions or even humorous "sessions gone wrong" (http://www.youtube.com/watch?v=qhCz067QWP4&feature=youtu.be) can assist new CV providers in adoption. Providing staff with practical guidelines relevant to CV [See 7, 13, 28, 30] and specific to their professional discipline will help them to feel and be competent with the medium. Of course, we recommend that clinicians become familiar with the chapters in the second portion of this volume, and especially Chap. 10 regarding therapeutic alliance via CV for clinicians who may be particularly concerned about providing CV services.

Referring staff to an established review of the extant literature regarding CV establishes an empirical basis for CV intervention and facilitates discourse regarding provider concerns [3, 27]. CV administrators must speak to the modality's strengths and limitations nondefensively to demonstrate their credible commitment to patient care first and technology second. Providing clinicians with data that review increased patient care access/reduced costs [16, 20], high rates of patient satisfaction [10, 29], and comparable outcomes to in-person care [16, 26] builds a foundation through which attitudes may change.

In clinics where demand on provider's time is already at a capacity level, adding "additional" duties by being asked to deliver services via telehealth modalities may cause providers to find ways to decline the opportunity to engage in telehealth. At the Portland VA Medical Center, providers were not asked to add additional duties by providing services via telehealth, but rather asked to identify patients from their existing panel to determine who may be suitable for receiving care at a distance. The patients that converted to telehealth were no longer traveling great distances. When management took an "instead of" vs. "in addition to" approach to their providers, it was met with enthusiasm.

In the authors' experiences, providers often cite behavioral and medical emergencies in unsupervised clinical settings as a major point of concern. Several key studies [8, 14, 15] may help allay those fears with recommendations regarding how best to mitigate and manage these risks. In addition, emphasizing the personal benefits of CV adoption for providers, including provider safety [4], increased infection control for provider and patient, and natural partnership with telework may highlight the manner in which the modality stands to improve the provider's work satisfaction. Table 5.6 provides samples of providers' frequently asked questions and possible responses.

Conclusions & Pulling It All Together

Establishing a new CV service requires CV administrators to consider a myriad of factors. Successful administrators and managers consult the literature, seek consultation, and make educated guesses regarding what might work best when other information is unavailable. Table 5.7 provides a brief overview of the questions covered in this chapter.

Table 5.6 Answers to frequently asked questions by providers new to CV

What is Clinical videoteleconferencing (CV)?
CV refers to the use of teleconferencing equipment to communicate with patients over a distance. Typically, the patient is located in his/her home or at one of our partner clinics with videoconferencing equipment.
How is it different from in-person care?
Although the technology used to deliver care is new, the services you provide are not. Scientific studies conducting in typical healthcare settings uniformly support the use of CV.
Is it safe?
Yes. Research shows that CV care—correctly administered—is safe. You will work with your patients and colleagues to ensure that you have a comprehensive safety plan prior to delivering care. We will work together to make sure you are comfortable with and have input on the safety plan.
Do patients like it?
Yes. Research overwhelmingly shows that patients experience CV positively and establish good rapport with their CV care provider.
What will it be like for me?
Research and clinical experience demonstrate that clinicians report high levels of satisfaction with providing CV services. Clinicians report satisfaction with lower no-show rates and being able to provide services that are more convenient for patients as well as being able to provide services to people who otherwise might not be able to access care. Some providers like not having to physically retrieve patients from waiting rooms. Some providers do report an increased feeling of isolation in the workplace if much of their caseload is via CV, a situation that can be resolved by maintaining a mixed caseload and prioritizing team meetings, shared lunch, or team cohesion in other ways.

While there are a number of technological, logistical, legal, and policy-related hurdles to overcome in establishing CV, ultimately, the clinicians and managers implementing CV are responsible for the care delivered to patients. Solutions must work and make sense to them. Advocating for and implementing what works for managers, providers, and patients need not be overwhelming if an organized approach is used. Examining the intersection of a detailed conceptualization of the prospective services and the practical factors that will likely impact service feasibility before implementation will save CV administrators from innumerable challenges down the road. In CV implementation, the devil may be in the details, but the devil you know will cause significantly fewer problems.

Table 5.7 An overview of relevant questions informing the logistics of CV program implementation

Topic area	Questions to be addressed
Needs assessments	Who are the potential clients (diagnosis, stability, access, location?)
	What services are required?
	What resources are available in the identified geographic area?
Laws and policies	What are the provider licensing requirements?
	Will insurance panels and malpractice insurance provide coverage?
	What laws and regulations impact the types of services?
Settings	*Supervised settings*:
	Who are your stakeholders?
	What is your emergency plan?
	How will you document partnerships?
	How will you share space, equipment and records?
	Unsupervised settings:
	Does the patient possess adequate technical expertise and equipment?
	What is your emergency plan?
	What resources are local to the patient?
	Is there a support person to assist as needed?
Service provision	What specific services will you provide?
	What is the planned lifecycle of care?
	How will you communicate securely with remote clients?
	How will you recruit and train providers in telehealth?

Appendix 5.A

Memorandum of Understanding Template

Purpose

This Memorandum of Understanding (MOU) identifies specific clinical, business, and technical details of telehealth services between the patient and provider sites. The document identifies stakeholders, responsibilities and other practical details.

Service and Locations

a. Telehealth service
b. Originating, (Patient) site: Primary Contact:
c. Distant, (Provider) site: Primary Contact:

d. The following services will be provided:
e. How will consults be submitted to provider site:
f. How will patients be screened for appropriateness:
g. Admissions/Discharge policies of patient location:
h. Emergency Management:

    1. Urgent/Emergent events:

        – In the event of a patient medical or behavioral emergency during a tele-health visit, what actions will be performed by provider and patient locations?

Originating, (Patient) Site

Signing Official Date

Distant, (Provider) Site

Signing Official Date

Appendix 5.B

Important Contacts at Patient and Provider Sites

Role	Name	Phone number	Email
Distant (Provider) Site			
Provider			
Technical champion			
Telehealth clinical support technician			
Scheduling staff			
Supervisor (clinical)			
Program champion			
Emergency contacts			
Originating (Patient) Site			
Program champion			
Technical champion			
Telehelath clinical support technician			
Onsite security staff			
Referral source			

References

1. Adams Larsen MA. Legal and ethical issues on the digital frontier. Paper presented at the Idaho State Psychological Association Annual Conference, Sun Valley, ID. 2013 May.
2. American Psychological Association Practice Organization. 2013. Telepsychology 50 state review. http://apapracticecentral.org/advocacy/state/telehealth-slides.pdf. Accessed 30 Nov 2013.
3. Backhaus A, Agha Z, Maglione ML, Repp A, Ross B, Zuest D, Rice-Thorp NM, Lohr J, Thorp SR. Videoconferencing psychotherapy: a systematic review. Psychol Serv. 2012;9(2):111–31. doi:10.1037/a0027924.
4. Batastini AB, McDonald BR, Morgan RD. Videoteleconferencing in forensic and correctional practice. In: Myers K, Turvey CL, editors. Telemental health: clinical, technical and administrative foundations for evidence-based practice. Waltham: Elsevier; 2013. pp. 251–71.
5. Glueck D. Telepsychiatry in private practice. Child Adolesc Psychiatr Clin N Am. 2011;20:1–11. doi:10.1016/j.chc.2010.08.006.
6. Glueck D. Business aspects of a telemental health practice. In: Myers K, Turvey CL, editors. Telemental health: clinical, technical and administrative foundations for evidence-based practice. Waltham: Elsevier; 2013. pp. 109–34.
7. Grady B, Myers KM, Nelson EL, Belz N, Bennett L, Carnahan L. American Telemedicine Association Telemental Health Standards and Guidelines Working Group. Evidence-based practice for telemental health. Telemed J E Health. 2011;17:131–48. doi:10.1089/tmj.2010.0158.
8. Gros DF, Morland LA, Greene CJ, Acierno R, Strachan M, Egede LE, Tuerk PW, Myrick H, Frueh BC. Delivery of evidence-based psychotherapy via video telehealth. J Psychopathol Behav Assess. 2013; 506-21. doi:10.1007/s10862-013-9363-4.
9. Harris E, Younggren JN. Risk management in the digital world. Prof Psychol Res Pract. 2012;42(6):412–8. doi:10.1037/a0025139.
10. Holden D, Dew E. Telemedicine in a rural gero-psychiatric inpatient unit: comparison of perception/satisfaction to onsite psychiatric care. Telemed e-Health. 2008;14(4):381–4. doi:10.1089/tmj.2007.0054.
11. Kramer GK, Ayers T, Mishkind M, Norem A. DoD telemental health guidebook. 2011. http://t2health.org/sites/default/files/cth/guidebook/tmh-guidebook_06-11.pdf. Accessed 30 Nov 2013.
12. Kramer GK, Mishkind MC, Luxton DD, Shore JH. Managing risk and protecting privacy in telemental health: an overview of legal, regulatory, and risk management issues. In: Myers K, Turvey CL, editors. Telemental health: clinical, technical and administrative foundations for evidence-based practice. Waltham: Elsevier; 2013. pp. 83–108.
13. Leenknecht CK, Winters JM, Antoniotti N. Expert consensus recommendations for videoconferencing-based telepresenting. 2011. http://www.americantelemed.org/docs/default-source/standards/expert-consensus-recommendations-for-videoconferencing-based-telepresenting.pdf?sfvrsn=4. Accessed 30 Nov 2013.
14. Luxton DD, Sirotin AP, Mishkind MC. Safety of telemental healthcare delivered to clinically unsupervised settings: a systematic review. Telemed J E Health. 2010;16:705–11. doi:10.1089/tmj.2009.0179.
15. Luxton DD, O'Brien K, McCann RA, Mishkind MC. Home-based telemental healthcare safety planning: what you need to know. Telemed J E Health. 2012;18:629–33. doi:10.1089/tmj.2012.0004.
16. Morland LA, Greene CJ, Rosen CS, Foy D, Reilly P, Shore J, Frueh BC. Telemedicine for anger management therapy in a rural population of combat veterans with posttraumatic stress disorder: a randomized noninferiority trial. J Clin Psychiatry. 2010;71:855–63. doi:10.4088/JCP.09m05604blu.
17. Myers KM, Vander Stoep A, McCarty CA, Klein JB, Palmer NB, Geyer JR, Melzer SM. Child and adolescent telepsychiatry: variations in utilization, referral patterns and practice trends. J Telemed Telecare. 2010;16(3):128–33. doi:10.1258/jtt.2009.090712.

18. Nelson EL, Bui T, Sharp S. Telemental health competencies: training examples from a youth depression CV clinic. In: Gregerson M, editor. Techniques and technologies for medical and graduate education. New York: Springer; 2011. pp. 41–8.
19. Perle JG, Langsam LC, Randel A, Lutchman S, Levine AB, Odland AP, Marker CD. Attitudes toward psychological telehealth: current and future clinical psychologists' opinions of internet-based interventions. J Clin Psychol. 2012;69:100–13. doi:10.1002/jclp.21912.
20. Rabinowitz T, Murphy KM, Amour JL, Ricci MA, Caputo MP, Newhouse PA. Benefits of a telepsychiatry consultation service for rural nursing home residents. Telemed J E Health. 2010;16(1):34–40. doi:10.1089/tmj.2009.0088.
21. Shore JH, Manson SM. A developmental model for rural telepsychiatry. Psychiatr Serv. 2005;56(8):976–80. doi:10.1016/j.genhosppsych.2007.01.013.
22. Smucker Barnwell SV. Clinical issues on the digital frontier: how Scottie beams us up and other practical applications. Paper presented at the Idaho State Psychological Association Annual Conference, Sun Valley, ID. 2013 May.
23. Smucker Barnwell SV, Juretic MA, Hoerster KD, Van de Plasch R, Felker BL. VA Puget Sound Telemental Health Service to rural veterans: a growing program. Psychol Serv. 2012;9:209–11. doi:10.1037/a0025999.
24. Spargo G, Karr A, Turvey CL. Technology options for the provision of mental health care through videoteleconferencing. In: Myers K, Turvey CL, editors. Telemental health: clinical, technical and administrative foundations for evidence-based practice. Waltham: Elsevier; 2013. pp. 135–51.
25. Speedie SM, Ferguson AS, Sanders J, Doarn CR. Telehealth: the promise of new care delivery models. Telemed J E Health. 2008;14(9):964–7. doi:10.1089/tmj.2008.0114.
26. Tuerk PW, Yoder M, Ruggiero KJ, Gros DF, Acierno R. A pilot study of exposure therapy for posttraumatic stress disorder delivered via telehealth technology. J Traumac Stress. 2010;23(1):116–23. doi:10.1002/jts.20494.
27. Turvey CL, Myers K. Research in telemental health: review and synthesis. In: Myers K, Turvey CL, editors. Telemental health: clinical, technical and administrative foundations for evidence-based practice. Waltham: Elsevier; 2013. pp. 397–431.
28. Turvey C, Coleman M, Dennison O, Drude K, Goldenson M, Hirsch P, Zucker ML. ATA practice guidelines for video-based online mental health services. Telemed J E Health. 2013;19(9):722–30. doi:10.1089/tmj.2013.9989.
29. Wilson JAB, Onorati K, Mishkind M, Reger MA, Gahm GA. Soldier attitudes about technology-based approaches to mental health care. Cyberpsychol Behav. 2008;11:767–9. doi:10.1089/cpb.2008.0071.
30. Yellowlees P, Shore J, Roberts L. Practice guidelines for videoconferencing-based telemental health. Telemed J E Health. 2010;16(10):1074–89. doi:10.1089/tmj.2010.0148.

Chapter 6
Program Evaluation and Modification: Supporting Pragmatic Data-Driven Clinical Videoconferencing (CV) Services

Donald M. Hilty, Peter M. Yellowlees, Peter W. Tuerk, Sarah E. H. Nasatir-Hilty, Erica Z. Shoemaker, Barb Johnston and Michele T. Pato

Chapter Summary

Purpose This chapter discusses the prioritization of desired outcomes and ongoing program evaluation in the provision of clinical videoconferencing (CV) services. It provides an overall organizing framework to consider program evaluation from the very early stages of planning. Emphasis is placed on crafting evaluation fitted to specific needs and available resources.

Context Understanding the fundamentals of program evaluation is necessary for clinical managers, clinicians, and telehealth experts because the processes of sound evaluation are essential for goal-directed programming and innovation with new CV services. Program evaluation may require a fundamental shift in philosophy—from measuring what happens with services, to planning for specific desired outcomes, and then gathering support for and designing services around those specific outcomes—in advance. The foundation for high-quality evaluation is a program with organizational support and an interdisciplinary team that shares responsibilities for overlapped roles.

D. M. Hilty (✉) · E. Z. Shoemaker · M. T. Pato
Department of Psychiatry, Keck School of Medicine at USC,
Los Angeles, CA, USA
e-mail: hilty@usc.edu

P. M. Yellowlees
UC Davis Department of Psychiatry, Health Informatics
Fellowship Program UC Davis, Sacramento, CA, USA

P. W. Tuerk
Department of Psychiatry and Behavioral Sciences, Medical University of South Carolina;
Mental Health Service, Ralph H. Johnson VA Medical Center, Veterans Health Administration,
Charleston, SC, USA

S. E. H. Nasatir-Hilty
Department of Psychiatry, Keck School of Medicine at USC, Los Angeles, CA, USA

B. Johnston
HealthLinkNow, Sacramento, CA, USA

© Springer International Publishing Switzerland 2015
P. W. Tuerk, P. Shore (eds.), *Clinical Videoconferencing in Telehealth,*
Behavioral Telehealth, DOI 10.1007/978-3-319-08765-8_6

Tools   The chapter provides a number of concrete tools to assist in planning for
            and implementing CV program evaluation. Included is a list of team-
            based resources which should be evaluated during the program develop-
            ment stage; a list of team qualities that can be planned for and assessed;
            examples for identifying multidimensional goals and alignment of goals
            across facilities; resources highlighting types of cost analyses; a list of
            cost-related outcomes and questions relevant to CV programming; a list
            of satisfaction-related CV outcomes for patients, providers, and support
            staff; examples of relevant process-oriented evaluation measures; a table
            organizing different types of reference groups for comparing CV program
            outcomes; and a list of program evaluation do's and don'ts. References and
            resources for information are also provided for further review.

6.1 Introduction: Changes in Health Care and Contemporary Program Evaluation

The Affordable Care Act and other trends in health care are reshaping services significantly. The proportion spent on health care in the gross national product (GNP),
trouble balancing budgets, and recession all have been partially responsible for the
need to reexamine how health care is conducted and paid for. More accountability is
expected of clinicians, clinics, and health systems—by both consumers and payers.
Focus is being placed on accessible, safe, quality care when the consumer wants or
needs it, with efficiency and integration and the elimination of waste. New models
move efforts to improve quality from a desirable, though perhaps peripheral, part of
the care process to a central piece of it. Increased emphasis is also being placed on
mid-level practitioners, as high-level trained clinicians cannot do it all. Overall, we
are presented with more opportunities to integrate medical and mental health (MH)
services. Of course, the potential role of CV to help advance these efficiencies and
improve care cannot be overstated.

Yet designing new CV programs without building in thoughtful program evaluation and measurement of effectiveness misses the mark and threatens to replicate
our existing inefficiencies and shortcomings, albeit in a new medium of care [1].
Behavioral CV services are being increasingly integrated into primary care, just as
their in-person predecessors were, in the form of consultation to primary care or
collaborative care models [1, 2, 3, 4]. Additionally, web-based data management,
electronic health records (EHR), stepped models of care, and other innovations are
facilitating increased reliance on CV methods. Wider availability of services and
providing something better than usual care make CV services helpful—this necessary integration may change our decision-making about how to best to provide care
in general. However, rarely in life, and even less so in health care, do good ideas
translate into effective change without trial and error and ongoing evaluation.

Even so, program evaluation and outcome work is still *a substantial shift* in
philosophical approach for some. Usually in medicine, we assess and treat patients

and then look at outcomes—we assume doing evaluation at the end will suffice. This is akin to the old style of education, in which we taught developed curricula, with the assumption that mastery enabled a learner to succeed. Program evaluation was often cursory and added on at the end. The contemporary view of education is different—it is learner-centered and outcome-centered, whereby the end product determines what is built or put in place. Though "teaching to the test" can be a divisive idiom among educators, in medicine, it is our goal; we want the process of treatment to lead to predefined and quantifiable outcomes. Accordingly, the contemporary philosophy of program evaluation incorporates programmatic changes based on iterative evaluations and trials.

As CV enters its sixth decade, it has increased access to care and both patients and providers are very satisfied with it for a wide variety of services [5] for adults [6], children/adolescent [7, 8], and geriatric patients [9, 10]. A new generation of studies on telehealth and CV has replaced the "primary" view of CV as a new and different way of providing health services to a contemporary view that it is a vehicle for providing care that is here to stay and an integral part of modern health care. Whereas the primary view of CV often sought to assess the feasibility, acceptability, or patient/provider satisfaction with the modality, the contemporary view seeks to assess the actual desired outcomes of services delivered. An earlier review of CV's effectiveness considered it effective in terms of providing access to care, being well-accepted, and having good educational outcomes [5]. Most studies and programs today are moving beyond general satisfaction measures to issues of reliability, cost/economics, and clinical outcomes. Accordingly, a more recent review focused on clinical effectiveness as a bottom line way to evaluate CV [1], and concluded that the current evidence base generally supports the *assumption* that a broad array of face-to-face services can be replicated effectively via CV. Yet we must remain cognizant of this assumption and therefore not gear program evaluation to answer the question, "are CV services effective?," but rather, to answer "are CV services effective to do 'what' for 'whom,' 'when' and 'at what' financial, administrative, and clinical, costs?"

6.2   Program Evaluation Basics

At the root, the point of program evaluation is to improve upon, innovate, expand, justify, or secure resources for clinical services. As such, program evaluation is a broad term that can be applied to almost every aspect of clinical programming and every aspect supporting clinical programming. This broad conceptualization should be limited by a program's specific goals and careful consideration of what is crucially important to evaluate, given limited resources and time. To help organize and get a handle on the potentially daunting task of designing an effective CV evaluation strategy, we offer several nonmutually exclusive domains we believe to be crucial to managing high quality CV services: (1) Program and team development; (2) economic cost and value; (3) satisfaction (e.g., patient, provider, staff); (4) clinical outcomes; and (5) process-oriented parameters (administrative and clinical). These domains are by no means exhaustive and they necessarily overlap. The particular taxonomy of these overarching categories, as presented, is less important than making sure we consider and judge the specific contents based on specific goals and the goals of your CV collaborators. For example, the technical usability of a CV system could easily be its own domain, rather than being subsumed under the category of satisfaction, likewise, many process-oriented parameters (e.g., wait times, number of medication corrections) could also be considered clinical outcomes depending on the circumstances. The chapter is less concerned with organizing and categorizing domains of evaluation, than it is with familiarizing the reader with all the relevant individual components of CV assessment, identifying targets of measurement that might seem idiosyncratic to those new to CV programming, providing examples, and discussing relevant conceptual frameworks to assist with adequate program evaluation and high-quality services. Hopefully we can do so with parsimony and in a user-friendly manner. The point of the chapter is to simplify the process, not overwhelm.

6.2.1 Formal vs. Informal Assessment

Before we consider the first steps of program evaluation it may be helpful to highlight the importance of flexibility and creativity in assessment procedures. In order for assessment of any important construct to be useful, it has to be pragmatic and achievable. Ultimately, there is a range of how ambitious a program's goals are, its funding, skills of team members, and the level of support from administration. Deciding on the depth and breadth of CV program evaluation depends on a program's limitations as much as its goals. Informal, semiformal, and formal assessment procedures can be chosen or mixed and matched to meet a specific program's needs. Here it should be noted that *informal* assessment is not synonymous with *ineffective* assessment; well-planned informal procedures (such as conversations with staff, group-based identification of weekly struggles and successes, etc.) can be powerful tools to help guide ongoing implementation. Additionally, formal assessment need not be lengthy; a well-targeted four-question survey may be quite efficient and effective depending on the information needed and what you plan to do with the information. Issues of measurement validity and reliability will be addressed later in the chapter, for now it is enough to note that the most valid and reliable evaluative measures are useless if they go unused or unanalyzed due do to not being practical enough for a given situation.

6.2.2 Feasibility and Program Evaluation

Ultimately, programs and program evaluation must be feasible. Feasibility may be described in terms of operational, economic, technical, market, resource, cultural, or financial feasibility. In general, feasibility studies aim to rationally uncover the strengths and weaknesses of an existing or proposed venture, opportunities and risk, resources required, and ultimately the prospects for success. Often the term "feasibility" is used to distinguish such evaluations from evaluation aimed at investigating clinical outcomes. As the name suggests, demonstrating the feasibility of a program would come before demonstrating the clinical effectiveness of a program.

Feasibility parameters are often descriptive or qualitative and include a description of the product or service, details of the operations, descriptions of how well a proposed system solves current problems and takes advantage of opportunities, or fits in with existing business environments, policies, and overarching goals. Quantitative aspects of feasibility are often based on needs identified in historical data, financial or service utilization projections, or measures of how desirable the planned services are to patients, providers, managers, and stakeholders.

Most aspects of program feasibility will be subsumed under the process of performing a formal needs assessment before program planning and implementation (Chap. 2). To assess ongoing or operational feasibility, i.e., based on actual data collected during implementation, many research-funded projects incorporate a pilot program. Within the parameters of real-world program development and implementation, it may be wise to integrate the pilot project framework by starting small and building out with ongoing assessment.

The general groundwork for CV feasibility has already been laid and so current program evaluation of feasibility should be geared specifically to the nuances of the proposed services provided. The developed evidence-base related to CV feasibility is generally focused on satisfaction and usability of CV services (covered below). Circa 1995, technical issues were prominent in the feasibility literature (e.g., poor visual images, pixilation, "drops" of conversations, audio delay)—all due to low bandwidth. From there feasibility studies moved on to focus on the overall experience and acceptability of CV modalities to clinicians and patients.

As noted, Chap. 2 provides a thorough review of the needs assessment and initial feasibility process. For our purposes in considering ongoing program evaluation, the concept of feasibility will remain important at every new phase of program development and evaluation. That is, before asking if we have been successful with an identified goal, we must know that the identified goal addresses a real need and is possible. As basic as that sounds, not challenging unidentified assumptions in program development and evaluation often leads to unnecessary duplication of labor, role confusion, waste, and staff frustration. Accordingly, as applied to program evaluation, ask "does this evaluation goal address a real need in my program, and is it feasible to measure?"

6.3 Assessing Program Development: Begin Evaluation Immediately

Developing a new CV program is a much more difficult task than keeping an established one going. Accordingly, if you are committed to ongoing and meaningful program evaluation for the improvement of services, it makes little sense to do the hard part (i.e., building those services) without the benefit of a thoughtful stepwise evaluation. While it is tempting to want to build something and then see how it works, we would encourage the immediate engagement of an evaluation framework in the earliest stages. *Here we are not meaning merely building in the capacity for program evaluation at some point, but rather, we are promoting active and thoughtful assessment of how you are going about building the resources and collaborations that will become your CV program.* This is a process that we all do, on some level, when trying to get anything done, so really what we are discussing is operationalizing and expanding that internal evaluative process into an external, defined, and measurable set of hypotheses and goals. Committing to this creates an awareness that can help managers move from an initial internal thought, "Well that didn't go well," to an understanding (or hypothesized understanding) of how and why it did not go well, what to try differently in the future, and how to know if there was positive movement.

6.3.1   Time as a Basic Measure

Ultimately, responsible and conservative implementation with assessment built in is safer than doing too much at once. A basic plan with an option or two for expansion can work well. Program development will depend on identifying needs (Chap. 2), understanding established guidelines (Chap. 3), creating policy (Chap. 4), choice of available technologies (Chap. 1), and the logistics of implementation (Chap. 5). In relation to program evaluation, establishing and evaluating timelines for the development of all these milestones is crucial for the sake of urgency and to keep focus on being productive. Establishing, meeting, failing, and documenting the reasons for failing predetermined timelines will help you to identify and address process-, people-, and content-related patterns/problems in your program development.

6.3.2   Assessing Conflict and Resolution

Any new programming brings conflict and unexpected difficulties; expect, plan for, and assess how you deal with bumps in the road. In program development there will be layers of complexity, problems, complications, and other untoward events that are not foreseen. Resolution of a specific problem is key, but being effective at conflict resolution in general is essential. Because CV programs necessarily involved two or more sites of care, there is more opportunity for conflict, opposing views, and mismatched goals. Because scheduling between facilities involves not only patient and therapist availability, but also the availability of CV equipment and/or limited room space that the equipment is in, there is natural conflict built into the model. A common example is the tension between a scheduler's need for simplicity and organization (i.e., blocks of room and equipment time at a remote site allotted to a specific therapist) and a program manager's need for productivity and flexibility (i.e., limiting flexibility in a therapist's schedule might make staying

Table 6.1 Team-based resources to be evaluated during CV program development

1. Leadership staff
2. Clinical staff
3. Patient-side clinical support staff: walk patients to CV rooms, administer measures
4. Patient- and provider-side referral sources: clinical staff to provide referrals for CV
5. Patient- and provider-side technical support: hands-on responsive personnel
6. Administrative support: business manager, scheduling staff, clerks
7. Data entry support: for program evaluation
8. Statistician/analyst: to investigate data
9. Protected team time: meetings to celebrate success, review, and problem solve
10. Protected clinician time: adequate time for clinicians to manage CV encounters
11. Time for resource protection: to effectively convey evaluation results to stakeholders
12. Evaluation resources: assessment plans, clinical measures, process-oriented measures

busy more difficult depending on when and where patient flow is coming from). Additionally, CV rooms at patient-side sites are often in shared clinical space, and so there is more opportunity for conflict over the scarce resource. This problem can be compounded at the beginning of a program as it often takes time to build up appropriate remote-site referral streams and so blocked off time with no referrals can be seen as an unacceptable waste by others wishing to occupy the clinical space.

Accordingly, planning for, assessing, and modifying how you deal with built-in conflict based on the incoming data is no minor detail. Without a framework for assessment (formal or informal), it is often easy to conclude that particular schedulers, clinicians, or managers are just "difficult people." Such conclusions leave little room for pragmatic solutions and are a good sign that you are on "autopilot" with regard to actively evaluating your program development and ability or overcome barriers to change.

6.3.3   Personnel, Resources and Team Qualities

Good evaluation of outcomes related to CV begins with a program and its fitness: organization, function, leadership, team members, experience, and many other parameters. If one were thinking more broadly, the approach to evaluation would start with how to set up a good team. When designing a program, thought should be given to team members, affiliations, personnel competencies, level of on-site and remote-site buy-in, and resources, all in relation to specific and measurable program goals. A brief analysis of setting up a team well suited for ongoing program evaluation will be helpful. Each component of a high-functioning CV team should have a plan for evaluation, and plans can be as simple, involved, formal, or informal as you think necessary, as long as evaluation and feedback (positive and negative), and/or acquiring the needed team component is on your radar. Table 6.1 identifies the team-based resources that should be evaluated during the program development stage.

In regard to point 12 on Table 6.1, it is not insignificant that even our methods of evaluation should be evaluated, and discarded or improved upon if called for.

Table 6.2 Qualities of a high-functioning CV team

1. Unified goals
2. Vitality, purpose and sense of professional well-being
3. Interdisciplinary collaboration: ability to share knowledge and respect varied experiences and skill-sets
4. Role definition with overlapping/interchangeable responsibilities (see Chap. 5, Table 5.2 for list of personnel roles regarding CV programming)
5. Clear non-defensive communication
6. Personal support
7. Stability
8. Productive conflict resolution

Often the initial process of evaluation opens our eyes to aspects of programming that are not being adequately evaluated to meet our goals. The opposite is also true, in that an initial evaluation might make it clear that we are collecting data on and evaluating too much. Sometimes answers or processes are simpler than we suppose. Sometimes the need for and complexity of evaluation ebbs and flows with staff turnaround and program fluctuation.

Having a responsive team that can adapt to and create change is key. An underidentified area of program evaluation is in attending to team characteristics and mores that promote responsiveness and effectiveness. Assessing shared team processes, in addition to the individual staff and resources listed above, promotes efficiency in leadership and course correction. A high-functioning CV team will display the qualities listed in Table 6.2, all of which can be planned for, fostered, assessed, and improved.

As can be inferred from this list, successful programs and program managers plan for creating an environment with these qualities, and when such qualities are achieved on a team, it is by no mistake or arbitrary good fortune. Fostering and assessing such intangible, but meaningful, team characteristics can be challenging, which should underscore the importance of forethought when choosing CV personnel, team procedures, and program goals.

6.4 Assessing Alignment of Goals

In program development and evaluation it is important to understand from the beginning, or as soon as possible, how the CV program is aligned with the overall organization's goals and the goals of collaborating partners. Here we take it for granted that all parties are interested in facilitating meaningful clinical services to patients and instead focus on alignment of specific interests (i.e., clinical, administrative, technical, physical, and financial) within that larger mission that might impact the CV collaboration.

Alignment of goals involves multiple levels. First, consider the overlapping missions of the program and its parent organization, and then consider the goals of

Table 6.3 Example of aligned and non-aligned CV goals among institutional stakeholders. (Source: Tuerk et al., available at: http://behavioraltelehealth.org/v1/c6/goals)

	Parent institution or medical center	Specialty clinic providing CV services	Rural health center receiving CV services
Aligned goals	Expand patient catchment area	Demonstrate clinician productivity	Handle patient overflow
Aligned goals	Maximize use of highly developed resources	Develop referral streams for specialized services	Fill critical gap in existing services
Aligned goals	Cut down on travel reimbursements to qualified patients driving long distances for care	Lower the rate of missed or rescheduled appointments per therapist	Provide convenient care to current patients
Nonaligned goals	Rules focused: promote institutional organization; minimize liability by maximizing procedural standardization across services	Patient-flow focused: Minimize disruption to in-person services by maximizing procedural creativity to fit in new CV services; maximize CV patient scheduling flexibility via fluid resource sharing and ongoing responsive collaboration with rural site	Resource focused: Guard existing limited resources, reduce additional administrative work load on support staff by minimizing responsive ongoing collaboration, and maximizing fixed schedules and rigid collaborative procedures
Nonaligned goals	Seeks to meet evolving and often competing process-oriented benchmarks	Seeks to treat referrals with a specific diagnosis for specialized services with a specific clinical benchmark	Seeks to refer a wider, more general sampling of patients and problems to help with local backlog

the collaborating sites or organizations. Though we are interested in overlapping goals it is probably most important to understand where and how missions and motives might be at odds. Often these conflicts come into focus only after program implementation. Inconsistencies or resistance in the behaviors of collaborators are often tied to competing goals, and discerning or inferring those motives or goals can be difficult if communication is not open. Once identified or hypothesized, it can be helpful to use Venn diagrams or lists to delineate aligned and nonaligned goals. Table 6.3 provides a real-world example based on a mental health specialty clinic in an urban medical center providing services to a rural community clinic under.

Key demonstrations of alignment are in negotiated contract or service agreements, as noted by the agreed upon respective responsibilities to the collaboration. Often service agreements codify overarching alignment but are inadequate to address predictable logistical conflicts that might arise during implementation. Accordingly, because "the devil is in the details," it is wise to enter into CV partnerships with as much understanding as possible about potential stressors to the program. Doing so can help to make the service agreement or contract adequately specific as well as to highlight previously underidentified areas for assessment.

Table 6.4 Brief overview of popular cost analysis frameworks related to CV programming

Type of cost analysis	Function/purpose of analysis in CV context
Cost offset analyses	Investigates if treating mental conditions via CV may reduce other health costs, to offset the expense of new CV programming. Cost offset analyses are widely used
Cost minimization analysis	Same as cost offset framework, but searches for different (lower) costs in specific domains
Cost-effectiveness analyses	Investigates CV intervention costs compared to relevant alternative expenditures for similar clinical or administrative outcomes
Cost–utility analyses	Same as cost-effectiveness framework but adds data on quality-of-life measures related to treatment in CV contexts
Cost–benefit analyses	Investigates all factors in economic terms. This method calls for standardizing health inputs and outcomes by monetary units. It is useful for evaluating interventions that appear far too expensive at face value, but not longitudinally, e.g., a transplant helps someone live an additional 50 years; or PTSD remission helps someone go from being unemployed to working

PTSD posttraumatic stress disorder

6.5   Evaluating CV Cost/Economic Outcomes

With regard to assessing cost outcomes, the most straightforward and conservative approach is to involve a health economist with specialized expertise. In many cases resources will be too limited to hire expert analysts. However, an expert does not necessarily have to be involved over the whole course of programming, but can be consulted with beforehand to come up with a feasible plan for and your team to follow. In cases where no help is available, there is benefit to understanding and delineating between differing types of cost analyses [11]. Table 6.4 provides a brief overview of common frameworks applicable to CV programming evaluation. No one framework is likely adequate for a given program, rather the types of analyses are meant to vary by the relevant questions related to particular metrics or measures.

The ATA has thoroughly evaluated specific dimensions [12] of cost frameworks and concluded that standardized metrics and clear definitions do not exist for many of the cost structures. This may be appropriate as costs are derived and perceived differently across contexts. However, there are several cost factors that were identified as important to measure objectively, compiled by the ATA [13] and available at: http://www.americantelemed.org/resources/standards/ata-standards-guidelines/a-lexicon-of-assessment-and-outcome-measurements-for-telemental-health#.U2b-G2xYrfdk.

Typically, there are many resource-related costs and benefits to CV programming worth tracking for program evaluation. Cost assessments and value assessments overlap [13] and a systematic plan for evaluating both in relation to a program's predefined goals can aid a program significantly. Generally, programs vary in what they value and calculate in terms of cost. For example large institutions may choose to operate specific CV programs at a (comparative) loss to meet some larger clinical mandate, while smaller programs, or individual practices may be utilizing CV modalities specifically to increase revenue streams.

Table 6.5   Cost-related issues, outcomes, and questions relevant to CV programming

1. Cost constructs can considered for financial, time, space, travel, clinical, and any resource-related unit, outcome, benefit, or drawback to CV services
2. Cost constructs should be stratified by institution, program, clinician, patient, and community
3. Distinguish between:
a) Cost (how much?)
b) Value per cost (worth or desired outcome by units of cost)
c) Cost reduction (how much saved?)
d) Cost avoidance (how much costs prevented?)
4. Consider measuring cost avoidance rather than cost reduction. Although cost reduction is often confused with cost avoidance, cost avoidance is generally much easier and cheaper to estimate because it focuses on specific domains. For example, it is easier to estimate road miles saved per encounter over a clinical year and the related avoidance of institutional travel vouchers for eligible patients than it is to get to the bottom line of money saved by the institution after factoring in all the necessary inputs of cost outlay for the CV program
5. Are clinicians able to be more productive with CV services, i.e., have more clinical encounters due to CV implementation? Note: This applies both to remote specialty providers actually engaged in CV services and also to local patient-end referring providers who may be able to service/screen more patients in general settings due to the added availability of having specialty care providers to refer to via CV
6. Did clinicians experience fewer no-shows and cancelations via CV modalities? If so, what is the associated cost avoidance (or waste avoidance) in unproductive person hours?
7. Cost of travel, missed work, and hotel accommodations avoided by patients due to the availability of CV services locally
8. Did patients utilizing CV services experience shorter wait-times than usual for a given area/ patient population (worth/value)?
9. Did patients have access to and utilize more services appropriately with CV implementation?
10. Did patients utilize fewer services inappropriately with CV implementation? Service utilization is both a positive and negative outcome depending on clinical context [13]. For example we may want to use CV modalities to increase utilization of specialty care services for patients with a particular diagnosis, and at the same time decrease their utilization of general health services over the long term (ostensibly due to the specialty care amelioration of targeted problems)
11. Cost of administrative and technological CV infrastructure per clinical encounter. This can be compared to cost of in-person encounters or to additional revenue created by CV development. Note: distinguish start up costs/initial investment from ongoing program costs
12. Cost avoidance, or compounded cost avoidance over time, related to providing timely and clinically matched services to patients who otherwise would have gone un- or underserved in the early stages of a diagnosis
13. Comparative ratios of cost to clinical encounters
14. Comparative ratios of cost to desired outcome, i.e., diagnosis remission or quality of life. If you know ongoing program costs per time unit of capture (i.e., quarter or year), you can relate that to number of diagnoses in remission due to CV treatment over same period of time. That can be a broader calculation using all program costs, or more specific, prorating by just the number of patients who benefited

Table 6.5 provides is a summary list of cost-related outcomes and questions relevant to CV programming. It would be labor-intensive and unnecessary to measure and assess all of them. The checklist is provided to help managers think about what is most important for their specific programs.

In all cost-related CV evaluation, it is important to note or factor in that CV is associated with a greater time burden on providers. This is a fact that is often overlooked by leaders at higher levels of clinical administration. In CV services, it is tempting (though incorrect) to assume that providers of point-of-care services are a standard "X," that can be dropped into a telehealth equation. Even if an initial CV infrastructure and administrative staff is budgeted for, CV modalities are associated with more complex coordination, administration, communication, and technical difficulties for providers, before, during and after the actual point of care. Providers working with programs that do not plan for this extra time are often pressed for time or have to work late to finish clinical notes or other duties. The productivity lost in fewer scheduled billable slots per CV provider can be offset with fewer actual no-shows related to the provision of services that are more convenient for patients. Regardless, in cost evaluation it is important to remember that nothing is free, and providers' extended responsibilities are no exception. New technologies like asynchronous telepsychiatry [14] or implementation of low-cost, web-based clinical trial management system for community studies [15, 16] may be desirable. For an additional resource summarizing published cost-related studies in the field of CV see [1, 13].

6.6   Assessing Satisfaction

In general, the CV evidence-base for satisfaction and quality consistently documents superior ratings of both (see Chap. 10 for a review). In fact, although product satisfaction in general is typically impacted by consumers' states, traits, and past experiences, many studies on the impact of these potential moderators of satisfaction with CV modalities, such as depression, personality, and other dimensions as they relate to CV were aborted or never done, because satisfaction ratings were so high; studies in special populations like children and adults are positive, too [17]. Perhaps ironically, patient and provider *expectations* of CV are easier to meet than ever, as new generations who use Skype and other technologies to connect with loved ones across the world have increased familiarity with the technology and are used to delayed audio and occasional dropped or disrupted calls. At the same time CV infrastructures and technologies are becoming, faster, more stable, and easier to use.

Accordingly, given the already established and robust evidence base for CV satisfaction, increased public comfort with the modality, and ever-evolving product quality, there may be little scientific value in assessing CV satisfaction as a major component of CV program evaluation. Moreover, satisfaction should never be used as a primary program evaluation outcome unless the target population is dramatically different from typical treatment seeking populations in some relevant way, e.g., samples with highly impaired language, schizophrenia or other serious mental illness, or with a culture, condition, or disability that could reasonably impact comfort or ability to see, hear, and comprehend CV communication.

Even so there may be many good reasons to include measures of satisfaction within a larger program evaluation framework. First, not all stakeholders are aware

Table 6.6 Patient-related items often assessed in CV satisfaction surveys

1. Patient's overall subjective satisfaction
2. Patients' experience with the CV service provided
3. Patient–provider communication
4. Convenience of receiving care via this approach
5. Ability of CV services to meet specific health needs
6. Would patient use CV services again?
7. Would patient refer others to this service?
8. Ease of use
9. Preference
10. Comfort using the CV modality
11. Fit of or readiness for the CV modality
12. Simplicity of use
13. Availability of technical help
14. Clarity of transmission signal and volume
15. Interruptions in transmission signal
16. Ability to establish personal connection with provider
17. Therapeutic alliance
18. Comfort of clinical space
19. Missed work time avoided
20. Miles of travel avoided
21. Access to care
22. Open-ended questions to allow for patient-initiated feedback
23. Cultural acceptability

of the scientific CV literature and so demonstrating high satisfaction ratings may help to bolster a program's support base or resources. Second, satisfaction may be a very good measure when testing out new experimental CV technologies, treatment to low-bandwidth areas of the globe, or in ever-evolving contexts, for example, on smaller handheld devices or with a product like Google glasses. Third, as CV modalities become more widely accepted and are used in more diverse treatment ecologies, with varying target populations, disorders, and with new treatments, it may be wise to continue to assess satisfaction with the modality as a moderator of treatment outcomes. Fourth, a program may have resource limitations that might reasonably impact some dimension of satisfaction. Fifth, perhaps providers' attitudes and satisfaction with CV modalities will vary as more and more of their caseload expectations shift over to CV contexts. Sixth, assessing support staff satisfaction, and especially remote (patient-end) support staff satisfaction can be crucial to ongoing relationships and programming functioning. These are just a few of the reasons why measuring satisfaction may be helpful depending on a program's context.

When assessing CV satisfaction, use of validated measures such as the Telemedicine Satisfaction Questionnaire [18] is strongly encouraged. However, there may be circumstances where only a few aspects of satisfaction are relevant or targeted for assessment. Although it is not possible or useful to denote all potential aspects of programming open to satisfaction, Tables 6.6, 6.7, and 6.8 summarize some common patient-related, provider-related, and support staff-related elements,

Table 6.7 Provider-related items often assessed in CV satisfaction surveys

1. Ratio of negatives vs. positives regarding the modality
2. Therapist retention
3. Therapist recruitment
4. Sense of efficacy as a provider
5. Positive endorsement of patients' experiences, i.e., how do your patients like the CV modality?
6. Ease of integration into clinical workflow
7. Ease of physical transition between in-person and CV modes of care during work day
8. The extent to which the provider values telehealth encounters when interacting with patients
9. Aspects of in-person care the provider "misses" and/or the overall value of missed aspects
10. Satisfaction with plan for handling clinical emergencies
11. Avenues of communication: can clinical staff reliably reach support staff?
12. Satisfaction with ability to provide program input or feedback
13. Technical competency
14. Perceived value of better diagnosis, treatment or disease management
15. Sense of isolation during workday
16. Effect if any of increased "screen time" during work day
17. Open-ended questions to allow for clinician-initiated feedback

Table 6.8 Support staff-related items that should be considered for CV satisfaction surveys

1. Ease of scheduling
2. Ease of rescheduling in case of provider absence
3. Disruption to previous responsibilities
4. Comfort with operating in a more clinical realm than normal, i.e., walking patients to rooms, addressing potential clinical issues or questions
5. Comfort/satisfaction with plan for handling clinical emergencies
6. Avenues of communication: can support staff reliably reach clinical staff?
7. Ability to see and solve problems to affect administrative change?
8. Open-ended questions to allow for support-staff initiated feedback

which might help readers to identify the most relevant factors for their particular planned programming.

The list above identifies the assessment of culture as it relates to CV. A plan for assessment of ethnic, cultural, and language issues is essential in contexts where heterogeneity of culture cannot be ruled out [19]. In fact, the impact of culture on CV acceptance and effectiveness may be an overriding concern depending on context. The degree to which an individual perceives the mode of delivery to align with cultural beliefs and expectations is important and may be more malleable than many other culture-based beliefs, simply because CV contexts may be a relatively new idea to patients and so standard cultural perspectives on it might not be widely developed or shared. Accordingly, the impact of culture should be discussed and not assumed. Assessment of this should include cultural understanding of technology and expectations of interpersonal communication. For example, in cultures where too much eye contact is not the norm, CV modalities might actually amplify provider/patient differences. At the same time, CV modalities which increase outreach of services geographically also increase the chances of providers coming into contact with populations or cultures they are not familiar with. Assessment of cultural access, should also consider how technology might better connect cultural expectations, e.g., providing access to the patient's primary language or same-culture providers. Populations studied include, but are not limited to, Asian, Eastern European, Native American, and Latino American groups [19, 26].

The following items/techniques are often employed when assessing *provider* satisfaction with CV modalities:

Support staff often gets the "short shrift" in the telehealth literature. All telehealth managers know that successful programming relies on good relationships with patient-end support staff. Often, published findings related to successful CV outcomes take the time to discuss the importance of building patient-end staff buy-in and relationships [27] with site visits, lunches, or other techniques. Less often do managers outline the importance of taking the time to survey the valuable opinions of front-line support staff. If we objectify support staff as a potential barrier to be "dealt with" or "brought along" or "bought-in," we miss valuable opportunities to capitalize on the perspectives of people who see many aspects of our conceived programming from a completely different (and often times more well informed) perspective than we do.

Most aspects of program evaluation should be conducted frequently and with an emphasis on program improvement, however measures of satisfaction may be particularly salient to assess early. This is not only because satisfaction will impact patient/provider acceptance of the modality but also because many aspects of satisfaction are easily solved or manipulated. In program evaluation, and satisfaction particularly, we want to "fail often and fail quickly" so as to identify and improve problems in an efficient manner.

6.7 Evaluation of Process-Oriented Parameters

Evaluation demonstrates the value of services and is key to improving and protecting those services. Ultimately, even the most effective, evidence-based health care is not sustainable unless it meets the minimum acceptable level of success across a myriad of process-oriented outcomes. Indeed, because of the complexity of health care delivery, management, and remuneration, in many realms, process-oriented outcomes are valued above clinical effectiveness. Regardless of how much we may agree or disagree with what is valued when, and in which context, the process of health care is important and there is no doubt that every clinical context is subject to standard or idiosyncratic process-oriented benchmarks. Accordingly, crafting a custom evaluation plan to assess and define those benchmarks in CV-contexts is essential.

CV has the ability to help managers meet and improve both the process and the outcome of health care, yet these goals are often at odds. Moreover, it frequently is

Table 6.9 Examples of process-oriented domains and measures relevant to CV services

Type of process	Specific measure
Access to services	Average wait times for initial evaluation
	Average wait for follow-up appointment
	Number of patients seen/number of new patients seen
	Number of referrals made
	Percentage of encounters where patients chose follow-up date
	Number with specific diagnosis receiving specialty care
	Average number of appointments in episode of care
Missed opportunities	Reduction or number of canceled appointments
	Reduction or number of no-shows
	Reduction or number of rescheduled appointments
	Reduction in clinician "down-time"
	Reduction in CV equipment/room "down-time"
	Number of canceled in-person appointments facilitated by CV
Patient-oriented care	Number of after-hours encounters accommodated
	Number of home CV encounters, or encounters offered
	Percentage of offered/accepted CV appointments to facilitate desired appointment date
Guideline-oriented	Number patients with diagnosis receiving specifically earmarked care
	Number of patients screened with identified and tracked measures, e.g., substance use, suicidality, smoking
	Time between screens: for screens which reoccur
Technology	Percentage of successfully completed connections
	Percentage of dropped calls
	Average downtime during dropped calls

the case that "solutions" in one realm cause unintended consequences in another. For example, improving clinical outcomes by initiating an evidence-based medication management protocol that adds 15 min to each appointment, may negatively impact patient wait-times for services. The CV context can complicate matters by, for example, increasing access to intake and evaluation services, without necessarily increasing other "downstream" services in the ecology, such as labs, medication management, or emergency services. Every manager knows there is a "balancing act" to administrating clinical services. In the case of new CV program development, attending to the measurement of process-oriented outcomes not only helps day-to-day decision-making "in the trenches" but can also help to define what is considered important to hospital administrators.

6.7.1 Specific Process-Oriented Measures

As noted above, it is not helpful to try to denote all the relevant outcomes here, but examples of some common CV-related process outcomes, provided in Table 6.9, may help to frame evaluation issues, or help for thinking creatively about what is possible and useful to measure in a given ecology. Note that many of the economic and satisfaction metrics already identified in this chapter also could fall into the category of "process-oriented."

Wait time is an item in Table 6.9 that is worth further discussion. Operationally this means the time to next available appointment, when scheduling, and when the patient actually presents for care. For CV requiring a referral, wait time could be measured as the difference in the referral date and the date the patient was seen. Wait time may differentially affect patients and providers, and for patients, it may vary with regard to seeing the preferred provider versus any provider. Because CV makes access to care easier for rural populations, evaluation of wait times should be carefully considered prospectively and comparison benchmarks identified early.

6.8 Clinical Outcomes

CV appears to be as effective as in-person care for most behavioral treatments and assessing clinical outcomes is imperative for program evaluation. Many illnesses have been studied such as depression [3, 4, 27, 28], PTSD [3, 29], substance use [29 30 31], and developmental disabilities [32, 33]. CV clinical results regarding population parameters are also encouraging; age, disorder, and ethnic population seem to have little effect on CV clinical outcomes compared to in-person treatment [1]. Accordingly, assessing clinical outcomes of CV programming is not only an ethical imperative, but is also a good opportunity to showcase and support your programming. In many cases, doing so effectively might also mean bolstering clinical outcomes assessment in normative programming so that there is a metric to compare to (see following section).

Although effective program evaluation includes broad assessment across multiple dimensions of programming, the assessment of clinical outcomes should be the cornerstone of program evaluation. Chapter 10 provides a thorough and in-depth review of clinical outcome methods, and so we will not cover them here. For our purposes it is important to note that program evaluation does not occur in silos and efforts should be made to incorporate or reflect clinical outcomes across all the dimensions of program evaluation. For example, number of dropped calls or hours of support staff time both could be standardized by positive clinical outcomes (i.e., number of clinical encounters or dropouts per diagnosis remission). This technique can add a helpful perspective and can orient (or reorient) people to the true mission of CV programming or service expansion.

6.9 Assessment Comparisons and Benchmarks: Realms of Reference

With respect to many of the areas of assessment discussed in this chapter, it is helpful to clearly decide beforehand what the appropriate comparison group or realm of reference is that you are most interested in. Many CV program evaluations use

Table 6.10 Reference groups or realms for comparison in CV assessment: examples, pros, and cons

Realms of reference for CV comparison and example	Primary pro	Primary con
In-person services: Comparison of CV and in-person outcomes on the BDI-II for patients with diagnosis of depression receiving course of CBT	Provides comparison to known services; develops understanding that can be easily conveyed to patients and funders	Can be problematic if in-person services are inadequate. Non-random assignment to conditions complicates interpretation
Pre-defined benchmark or standard: Percentage of CV patients with HbA1c in nonclinical range after 6 months of treatment, goal 80 %; percentage of canceled or skipped appointments, goal 10 %; number of travel miles to clinic avoided per year; goal 10,000 miles	Clinically/administratively rigorous method; provides exact information on metrics identified as important beforehand	There are so many potentially important parameters that getting full picture can be complicated; the method may obscure important incremental gains lost by dichotomizing outcomes
No services: A new CV program seeks to extend specialty care for PTSD to a rural clinic where no specialty services were previously available	Frames programming in terms of new services not otherwise offered to convey true sense of impact	Not very rigorous; any service or metric over 0.0 can be considered a program success
Other telehealth or e-Health services: In-home CV consultation for medication management becomes available in a rural wintery area where phone consultations were previously used	Helpful for discerning comparative effectiveness of various CV platforms, or for helping to guide investment decisions	Unless comparison service is widely known, strongly vetted, or previously assessed on its own merits, it may be difficult to make comparative conclusions
Time: A new CV program assesses clinical outcomes over a 12-session course of ERP for OCD	Provides longitudinal assessment of specific clinical outcomes; rich data for assessing trajectories and dose responses	Open to regression to the mean or with time only those who did not dropout out provide data, skewing results

BDI-II Beck depression inventory-II, *CBT* cognitive behavioral therapy, *PTSD* posttraumatic stress disorder, *ERP* exposure with response prevention, *OCD* obsessive compulsive disorder

existing in-person services as a standard comparison. However, some aspects and processes of care should be measured against benchmarks rather than the quality of in-person services, which are often suboptimal. Alternatively, CV is often used to reach a subpopulation of underserved or at-risk individuals and so we might expect differential outcomes when compared to more general clinical populations. Accordingly, when CV services are compared to in-person services, it is critical to choose a similar clinical setting and patient population.

Comparison to in-person settings can be very helpful but it should not be the "knee-jerk" frame of reference for CV program assessment. Typically, but not necessarily, realms of references can be grouped into five broad categories, identified in Table 6.10. Importantly, separate items in the same assessment process might have different realms of reference for comparison of outcomes, or one item might have a few. Considering these realms is a good exercise to think creatively about assessment and ongoing program goals.

Considering this table can help you decide the appropriate scale and scope, depending on goals and budget of your program assessment. A very simple and elegant design using one very important metric and one frame of reference (i.e., percent or number of hospitalizations per year in chronic population, compared to the percent or number in the year previous to CV implementation) could be informative and adequate to assess the benefit of a program. While, a mix and match design for a more resourced program might be more appropriate to assess and guide complex management of personnel and resources (i.e., a longitudinal assessment of clinical outcomes for CV, in-person, and no-services; assessment of utilization across the three arms and potential impact of patient geography factors on both service utilization and clinical outcomes).

6.10   Validity and Reliability

No matter what you are measuring in program evaluation or what the reference group may be issues of measurement validity and reliability should be considered. The validity of a measurement tool is high if it measures what it claims to measure. There are a variety of subtypes of validity, most prominently: construct, content, convergent, criterion, discriminant, predictive, and face validity. Effective program evaluation does not depend on mastering these definitions, though it would not hurt. These terms are easily searchable on the internet and becoming familiar with them might help one to think critically and creatively about program evaluation measures.

In program evaluation threats to measurement validity vary depending on whether a psychological construct is being measured (e.g., satisfaction, depression) or if a more tangible statistic is being measured (e.g., number of appointments, percentage of dropped calls). When measuring a construct, the classification of validity types and psychometric properties of the items on the measure are important factors, which is why we recommend using published and validated measures. When examining statistics of program functioning, the precision and scope of definition, complexity of coding, heterogeneity in methods of pulling information from electronic medical records data bases, and simple miscommunication between managers, data technicians, and clinicians pose very real threats to the validity of the statistic. Most seemingly simple metrics in this context require careful consideration in conceptualization and execution.

Let us consider tracking of the number of dropped calls during patient care. If a patient is seen for four 60 min appointments and is disconnected three times in one appointment due to a consistently poor connection, will that be counted as one dropped call (in which case the number of sessions is an appropriate denominator, i.e., one disruption out of four appointments), or as three dropped calls (in which case the number of total treatment minutes is the appropriate the denominator, i.e., three disruptions over 240 min of treatment)? Ideally, the evaluator thought about this issue beforehand, clearly communicated how to track the measure to clinicians, and could choose which version of the metric to use depending on interest. Less ideally, the evaluator will be forced to use one or the other definition after realizing the ambiguity in data monitoring. Even less ideally, the evaluator realized the ambiguity but has no way of sorting out which event was coded when and by whom and so chooses not to use the data. The least ideal scenario is that the evaluator never discovers or realizes that there was heterogeneity in how the measure was recorded and so is using and making conclusions on an invalid statistic that is proposed to be a "fact."

In psychometrics, reliability is used to describe the overall consistency of a measure. A measure is said to have a high reliability if it produces similar results under consistent conditions. For conceptual constructs, a common example of a measure with poor reliability is the widely used global assessment of functioning (GAF [34]) scale; the same patient on the same day might elicit very different scores depending on provider. In program evaluation a common threat to the reliability of measures is related to inconsistencies in how data are tracked, i.e., some providers may be more reliable than others in tracking or entering a particular measure. Reliability of measures is also related to inconsistencies in how data are pulled from the system once already tracked and entered. For example, clinician productivity is often measured over a certain period of time as a ratio. If data managers sometimes report productivity as a function of a month and sometimes report it as a function of a quarter, the measure is not reliable. Regardless of timeframe, a common threat to both the reliability and validity of clinician productivity is that often calendar time frames are used as the denominator, not taking into account actual work days. Months vary in the number of days and holidays, and clinicians vary in the number of sick or vacation days taken.

Reliability does not imply validity; a clock that has stopped working is highly reliable but not valid (except, as the joke goes, two times a day). However, a lack of reliability does place limits on the overall validity of a test. A test that is not perfectly reliable cannot be perfectly valid, either as a means of measuring attributes of a person or as a means of predicting scores on a criterion.

6.11   General Dos and Don'ts of Evaluation

There are some very effective dos and don'ts of evaluation. Initial evaluation should unfold according to a plan and reevaluation should occur periodically as things move forward and questions arise about priorities, options, scope, and practical issues (e.g., how much data to collect). The following tips are helpful in constructing a custom evaluation plan regardless of the agreed upon scale and depth of assessment. Tables 6.11 and 6.12 identify methods to be avoided or incorporated into CV assessment procedures.

Table 6.11 The "Don'ts" of CV assessment

1. Don't use patient or clinician satisfaction measures as your primary program assessment. Such measures are often "straw man" metrics and the literature has already demonstrated repeatedly that behavioral CV interventions are well tolerated and widely accepted by patients and providers (see Chap. 10 for review of the CV satisfaction literature)
2. Don't collect "extra" data. If it is not immediately relevant, do not spend time on it. Providers are often asked to put too much in front of patients to self-report, and providers themselves often have to fill out too many needless surveys, and/or have too much data—so much—they often never get around to analyzing them
3. For telehealth grants, don't ignore even minor evaluative expectations of the grant agency. Use the granting agency's language, as identified in the request for proposals (RFP) wherever possible
4. Don't "over correct" by trying to respond to changes or new measures in the literature in real time; updating everything with the latest and the best is not always necessary. Additionally, there are benefits to allowing the field to vet a new measure with true clinical populations
5. Don't automatically assume that in-place electronic health records (EHR) and other ecological processes can easily be used for evaluation to save time/money, as noted, retrospective assessment is both less accurate and more labor-intensive

Point 11 in Table 6.12 suggests the use of specific measures. This is applicable to non-CV settings as well; however, because the field of CV is expanding and existing treatments are being conducted over a new medium, we may miss opportunities to identify areas where CV may be especially effective, if our measurements are not specific enough. For example, the feasibility, acceptability, and sustainability of clinical video for children and adolescents and for those with attention deficit hyperactivity disorder [17, 35, 36] have been shown to be particularly robust. It has been hypothesized that this approach may be better than in-person care for some disorders or patients, such those with autism spectrum patients [33]. A qualitative study of young people's revealed that the sessions were helpful, they felt a sense of personal choice during the consultation, and they generally liked the technology [17].

6.12 More vs. Better: Models of Services to Primary Care and CV Evaluation

Quite often CV care is seen as a method to increased access to care at an end-point, or to increase the availability of specialty care for a specific population, or to overcome barriers that limit treatment, or just to expand a practice's ability to service more patients. All of these are examples of "more." However, telehealth and more specifically, CV, is also being used to provide better care, not just more care. Past studies showed positive outcomes for patients when using a consultation model of care into primary care sites. In one study, specialists changed the diagnosis and medications in 91 and 57 % of cases, respectively, and the interventions led to clinical improvements in 56 % of cases [5]. Other studies have demonstrated that

Table 6.12 The "Do's" of CV assessment

1. Get your funders, stakeholders, and team on board with your board assessment plan, look for buy-in and opportunities to highlight and incorporate team values
2. Design and implement data collection and evaluation prospectively rather than retrospectively. Not only does retrospective (i.e., chart review only) data collection lead to "holes" in what was collected and might not meet the needs of the assessment you really want, but nonintuitively, looking back, organizing, cleaning, and analyzing data via chart review actually doubles or triples or your administration/staff time
3. Make sure you know (or someone knows) what you are doing. If you need an academic evaluator, or statistician, get them involved earlier, not later. The time is worth the money every time
4. Integrate staged evaluation so if you fall short or get unexpected results, you will know where in the process a breakdown occurred
5. Measure staff-related factors
6. Distinguish between patient-end and provider-end. A program may seem to be running well on one side of the equation but be an administrative nightmare on the other side (i.e., unsustainable)
7. Measure provider-related factors and distinguish between referring providers and treating providers
8. Measure providers in the ecology who have nothing to with the CV program. Do they know about it? Would they like a similar resource in their realm/practice?
9. Where possible, adopt standardized clinical measures already used, or published on. They typically have undergone multiple iterations, levels of review, and sometimes psychometric testing
10. Use patient self-report measures. This comes down to time and money. For example, the clinician administered alcohol 4-item CAGE [38] may be better than the AUDIT [37] for assessing substance use, but patients can fill out the latter one
11. Use specific measures unless generalized measures provide the minimum adequate information more efficiently. For example, it is desirable to use population-specific outcomes measures (e.g., children or adolescents [7, 8, 17, 35, 36]; geriatric patients [9, 10]) if they exist and have been well-assessed, or diagnostic-specific measures to assess specific service effectiveness, (e.g., the BDI-II [39, 40] for depression; the Y-BOCS [41] for OCD)
12. If employing a clinical measure to be used throughout the whole CV program to promote standardization of outcomes and convenience regardless of diagnosis, consider a measure of general functioning (e.g., the SF-36 [42], or SF-12 [43]), rather than specific symptom measures (e.g. BDI-II). See Chap. 9 for in-depth review of clinical assessment in CV contexts
13. Check for overlap of proposed measures. For example, in PTSD samples undergoing treatment, the PTSD checklist [44] and BDI-II [40] are highly correlated, and so there are diminishing returns for using both
14. Measure enough to compare "apples to apples." Using a clinical outcomes questionnaire and comparing across CV and in-person samples might obscure the benefits of CV outcomes if you do not also include measures of dropout and treatment adherence. CV groups might evidence less improvement overall than in-person groups if the dropout was double for the in-person sample. This is known as a "suppressor effect" [45] and is highly relevant to CV program evaluation. For example, if driving to the main medical center represents such a burden that patients "on the fence" about treatment stop coming, then the in-person comparison group will "select for" individuals more motivated to get better

AUDIT alcohol use disorders identification test, *BDI-II* Beck depression inventory-II, *Y-BOCS* Yale–Brown obsessive compulsive scale, *OCD* obsessive compulsive disorder, *PTSD* posttraumatic stress disorder patient-side provider knowledge, skills, and complexity of questions improve over time with CV consultation, particularly in rural primary care settings [2, 3, 27]. The most intensive model of consultation to primary care is collaborative care [46], which has now been deployed via telemedicine [3, 4, 28] with encouraging results. The virtual collaborative care team was able to produce better outcomes than the traditional "gold standard" methodology of primary care psychiatry [3].

When designing program evaluation for CV services, it may be worthwhile to contemplate which aspects of the services are related to "more" and which are related to "better." In many situations, assessing the effectiveness of "better" can be quite straightforward, as it is facilitated by the historical patient record. While it is not always easy to get information out of the patient record, these types of assessments, built into a larger program evaluation, can be very enlightening and powerful because they have intrinsic meaning (e.g., "changed the diagnosis and medications in 91 and 57 % of cases, respectively"). Some more examples of telehealth-related models of "better" care that have been thoroughly evaluated and well-articulated are listed in Appendix 6.A.

Conclusion

This chapter addressed the prioritization of desired outcomes and evaluation in the provision of CV services. Process, procedures, levels of depth and dos and don'ts were offered to give the reader options to learn basic or advanced approaches to CV, program change, and evaluation/outcomes. Clearly, the best standard for program evaluation is a simple yet elegant plan, and one that is practical, efficient, systematic, and grounded in the evidence base. This chapter attempted to convey that varying levels of evaluation quality, scope and depth may be employed depending on the situation, but that any evaluation should be grounded in and facilitates program improvement. Why ask the question if you do nothing with the answer? Accordingly, an efficient plan could be centered on just a few variables sufficient to get to the next better place incrementally. The important thing is that those few variables be chosen with thought, with broad agreement among players, and be measurable with the means available.

Acknowledgements American Telemedicine Association, and in particular, the Telemental Health Interest Group, Department of Psychiatry and Behavioral Sciences of the Keck School of Medicine at the University of Southern California, the UC Davis School of Medicine Center for Health and Technology of the UC Davis Health System.

Appendix 6.A

Examples of telehealth care that have been thoroughly evaluated and well-articulated

1. Randomized controlled trial (RCT) for depression in adults [27].
2. Phone and email physician-to-provider consultation system using a 24 h "warm" line [47].
3. Telepsychiatric consultation (phone, email, or video), with continuing medical education (CME) [48].
4. Cultural consultation to rural primary via telemedicine [2].
5. Collaborative care via telepsychiatry, coprovision of medication for primary care patients by the telepsychiatrist and primary care provider in rural communities for adults [3, 4] and children [28].
6. Asynchronous telepsychiatry (ATP) [14], formerly known as store-and-forward services, used at the patient end (video recording local providers and patients, and uploading of videos for remote review and consultation. It is very cost-efficient) [14, 49].
7. Telepsychiatric emergency room evaluation [50, 52].
8. Integrated behavioral health by telepsychiatry [53].

References

1. Hilty DM, Ferrer D, Callahan EJ, et al. The effectiveness of telemental health: a 2013 review. Telemed J E-Health. 2013;19(6):444–54.
2. Hilty DM, Yellowlees, PM, Cobb HC, et al. Models of telepsychiatric consultation-liaison service to rural primary care. Psychosomatics. 2006;47(2):152–7.
3. Fortney JC, Pyne JM, Edlund MJ, et al. A randomized trial of telemedicine-based collaborative care for depression. J Gen Intern Med. 2007;22(8):1086–93.
4. Fortney JC, Pyne JM, Mouden SP, et al. Practice-based versus telemedicine-based collaborative care for depression in rural federally qualified health centers: a pragmatic randomized comparative effectiveness trial. Am J Psychiatry. 2013;1–12. http://ajp/psychiatryonline.org.
5. Hilty DM, Marks SL, Urness D, et al. Clinical and educational applications of telepsychiatry: a review. Can J Psychiatry. 2004;49(1):12–23.
6. AACAP Practice Parameter for Telepsychiatry with Children and Adolescents. J Am Acad Child Adolesc Psychiatry. 2007;47(12):1468–83.
7. Pesamaa L, Ebeling H, Kuusimaki ML, et al. Videoconferencing in child and adolescent telepsychiatry: a systematic review of the literature. J Telemed Telecare. 2004;10:187–92.
8. Yellowlees PM, Hilty DM, Marks SL, et al. A retrospective analysis of child and adolescent e-mental health. J Am Acad Child Adolesc Psychiatry. 2008;47(1):1–5.
9. Rabinowitz T, Murphy K, Amour JL, et al. Benefits of a telepsychiatry consultation service for rural nursing home residents. Telemed J E-Health. 2010;16:34–40.
10. Jones BN, Ruskin PE. Telemedicine and geriatric psychiatry: Directions for future research and policy. J Geriatr Psychiatr Neurol 2001;14(2)59–62.
11. Weinstein MC, Stason WB. Foundations of cost-effectiveness analysis for health and medical practices. N Engl J Med. 1977;296(13):716–21.

12. Yellowlees PM, Shore J, Roberts L. Practice guidelines for videoconferencing-based tele-mental health, American telemedicine association. Telemed J E-Health. 2010;16:1074–89. http://www.americantelemed.org/resources/standards/ata-standards-guidelines/practice-guidelines-for-video-based-online-mental-health-services#.U2bGexYrfdk.

13. Shore J, Mishkind MC, Bern Bernard J, et al. A lexicon of assessment and outcome measures for telemental health. ATA. 2013. http://www.americantelemed.org/practice/standards/ata-standardsguidelines/a-lexicon-of-assessment-and-outcome-measurements-for-telemental-health#UwF5Dv0_3-Y. Accessed 1 Feb 2014. http://www.americantelemed.org/resources/standards/ata-standards-guidelines/a-lexicon-of-assessment-and-outcome-measurementsfor-telemental-health#.U2bG2xYrfdk.

14. Yellowlees PM, Odor A, Burke MM, et al. A feasibility study of asynchronous telepsychiatry for psychiatric consultations. Psychiatr Serv. 2010;61(8):838–40.

15. Geyer J, Myers K, Vander Stoep A, et al. Implementing a low-cost web-based clinical trial management system for community studies: a case study. Clin Trials. 2011;8:634–44.

16. Unutzer J, Choi Y, Cook IA, et al. A web-based data management system to improve care for depression in a multicenter clinical trial. Psychiatr Serv. 2002;53:671–8.

17. Myers KM, Valentine JM, Melzer SM. Feasibility, acceptability, and sustainability of tele-psychiatry for children and adolescents. Psychiatr Serv. 2007;58:1493–6.

18. Yip MP, Chang AM, Chan J, et al. Development of the telemedicine satisfaction question-naire to evaluate patient satisfaction with telemedicine: a preliminary study. J Telemed Telec-are. 2003;9:46–50.

19. Yellowlees PM, Odor A, Patrice K, et al. Transcultural psychiatry made simple: asynchro-nous telepsychiatry as an approach to providing culturally relevant care. Telemed E-Health. 2013;19(4):1–6.17.

20. Nieves J, Stack KM. Hispanics and telepsychiatry. Psychiatr Serv. 2007;58:877–8.

21. Chong J, Moreno FA. Feasibility and acceptability of clinic-based telepsychiatry for low-income Hispanic primary care patients. Tele-Health. 2012;18(4):297–304.

22. Mucic D. Transcultural telepsychiatry and its impact on patient satisfaction. J Telemed Telec-are. 2010;16(5):237–42.

23. Moreno FA, Chong J, Dumbauld J, et al. Use of standard webcam and Internet equipment for telepsychiatry treatment of depression among underserved Hispanics. Psychiatr Serv. 2012;63(12):1213–7.

24. Lopez AM, Cruz M, Lazarus S, et al. Use of American sign language in telepsychiatry con-sultation. Telemed E-Health. 2004;10(3):389–91.

25. Shore JH, Brooks E, Savin D, Orton H, Grigsby J, Manson S. Acceptability of telepsychiatry in American Indians. Telemed E-Health. 2008;14(5):461–6.

26. Ye J, Shim R, Lukaszewski T, Yun K, et al. Telepsychiatry services for Korean immigrants. Telemed E-Health. 2012;18(10):797–802.

27. Hilty DM, Marks SL, Wegeland JE, et al. A randomized controlled trial of disease manage-ment modules, including telepsychiatric care, for depression in rural primary care. Psychia-try. 2007;4(2):58–65.

28. Richardson L, McCauley E, Katon W. Collaborative care for adolescent depression: a pilot study. Gen Hosp Psychiatry. 2009;31:36–45.

29. Frueh BC, Monnier J, Yim E, et al. Randomized trial for post-traumatic stress disorder. J Telemed Telecare. 2007;13:142–7.

30. Tuerk PW, Wangelin B, Rauch SAM, Dismuke CE, Yoder M, Myrick DH, Eftekhari A, Acierno R. Health service utilization before and after evidence-based treatment for PTSD. Psychological Services. Advance online publication. http://www.ptsd.va.gov/professional/articles/article-pdf/id39607.pdf. doi:10.1037/a0030549. Accessed 12 Nov 2012.

31. Tuerk PW, Yoder M, Ruggiero KJ, Gros DF, Acierno R. A pilot study of prolonged exposure therapy for posttraumatic stress disorder delivered via telehealth technology. J Trauma Stress. 2010;23(1):116–23. doi:10.1002/jts.20494.

32. Szeftel R, Federico C, Hakak R, et al. Improved access to mental health evaluation for patients with developmental disabilities using telepsychiatry. J Telemed Telecare. 2012;18(6):317–21.

33. Pakyurek M, Yellowlees PM, Hilty DM. The child and adolescent telepsychiatry consultation: can it be a more effective clinical process for certain patients than conventional practice? Telemed J E-Health. 2010;16(3):289–92.

34. Hall RC. Global assessment of functioning. A modified scale. Psychosomatics. 1995;36(3):267–75.

35. Myers KM, Vander Stoep A, McCarty CA, et al. Child and adolescent telepsychiatry: variations in utilization, referral patterns and practice trends. J Telemed Telecare N Am. 2011;20(1):155–71.

36. Myers KM, Palmer NB, Geyer JR. Research in child and adolescent telemental health. Child Adolesc Psychiatr Clin N Am. 2011;20(1):155–71.

37. Saunders JB, Aasland OG, Babor TF, et al. Development of the alcohol use disorders identification test (AUDIT): WHO collaborative project on identification and treatment of persons with harmful alcohol consumption, phase II. Addiction. 1993;88:791–804.

38. Ewing JA. Detecting alcoholism: the CAGE questionnaire. J Am Med Assoc. 1984;252:1905–7.

39. Steer RA, Rissmiller DJ, Beck AT. Use of the Beck depression inventory with depressed geriatric patients. Behav Res Ther. 2000;38(3):311–8.

40. Steer RA, Ball R, Ranieri RF, et al. Dimensions of the Beck depression inventory-II in clinically depressed outpatients. J Clin Psychol. 1999;55(1):17–28.

41. Goodman WK, Price LH, Rasmussen SA, et al. The Yale–Brown obsessive–compulsive scale. I. Development, use, and reliability. Arch Gen Psychiatry.1989;46:1006–11.

42. Ware JE, Kosinski M. SF-36 physical & mental health summary scales: a manual for users of version 1. Lincoln: Quality Metric; 2001.

43. Stewart AL, Ware JE, editors. Measuring functioning and well-being: the medical outcome study approach. Durham: Duke University Press; 1992.

44. Blanchard EB, Jones-Alexander J, Buckley TC, et al. Psychometric properties of the PTSD checklist (PCL). Behav Res Ther. 1996;34(8):669–73.

45. MacKinnon DP, Krull JL, Lockwood CM. Equivalence of the mediation, confounding and suppression effect. Prev Sci. 2000;1(4):173–81.

46. Katon W, Von Korff M, Lin E, et al. Collaborative management to achieve depression treatment guidelines. J Clin Psychiatry. 1997;58(Suppl 1):20–4.

47. Hilty DM, Ingraham RL, Yang RP, et al. Multispecialty phone and email consultation to primary care providers for patients with developmental disabilities in rural California. J Telemed E-Health. 2004;10:413–21.

48. Hilty DM, Yellowlees PM, Nesbitt TS. Evolution of telepsychiatry to rural sites: change over time in types of referral and PCP knowledge, skill, and satisfaction. Gen Hosp Psychiatry. 2006;28(5):367–73.

49. Butler T, Yellowlees P. Cost analysis of store-and-forward telepsychiatry as a consultation model for primary care. Telemed J E Health. 2012;18(1):74–7.

50. Shore JH, Hilty DM, Yellowlees PM. Emergency management guidelines for telepsychiatry. Gen Hosp Psychiatry. 2007;29:199–206.

51. Yellowlees PM, Burke MM, Marks SL, et al. Emergency telepsychiatry. J Telemed Telecare. 2008;14:277–81.

52. Sorvaniemi M, Ojanen E, Santamäki O. Telepsychiatry in emergency consultations: a followup study of sixty patients. Telemed J E-Health. 2005;11(4):439–41.

53. Neufeld JD, Bourgeois JA, Hilty DM, et al. The e-Mental Health Consult Service: providing enhanced primary care mental health services through telemedicine. Psychosomatics. 2007;48:135–41.

Part II
For Clinicians: Clinical Standards and Protocols to Support Effective and Safe Intervention

Chapter 7
The Informed Consent Process for Therapeutic Communication in Clinical Videoconferencing

Stephanie Y. Wells, Kathryn Williams, Kristen H. Walter, Lucy Moreno,
Ebony Butler, Lisa H. Glassman and Steven R. Thorp

Chapter Summary

Purpose: This chapter addresses important issues related to the process and content of informed consent when providing services via clinical videoconferencing (CV). Relevant differences between in-person services and CV services are highlighted for modifying the informed consent form (ICF) and consenting process. ICF modifications are also considered regarding the various settings and contexts within CV services. The chapter also highlights helpful ground rules for communication in CV contexts.

Context: The information contained in this chapter is necessary for providers because they have an ethical responsibility to provide patients with information regarding services and therapy, the potential benefits and risks of CV, and the differences between in-person services and services delivered via CV related to the unique medium of communication. The chapter also contains helpful information for providers new to CV regarding avoidable but common missteps in patient/provider communication.

S. R. Thorp (✉)
Center of Excellence for Stress and Mental Health, Mental Health Service,
VA San Diego Health Care System; University of California, San Diego/San Diego State
University Joint Doctoral Program in Clinical Psychology, San Diego, California, USA
e-mail: sthorp@ucsd.edu

S. Y. Wells
University of California, San Diego/San Diego State University Joint Doctoral Program in
Clinical Psychology, San Diego, California, USA; Mental Health Service,
VA San Diego Health Care System, San Diego, California, USA

K. Williams · K. H. Walter · L. Moreno · E. Butler
Mental Health Service, VA San Diego Health Care System, San Diego, California, USA

L. H. Glassman
Center of Excellence for Stress and Mental Health, Mental Health Service,
VA San Diego Health Care System, San Diego, California, USA

© Springer International Publishing Switzerland 2015   133
P. W. Tuerk, P. Shore (eds.), *Clinical Videoconferencing in Telehealth*,
Behavioral Telehealth, DOI 10.1007/978-3-319-08765-8_7

Tools: The chapter provides an overview of current recommendations for the informed consent process in CV, informed consent form (ICF) templates, a clinical note template for documenting the informed consent process, a liability waiver form, and web-links to legislation regarding conducting informed consent via CV. The chapter also includes tools to assist with establishing healthy and ethical CV communication with patients, including directions regarding establishing initial contact with patients, determining eligibility for services, specific procedures to avoid, common unintended consequences of patient behaviors in CV contexts, clinician boundary setting, and the intentional identification of various models of provider access. Lastly, the chapter also includes a "lessons learned" section (see Appendix G) informed by clinician experience.

7.1 Introduction

Prior to the start of traditional clinical services, clinicians should conduct the informed consent process with patients in real-time (e.g., instantaneous communication; Department of Defense [DoD]) [7, 12, 13]. The goal of the informed consent process is to allow patients to make an informed decision about participation in services. Therefore, the informed consent process should include all relevant information about the service provided, any risks or benefits of the services, any rules or expectations regarding the services, mandatory reporting laws, and the opportunity for patients to ask questions regarding the services. Typically, the provider or other staff member will meet with the patient in-person to review the informed consent form (ICF). The ICF is a written document that includes all necessary information that patients need to know prior to engaging in services. After explaining the content included in the form and allowing the patient to ask questions, the patient signs the form and the provider documents (in a progress note) that the informed consent process occurred and that the patient signed the ICF. The provider should provide the patient with a copy of the signed ICF to keep for future reference.

7.2 Informed Consent via Clinical Video

The informed consent process is a standard part of delivering psychosocial services, whether in-person or via telemedicine. According to the American Telemedicine Association [3], Telemedicine is defined as, "the use of medical information exchanged from one site to another via electronic communications to improve a patient's health status. Telemedicine includes a growing variety of applications and services using two-way video, email, smart phones, wireless tools, and other forms of telecommunications technology." Clinical videoconferencing (CV) or two-way video is one form of delivering telemedicine. CV allows the patient and provider to be at different locations, but conduct services in real-time or what's also commonly known as "synchronous" communication in the terminology of telemedicine (as opposed to e-mail or store-and-forward technologies, which are termed as "asynchronous").

The current literature provides several recommendations concerning key ICF components for care delivered via CV. Several authors have recommended that the ICF should describe how CV differs from in-person care, the potential risks and benefits of CV, safeguards to protect against the risks associated with CV, the structure of the services provided, privacy and confidentiality (and limits of confidentiality), mandatory reporting state laws, recording of sessions, emergency plans, documentation of patient information, transmission and storage of patient information, the patients' right to end treatment without penalty of care, alternative services, and conditions for termination of care delivered via CV [5, 7, 9, 11, 13, 17]. Each of these components and their importance will be discussed in further detail in this chapter (see Appendices 7.A and 7.B for modifiable ICF templates for office and home-based CV).

7.3   Clinical Video and Legal Considerations

Currently, the laws regarding informed consent for CV, and telemedicine more broadly, are limited; however, there are some extant guidelines. The DoD Guidelines recommend obtaining written informed consent prior to the initiation of services [7] and informed consent for CV should include all of the necessary information for traditional in-person care, as well as information specific to CV [5, 7, 13]. Some states allow electronic signatures to be used in place of written consent and other states do not have guidelines for how informed consent should be obtained. Due to the discrepancy in guidelines for the use of CV and the informed consent process, providers need to be aware of the state and national laws where patient is physically located during session [13]. See Appendix 7.E for helpful resources regarding CV regulations in general.

The CV literature is expanding, and researchers have highlighted potential issues (e.g., privacy, greater frequency of miscommunications, technological issues) associated with CV [5, 9, 17]. Providers should consider presenting these issues within the ICF. Providers must follow the Health Insurance Portability and Accountability Act (HIPAA; 1996) for all care delivered via CV [7]. Additional consent forms are sometimes required. Most notably, if a provider intends to audio record or video record sessions, the patient must sign a related written consent form [7]. In this case, the informed consent form should include information regarding viewing, storing, and discarding of the audio record/video record when it is no longer needed.

7.4   The Process of Informed Consent via CV

7.4.1   Initial Contact with the Patient

The person responsible for making the initial contact with patients may differ by treatment setting. For example, in private practice patients will likely contact the therapist directly, whereas in a community mental health practice or hospital, the patient may initially speak with an administrative assistant. We suggest that the therapist initiate contact with patients prior to the first treatment session, if possible, to begin to develop a therapeutic alliance.

Prior to beginning psychosocial services via CV, the person initiating contact with the patient should provide a brief overview of the treatments available, describe CV, provide risks and benefits of CV, describe the eligibility requirements for the clinic (or study), and determine eligibility for the specific treatment. Note, these are recommendations for initial contact, i.e., in addition to and before the formal informed consent process. Appendix 7.C provides a checklist summary of recommendations for initial contact. These components and their importance will be discussed in further detail in this chapter.

7.4.2 Suitability for CV Services

When determining suitability for CV services there are a few basic standards that are recommended. Individuals with the following conditions/symptoms may not be the best candidates for clinical video conferencing: (1) significant cognitive deficits (dementia, developmental deficits), (2) high-risk behaviors (imminently suicidal/ homicidal, i.e., more than ideation), (3) history of intoxication during treatment sessions, (4) acute psychosis or mania, (5) history of delusions regarding thought broadcasting via technology, or (6) sensory deficits that would preclude ability to initiate or communicate via CV. It should be noted, however, that sometimes CV mediums are particularly well suited for patients with sensory deficits given the right configuration of equipment. For example, patients who have auditory deficits may benefit from using headphones, or even noise canceling headphones, during CV. In such cases the ability to communicate may actually be enhanced by the amplification of a provider's voice not available in face-to-face settings.

7.4.3 Description of CV Process

After a verification of suitability for services, the individual initiating contact should clearly describe to patients what CV entails. For example, it should be clear that patients will communicate in real-time with the therapist via videoconferencing technologies. Additionally, patients should be informed about where he/she will use the CV technologies. For patients receiving treatment at hospitals or local outpatient clinics, it is likely that they will use the CV equipment in a hospital or clinic setting (i.e., office-to-office CV). However, individuals with limited access to care (e.g., patients in rural areas) may use CV equipment on their home computers (e.g., in-home CV) or mobile devices (e.g., smart phones or tablets). If individuals are using the CV equipment in their home, they need to be informed if they are responsible for purchasing and/or installing software or equipment necessary for CV (e.g., webcam).

The person initiating contact should describe the potential benefits of using CV. One of the major benefits of CV is that it is often more convenient than in-person care. For example, in-home CV reduces travel time and fuel costs, and this is often true of community-based office-to-office CV as well (rather than driving to a primary institution in the region). The risks of CV should also be reviewed by the person initiating contact. For example, patients should be made aware of potential technological difficulties. In cases of non-clinic based CV, individuals will need to be informed of the additional risk of receiving care in these settings (e.g., no professional staff available to assist in case of an emergency, software utilized may be less "secure" than software utilized in a clinic-based setting, and technical support may not be readily available). A more in-depth review of these issues will be provided in the ICF, but potential patients should be primed regarding the relevant issues relating to CV during the initial contact.

7.4.4   Obtaining In-Person Consent

Prior to delivering psychosocial services via CV, it may be helpful if the patient and provider can meet in-person to review the informed consent process. However, requiring an initial in-person visit may likely pose an unnecessary barrier to care, especially if CV services are being considered for patient-oriented reasons. If an initial in-patient visit is possible and non-burdensome to the patient, the provider can explain CV, demonstrate the use of the equipment, and then allow the patient to ask questions so that he or she understands the functionality, risks, and benefits of CV prior to receiving services in this modality. Once the informed consent form has been reviewed, all questions have been answered, and the patient agrees to participate in CV, the patient will sign the informed consent form and the provider will document this in the patient's medical record (see Appendix 7.F for a template). A copy of the informed consent form should be provided to the patient.

7.4.5   Obtaining Consent Remotely

If it is unduly burdensome for the patient to meet in-person to complete the informed consent process and sign the ICF, then the provider should conduct the informed consent process over the phone. The provider will review each component of the consent form and confirm that all of the patient's questions are addressed. If the patient agrees to receive services via CV, the patient must sign the informed consent form and send it back to the therapist. The patient and provider will determine the specific method of delivery, e.g., post it in the mail, fax, e-mail, or upload. Note, the use of a phone camera and mobile application (e.g., TurboScan) to convert the document into a pdf for convenient transmission to the provider often results in acceptable and even excellent image quality (see Chap. 10 for a more in-depth review of methods for exchanging materials in CV contexts). If the patient sends the ICF via e-mail or fax, the patient and provider should discuss whether an original or electronic signature can be used.

As always, therapists need to make sure to comply with all state and federal laws regarding transmission of ICFs. Optimally, the use of CV should be avoided until the patient signs the informed consent form; however, providers can assess if it is in the best interests of a patient to document verbal consent over the phone and proceed with treatment prior to receiving a hard-copy singed ICF.

7.5   The Informed Consent Form (ICF): What to Include

ICFs should include any specific information necessary for prospective patients to make a reasonably informed choice regarding the initiation of diverse services. Accordingly, ICFs often vary by treatment, treatment setting, provider, and other contextual factors. Even so, there are common and essential elements that we believe should be included in ICFs for CV services. As noted, Appendices 7.A and 7.B provide modifiable complete templates for ICFs for clinic-based and home-based CV services, the following section of the chapter reviews and discusses the essential elements captured in the templates.

7.5.1   Brief Overview of CV and Structure of Services

Similar to the initial contact with the patient, the ICF should begin with a brief description of CV. The overview should include how CV differs from in-person care and how CV works. The ICF should provide an overview of the structure of the services that will be provided. The structure of services will differ by provider and location so this information should be personalized based on the needs of the provider and patient.

7.5.2   Provider and Patient Expectations

It is important to educate patients about the expectations for both the patient and provider. The provider should clearly outline what his/her role will be and what is expected of the patient. For example, if providing psychotherapy via CV, the therapist should inform patients about the work that they will be expected to complete during therapy sessions and outside of sessions (e.g., homework, review or completion of documents, practice assignments). Clearly stating expectations at the outset of treatment can minimize confusion and inoculate against many future problems.

The ICF should also establish any boundaries relevant to treatment. Any patient–provider boundaries should be outlined in this section (e.g., appropriate dress, between session contact). Different providers will have disparate boundaries that they expect the patient to maintain, and these may also differ by setting. For example, therapists working in private practice may include when the patient should call the therapist's cell phone or whether and when to email the therapist. Further, the therapist may choose to state hours that they are available via cell phone, with the exception of emergencies. If the provider's institution has regulations that need to be followed, these should also be summarized in this section. For example, in some institutions, the use of personal e-mail in clinical care may be discouraged or prohibited. Therefore, it is crucial for providers in these settings to inform patients prior to treatment that he/she should call the clinic rather than e-mailing.

Services provided via in-home CV rather than in-office CV may pose unique considerations not faced in traditional in-office care. The use of CV in the home is rapidly expanding. With in-home CV, there may be expectations or boundaries that do not apply for in-office CV. For example, the provider may discuss the minimum technology standards necessary for CV to work adequately from home-based equipment. More specifically, the provider may request that patients have a certain bandwidth level to improve CV connectivity. The provider should emphasize the importance of privacy when receiving services via CV. For example, due to the sensitive nature of information that is often covered in psychosocial services, the provider may request that the patient be the only individual in the room when receiving services via in-home CV (to maximize privacy and ensure that loved ones or roommates are not overhearing the session). It is also important to discuss sound issues and troubleshoot ways to ensure privacy (use of headphones, or light noise at doors from white noise makers). In addition to audio/visual privacy, the provider should also clearly state that the patient cannot record this session for distribution or sharing on public domains. There have been cases where patients have posted session segments on social networking sites and video sharing sites without the provider's knowledge. In sum, every setting and provider will have different expectations that need to be determined and included in the ICF.

7.5.3 Benefits and Risks of CV

The ICF should include an objective description of the benefits and risks of CV [4, 14]. As noted, CV is often more convenient than traditional in-office care (e.g., less travel time). Additionally, if patients have a physical limitation (e.g., a wheelchair) that makes travel difficult (or that makes transportation in clinic parking lots, hallways, or offices unmanageable), patients may be able to use CV in their homes. The use of CV can increase access to care for individuals in rural areas or areas without access to sufficient services and providers. Furthermore, CV may encourage some patients to receive care they may not receive otherwise due to the fear of being stigmatized. For example, some patients resist sitting in mental health waiting rooms. Some patients have also voiced a preference for CV as a less intimidating approach to mental health care, expressing a greater feeling of safety and privacy during initial visits.

There are also risks that the patient needs to be aware of before engaging in services. The use of CV may introduce several technological issues such as dropped calls, pixelated images, delayed or frozen images, distortion or lack of sound, and slow connection speed. Although these issues may never arise during CV, patients should be made aware of these possibilities in order to make an informed decision about engaging in CV. Technological issues may be less burdensome for office-to-office CV because support staff are often available to troubleshoot problems with CV equipment, and often the teleconferencing equipment used in offices is more sophisticated than home equipment. However, for patients using in-home CV, the patient should be informed that it may be his/her responsibility to fix technological issues that may arise, with guidance from support staff as available. The patient and provider should have a back-up plan (e.g., conduct services over the phone or in-person) in the case of technological disruptions. This plan should be explicitly stated in the ICF. Finally, the provider should inform the patient about whether or not the technology is HIPAA compliant and about limits of confidentiality. These two issues are discussed in further detail below.

7.5.4   Privacy, Confidentiality, and Limits of Confidentiality

When conducting psychosocial services through CV, including the consent process, the Health Information Portability and Accountability Act of 1996 (HIPAA; Public Law 104-191) should be followed at all times to protect health information and maintain privacy and security (text of law available at: http://library.clerk. house.gov/reference-files/PPL_HIPAA_HealthInsurancePortabilityAccountability-Act_1996.pdf). HIPAA establishes federal security and privacy standards including the provision of telemedicine. The law commonly applies when providers file insurance claims or request payment from a third party [2], but also applies when using third parties to facilitate telemedicine (i.e., Business Associates, who are individuals or companies that help to provide health care activities). HIPAA, and the methods employed to comply with HIPAA law, should be included and discussed in the informed consent process.

Two particular rules, the Privacy Rule and the Security Rule relate to the delivery of psychological procedures, including through the use of CV. The Privacy Rule (summary at: http://www.hhs.gov/ocr/privacy/hipaa/understanding/summary/privacysummary.pdf), protects against intentional disclosures of protected health information (PHI) and covers verbal, paper, and electronic means of communication. Although there are no specific requirements for providers to follow regarding the privacy of PHI, the rule encourages that reasonable and appropriate safeguards be employed to maintain privacy of sensitive information. Thus, by not requiring specific safeguards, the rule allows for flexibility to account for organizational needs, infrastructure, costs, and potential risks to PHI.

The Security Rule was implemented to protect health information specifically transmitted through electronic means and highlights important considerations for CV (summary at: http://www.hhs.gov/ocr/privacy/hipaa/understanding/srsummary. html). There are distinct security concerns regarding CV and related electronic communication, including electronic transfer of information to unauthorized users, data tampering without knowledge, and the speed in which data can be accessed. Similar to the Privacy Rule, the Security Rule does not require the implementation of specific safeguards to address these risks. Instead, HIPAA allows for organizational flexibility and requires the implementation of reasonable safeguards related to administrative (e.g., risk analysis, security personnel, workforce training, information access management), technical (e.g., access control, audits, integrity control, transmission security), and physical (e.g., facility access, workstation/device security; HIPAA, 1996) aspects of programming. Furthermore, security mechanisms can include firewalls, passwords, data encryption, electronic signatures, disaster recovery plans, and back-up systems [8]. Providers should use safeguards whenever possible to protect patient information. See Chap. 1, Sect. 4.5.4 *HIPPA and FIPS 140-2,* for more information regarding HIPAA in CV contexts.

One safeguard against unauthorized access to electronically-transmitted PHI is the encryption of PHI in order to control access. HIPAA does not prohibit the use of standard e-mail in patient-provider communication; however, the encryption of electronic communication can be considered a reasonable safeguard for data security. Encryption is a process of converting data into a form that is not readable by those who are unauthorized to read the content. If encryption is utilized it may be prudent for it to meet recognized standards by the National Institute of Standards and Technology (NIST) for software and hardware used by the United States federal government to encrypt sensitive information. These established standards are referred to as the Federal Information Processing Standard (FIPS) 140-2 (available at: http://www.hhs.gov/ocr/privacy/hipaa/administrative/securityrule/fips1402.pdf) and provide requirements at four levels of increasing security for 11 requirement areas. An example of encryption that provides acceptable levels of security is Advanced Encryption Standard (AES), which is an algorithm used by the USA government. When utilizing encryption to protect the security of PHI, patients should be informed about the technologies employed in language that is easily understood by those without a technical background. Likewise, it is not necessary for providers or clinical managers to understand the technical details of encoding, but making basic inquires of potential hardware and software vendors to ensure that the CV product is "FIPS 140-2" compliant is an important aspect of choosing CV systems. When documenting and explaining encryption in an ICF it is prudent to include a statement acknowledging that security cannot be absolutely guaranteed, even with the use of such security measures. (See Chaps. 3 and 4 for more information regarding encoding, CV systems, and the use of widely-disseminated technologies such as Skype and Facetime).

7.5.5 Hardware and Software

Expectations for in-home CV equipment (e.g., webcams, speakers) should be stated within the informed consent. The quality of technological equipment and bandwidth speed could impact connectivity. Patients should also be informed that they may need to view videos or other stimuli via media players (e.g., DVD players or videos on a computer) as part of some treatments, and thus should plan for using their own equipment or that provided by the treatment team.

7.5.6   *Mandatory Reporting*

Maintaining patient confidentiality is an essential component of delivering effective psychological services, and adhering to the limits of confidentiality poses a unique challenge for clinicians who provide treatment remotely. Mental health professionals are often mandatory reporters, meaning that they are required to break patient confidentiality under certain circumstances outlined by law. Mandatory reporting laws for mental health professionals vary by state. For example, although most states require a clinician to breach confidentiality when patients pose a serious threat of harm to another individual, some states do not require a duty to warn in these circumstances [6]. Furthermore, states may differentially require actions to satisfy a clinician's duty to warn (e.g., involuntary hospitalization, notifying law enforcement, [6]). States also differ on the parameters for reporting and addressing imminent risk for self-harm [16]. All professionals, independent of whether they deliver services via telemedicine platforms or in-person, should make sure that they review and understand the mandatory reporting laws of their state(s) of practice (see Chap. 4 for relevant state by state information).

Although laws are state-specific, some form of reporting is always required when a clinician becomes aware of current child physical or sexual abuse, and many states require reporting in instances of childhood psychological abuse, neglect, or exposure to domestic violence [10]. Several states also require reporting in cases of elder abuse [15]. Importantly, requirements for how to report child and elder abuse and the threshold for warranting a breach of confidentiality (e.g., specific types of injury, serious injury, or when a clinician suspects abuse) also vary by state [15].

There are several aspects of mandated reporting and informed consent that are unique to telemedicine. First, the clinician and patient may not be located in the same state as one another. Unless the provider is working within a federal system where license mobility law is in place, the clinician must be licensed in the state where patient is situated during the session. As a mandated reporter, a clinician must be aware of the confidentiality rules in their own state of licensure, as well as the state where their patient is receiving services. A clinician may be mandated to report in both states, depending on the laws of each jurisdiction. Accordingly, the ICF should also note that mandatory reporting laws vary by state, and should contain language that allows a clinician to follow mandatory laws across all the USA States and other countries, as necessary. Furthermore, clinicians may wish to start each session by confirming the specific location of their patient (e.g., whether they are at home, or staying in a hotel room in another state) to ensure that they can identify which mandatory reporting laws they need to follow, as well as to identify which authorities should be contacted if an immediate breach of confidentiality is necessary to protect the patient and/or another individual. In some cases, providing services via telemedicine platforms may require broader knowledge of mandatory reporting laws and greater care regarding the implementation of these laws when necessary.

7.5.7 Transmission, Storage, and Documentation

Due to limited in-person contact when using CV, it is essential to have plans in place for the sharing of documentation between provider and patient. As noted, Chap. 10 addresses various methods of document exchange, for the purposes of informed consent it is necessary to include chosen methods of exchange in the ICF and in accompanying collaborative discussion.

Once initial paperwork and consent forms are completed, it is important to further explore how electronic communication will be utilized during treatment. Patients and providers will need to discuss and agree on if and when to use electronic communication in between sessions. For example, they should discuss if and when it is acceptable or not to use email (e.g., rescheduling an appointment versus an emergent situation).

The ICF should also describe how patient information (electronic and hard copy files) will be stored. Providers need to abide by HIPPA laws, facility policies, and any other state or federal laws when storing patient information. Providers who collect hard copy materials (e.g., assessment measures) need to ensure that all patient information is stored in a locked filing cabinet or other secure location. If possible, identifiable information should not be included on general patient forms, though of course some materials, such as the ICF or patient contact sheet, must do so. If patient information is going to be stored electronically, all documents should be saved on a secure drive that is password protected. Regardless of the method used to store patient data, the informed consent form must clearly state how data will be stored and follow HIPAA laws.

7.5.8 Clinical Notes

Documenting treatment services for clients will vary depending on the type of facility where services are rendered (e.g., large public facility versus private practice), context of the treatment, and the type of treatment. Documentation of services typically includes clinical progress notes. Depending on the treatment setting, clinical progress notes may be in handwritten or electronic form. Because documentation is such a vital part of psychosocial services, several factors should be considered for inclusion in the ICF.

First, the ICF may address what the provider will include in patients' clinical progress notes. Clinical progress notes typically include the name of the treating provider, as well as the time and date that services were rendered. It is also important to include a summary of the session, diagnosis (if applicable), mental status information, and continued treatment plans. One common practice is to follow the SOAP format (*S*ubjective, *O*bjective, *A*ssessment, and *P*lan), though different settings may use other organizational formats. The provider may want to include this information in the consent to ease any concerns patients may have about documentation.

During the initial appointment the provider will conduct the informed consent process. Immediately following this appointment, the provider should document the informed consent process, whether or not consent was obtained, and how the consent was obtained (e.g., written or verbal) in the patient's clinical notes. Describing the informed consent process within a clinical progress notes provides documentation that the client has been informed of and understands the treatment process.

7.5.9 Destroying of Patient Data

Finally, regardless of how the provider decides to store and document patient information, the ICF should include how or if the information will be destroyed. There are often state laws or institutional guidelines about how long data should be kept and how to destroy data, and this should be included within the ICF. When destroying patient information (e.g., chart files, video recordings) confidentiality laws should still be followed.

7.5.10 Safety and Emergency Procedures

Prior to engaging in CV for mental health, it is imperative to have clear, concise emergency procedures developed. Chapter 8 provides an in depth review of safety and emergency procedures for CV contexts. Regardless of which emergency management protocols and procedures are utilized, it is necessary for them to be clearly communicated in the informed consent process. Ideally, emergency plans should be collaboratively agreed upon by the provider and patient, rather than just presented to the patient. This aspect of informed consent is particularly salient in CV contexts because often (especially in home-based CV) emergency planning includes individuals or resources within the patient's natural ecology and therefore represent additional threats to privacy.

7.5.11 Termination or Changes in Care

Also of importance to communicate to the patient as part of the informed consent process is the issue of termination or changes in care. Patients may terminate care at any time and may decide to end care for several reasons. These reasons may include but are not limited to: a decrease in symptoms, improvement in functioning, dissatisfaction with the care or provider, or logistical reasons. However, the provider is also entitled to terminate care if it is no longer appropriate for the patient. One possible reason that a provider may terminate care is if the patient does not follow important instructions (e.g., if the patient does not follow through with referrals in the case of a life threatening emergency, or does not attend assessment or treatment meetings without notice). Additionally, the provider may end treatment if it is in the patient's best interest (e.g., if it appears that the treatment is causing harm or no longer demonstrating improvements). If the provider decides to end treatment, he/ she must inform the patient and discuss alternative treatment options.

CV can cause the provider to terminate care for unique reasons that are not faced in traditional, in-person care. For example, if the technology is continually failing, the provider may decide to see the patient in-person, if possible, or arrange for other services. If a patient becomes imminently suicidal, the provider may decide that in-person care is more appropriate to assure patient safety. We have also noted that the CV context leads some patients to assume that their provider will be able to "follow them" when they move, or when on extended trips, or when their housing situation is disrupted. Accordingly, it is important to clarify up front that this may not be the case, especially if the patient moves to a different state or is forced to reside in a less than optimal or safe situation. The ICF should include all expected reasons that care could be terminated so that the patient is aware of this prior to beginning services.

7.5.12   Billing and Insurance

Most states allow for billing of CV services with the use of additional modifier codes added to traditional procedure codes. If providing services that will be billed to insurance, a therapist will first select the proper current procedural terminology (CPT) code for the type of session and session length (e.g., assessment, individual therapy, group therapy, brief intervention, etc.). The addition of a CV modifier, "GT," stands for interactive audio and video telecommunications system, and is used by most insurance companies to indicate that the session occurred through the use of CV. In some states, the modifier is not necessary, as some insurance policies do not require a differentiating code between in-person or CV sessions. This varies by state as well as by insurance company. Chapter 4 discusses and provides a list of relevant CPT codes CV.

Prior to initiating services, it is important to discuss billing and payment policies with perspective patients. Regardless of billing procedures, therapists will generate billing statements for patients and must discuss how those statements will be conveyed to the patient. The CV context often creates potentially unidentified expectations of electronic communication in the minds of patients receiving CV services, and this expectation may be more pronounced in home-based settings. However, providers often have a set system of billing that they may not wish to deviate from based on service context. Accordingly, the ICF should include all billing procedures.

7.5.13   Voluntary Participation

Participation in services is entirely voluntary. The patient may refuse to participate or withdraw from services at any time without jeopardizing his/her other medical care that he/she may receive at the same facility. However, if a patient chooses to withdraw from services, the provider should invite the patient to meet a final time before ending services to ensure the safety and well-being of the patient and to discuss the plan for future treatment.

7.6   Settings

The ICF can be relatively uniform across settings. However, there are some settings where additional information may need to be included. This section will provide a brief overview of settings or treatment types that may require additional information to be included in the ICF.

7.6.1   In-Home CV

Special considerations should be made when services are provided via in-home CV because patients are in the comfort of their own home. The provider may need to set stricter boundaries and/or expectations with the patient. For example, the therapist may want to outline expectations regarding appropriate dress during sessions (e.g., dress as if the patient was going to see the provider in person). Additionally, the provider may want to ask the patient not to have the CV equipment in the bedroom. This helps to avoid an overly informal or intimate setting in which therapy will occur and promotes healthy boundaries. Patients may prefer to be in their bedroom (or in some cases, patients have used their bathroom) for in-home CV sessions, for privacy reasons, which are valid and should be respected. In these cases the provider should insist that a chair is brought into the bedroom if one is not otherwise available as CV sessions *should not be conducted from bed (unless the patient is bedridden)*.

In home-based CV contexts, it is sometimes the case (ironic as it may be) that a patient "no shows" to a home-based appointment. This may be due to poor organization or the patient's preference to terminate services. However, the home context introduces additional possibilities. The appointment may have become inconvenient or a threat to the patient's privacy due to unfolding situations in the patient's home (e.g., a surprise visit from a friend, or domestic argument). Accordingly, the informed consent process for home-based CV services should address and plan for this potential and for an alternative communication plan. As many seasoned providers can attest to, sometimes a missed appointment, even an unintentional one (e.g., provider sickness, vacation, or patient transportation problems), can sabotage momentum in treatment, engender embarrassment, or lead to unnecessary termination of otherwise helpful services. Hopefully, addressing and planning for missed sessions up front with a thorough consent process might reduce this possibility.

It is important that patients be focused on the session with as few distractions as possible. To ensure full engagement in the services, the provider should ask the patient to not engage in other activities (e.g., cooking, cleaning, surfing the internet) during the session. Additionally, patients should try to find a private area in the home to minimize distractions (e.g., other people) and maximize privacy. Finally, a patient should try to participate in services from his/her home, if it is possible, rather than public places (e.g., work office, hotel rooms, vehicles, etc.) to increase privacy. However, it is sometimes the case that a vehicle parked in the driveway provides a much more private setting than a small apartment, and such flexibility can be considered after a thoughtful discussion by all parties (e.g., there is less privacy when monitors can be viewed through car windows, so the setting is important).

In clinical facilities that provide in-home CV services, many programs have developed standardized liability waivers. The liability waiver usually refers to the agreed upon technology used for connections (e.g., Jabber, Vidyo, Doxy.me, etc.) and the impact it may have on the patient's computer or tablet. This waiver does not hold the provider or supporting organization responsible for any technological difficulties that may arise on the computer. In a private setting, providers are also encouraged to consider making their own standardized liability waiver documents.

Providers may also wish to expand the scope of the ICF for in-home CV contexts to account for the nature and mores of electronic communication. Electronic communications are often less formal than in-person communications, which can assist in building therapeutic alliance, but may also pose threats to formal patient–provider relations and the ethical principal of avoiding multiple relationships [1]. Moreover, the context of patients and providers engaging in services over the internet from home computers or tablets, may lead both patients and providers to feel more comfortable crossing lines that otherwise would be avoided (especially in relation to social media sites and services). As noted earlier, expectations and boundaries should be addressed within the ICF. For example, providers who receive a "friend request" on Facebook from one of their patients may find themselves in an awkward situation if they have not established ground rules and boundaries for electronic communication at the beginning of services. Likewise, email addresses are often readily available online for patients to access. Boundaries around logistical texting regarding scheduling, and even therapeutic texting regarding behavioral homework assignments, can be crossed as familiarity between patients and providers increases. Including information about the limits of electronic communication in the ICF gives providers an easy tool to refer back to if they feel boundaries are being blurred at any point in the therapeutic relationship. Additionally, providers should be mindful of their public online presence.

7.6.2   Office-based CV

During the CV encounter, patients are escorted to and left in CV-equipped rooms. Patients are advised that a support person will be available at any time during the session, and his or her physical location should be pointed out. A contact number for the designated support person will also be provided to each patient who is undergoing a CV encounter. The patient is instructed to call the support person with any questions or issues that arise during the session. The therapist that is at the remote site conducting the CV appointment is also informed and provided with the name and contact number for the support person who is coordinating the appointment.

We believe the best practice is to document everything in the IFC but to also make checklists or support numbers easily accessible and in plain view in the treatment room (e.g., posted near the CV equipment), as carrying around an ICF documenting medical or psychological care represents an unnecessary risk to PHI.

7.6.3   Group Psychotherapy

Providing mental health services through CV is a viable option for both patients and providers. As this modality of healthcare continues to grow and technology improves, the option of providing group therapy via CV is also gaining popularity. Group therapy delivered via CV raises potential concerns for confidentiality. Because a provider or support person might not be in the room, providers should consider the method by which required forms (e.g., safety forms) will be distributed to and received from patients. It is also important for providers to consider the extent to which confidentiality will be maintained, both within the group and via the internet. The informed consent should clearly state that confidentiality cannot be guaranteed. However, individual group members should be encouraged to respect others' privacy and not discuss group matters outside of the group.

Finally, providers may also want to include in the ICF the group attendance policy, sharing time, and especially relevant to group CV contexts, attention policies. Remote providers might not be able to see group members texting while others are sharing. In residential treatment settings where group CV is conducted, it is important to communicate to group members that information shared within the group setting remains in the group. This can be challenging within in-person group contexts when patients share the same domicile and see one another in multitude of areas within same setting. Because CV providers are not situated within the treatment ecology, may be unfamiliar with the general programming schedule, and are unavailable more broadly to monitor the ward, it is especially important to highlight the importance of keeping information within the one particular group. In considering such factors, providers are responsible for verbally informing clients of these aspects of group treatment and including them in the ICF.

Clinicians and clinical managers can modify the ICF templates provided in Appendices 7.A and 7.B to meet their specific needs. However, it may be the case that starting from scratch or integrating CV-specific components into existing ICFs will be more convenient or preferred. Accordingly, for convenience, Appendix 7.D summarizes the above ICF essential elements in a summary checklist.

Conclusion

The growing demand for mental health care in both rural and urban settings, coupled with the rapid gains in videoconferencing technologies, suggests that treatments via CV will continue to expand as a modality for mental health services. Fortunately, the bulk of the extant literature indicates that treatments by CV are generally as good as in person treatments with regard to symptom improvement, satisfaction, and therapeutic alliance, among other issues [4]. For those of us who are passionate about increasing access to mental health services, the future of CV looks promising. However, the path toward this novel territory should be approached thoughtfully. The informed consent process is central to properly guiding expectations, and it provides the perfect opportunity to provide information about problems that may be unlikely and yet have the potential for confusion or harm. Conducting the informed consent process early, and referring to it throughout treatment, is the optimal way to initiate and maintain good communication in the therapeutic context.

Appendix 7.A: Office-based Clinical Videoconferencing Informed Consent Template

[Note: These templates describe a treatment for PTSD, but any treatment for any disorder may be described.]

Jane Doe, Ph.D.
Center for the Treatment of Psychological Disorders
100 Sunshine Drive
San Diego, CA 92013

Informed Consent for Treatment

Overview of Services

I understand that the purpose of the treatment that Dr. Doe will be providing to me is to help reduce my posttraumatic stress disorder (PTSD) symptoms. Dr. Doe will be using Cognitive Processing Therapy (CPT), a treatment that has been shown to be effective at reducing PTSD symptoms. The purpose of CPT is to help identify negative thoughts that I am having about myself, the world, and others after experiencing the traumatic event. I understand that Dr. Doe and I will be working together on evaluating thoughts related to my traumatic event. I understand that I may experience an increase in anxiety and other symptoms at the beginning of treatment but that Dr. Doe will monitor this with me. I understand that I will be responsible for completing weekly practice assignments that I will have sessions via clinical video (CV) with Dr. Doe. CV includes the use of videoconferencing technology over a computer screen to meet with Dr. Doe. I understand that Dr. Doe will assist me with managing any distress that I may have and will work with me to try to improve my PTSD symptoms. I understand that I am expected to actively engage in the therapy in order to receive the most benefit.

I understand that I will be meeting with Dr. Doe over the next *12 weeks on Mondays at 3 p.m.* via CV software. I understand that I will go to the local Center for the Treatment of Psychological Disorders office and use the CV equipment that is in the office, and that Dr. Doe will be at a different site of the Center for Treatment of Psychological Disorders. So, we will be meeting via CV and not in-person. I understand that I can ask the front desk staff or other support person for help using the CV equipment if there are any technological problems.

I understand that I can reach Dr. Doe at her office between the hours of 9 am and 5 pm, Monday through Friday at (555) 555-5555. Also, I understand that I can call Dr. Doe on her cell phone for non-emergencies (e.g., scheduling issues) after these hours and on weekends at (444) 444-4444. I acknowledge that Dr. Doe prefers to communicate over the phone and does not use personal e-mail with clients. Additionally, I understand that I should call 911 in the case of emergency, such as if I am having thoughts of harming myself or others.

Risks and Benefits

I understand that when engaging in psychological treatment, there may not be benefits to me. However, I may end up experiencing an increase in my mental health and overall well-being. I understand that CPT could help decrease my PTSD symptoms and I could feel better. I understand that I may initially experience greater distress because I am talking about my traumatic event. However, I understand that Dr. Doe will help me work through this distress.

I understand that the use of CV for psychological treatment may have some limits of confidentiality. I understand that third parties could access information shared via CV without Dr. Doe or I knowing (e.g., if someone hacks into the computer system or server). However, Dr. Doe and the Center for the Treatment of Psychological Disorders have installed encryption software (i.e., software that allows only the intended recipient to view information) to help protect information that is shared via CV. All software complies with national and state laws (including HIPAA compliance) to protect information shared via CV.

I understand that CV can result in technological difficulties, such as dropped calls, frozen images, pixilated images, lack of sound, or distorted sound. Dr. Doe and I have agreed that if the CV equipment fails during therapy sessions, she will call me on the phone in the therapy room that I am in and we will finish the session over the phone. Dr. Doe and I have also agreed that if the CV equipment fails more than twice, we will meet in person so that I can have the best care possible.

Confidentiality

I understand that Dr. Doe will keep all of our conversations confidential, but that she must follow mandatory reported laws. I understand that if I reveal any information about child or elder abuse, Dr. Doe will need to report it. I understand that if I reveal any information that I am going to harm myself or others, Dr. Doe will need to report it.

I understand that only Dr. Doe and authorized staff members will have access to my files. Dr. Doe will keep all of my files stored in a locked cabinet in the office so that only she and authorized staff can access them.

Transmission of Patient Information

I understand that I am not to e-mail any personal information to Dr. Doe or any other staff, but instead I will call Dr. Doe and complete any forms in-person. Dr. Doe will not be audio- or video recording any of my sessions. I agree to tell Dr. Doe if I would like to audio record my therapy sessions. However, I agree to not share these audio recordings online or with the public. Dr. Doe will be documenting weekly clinical progress notes and I understand that I may request to see these. I understand that clinical progress notes will include a summary of my treatment sessions, mental status information, diagnoses, and treatment plans. Dr. Doe may need to fax forms to a different clinical site within the Center for the Treatment of Psychological Disorders, but she will use a cover sheet that states the information is confidential. I understand that both fax machines will be located in locked offices that only staff can access.

Emergency Plans and Safety

Dr. Doe and I have agreed that in between sessions, if I am in an emergency (e.g., feel like harming myself or others), I will call 911 immediately. If I am engaging in a CV therapy session and I feel particularly distressed, I agree to tell Dr. Doe and notify on-site staff to help me. I also understand that if there is a technological emergency (e.g., CV equipment failing) that Dr. Doe will call me on the office phone where I am located.

Termination or Changes in Care

I understand that all participation in services is voluntary and that I may decide to end care at any time without penalty (the decision will not affect my ability to access future services). I also understand that once I have completed the 12 weeks of CPT, Dr. Doe may decide to end therapy if my PTSD symptoms have improved. However, if she believes that I need additional sessions, we will continue to meet weekly via CV. I understand that if Dr. Doe believes that more intensive services are needed (e.g., inpatient) that we will stop therapy via CV and will make other arrangements. Dr. Doe will end care if she believes it is in my best interest (e.g., my symptoms are getting worse or the treatment is harmful). Also, I understand that if I skip more than four therapy sessions without notice, Dr. Doe may not provide therapy to me any longer and will give me a referral to another provider.

Billing and Insurance

Dr. Doe accepts Blue Cross Blue Shield and United Healthcare insurance. I have already confirmed that Dr. Doe is an approved provider within my insurance network and I realize that I am responsible for paying the copay of $ 20 at each therapy session. If Dr. Doe is not an approved provider through my insurance company, I do not have insurance, or I am choosing not to use insurance to cover these services, I agree to pay the full cost for these services out of pocket at each session at $ XXX per session. The staff at the clinic will provide me with a receipt of my payment for my records. Dr. Doe may use a sliding fee scale for individuals who have low-income or extenuating circumstances. If I think that I may be eligible for the sliding fee scale, I should discuss this with Dr. Doe prior to my first therapy appointment. Individuals who earn less than $ XXXX per year (before taxes) or are currently experiencing financial hardship (e.g., chronic illness, medical bills, unemployment) may be eligible.

Other Information

I agree to give Dr. Doe 24 h notice if I need to cancel or reschedule an appointment. Dr. Doe agrees to waive the fee for the first missed appointment without notice. However, if I miss a second appointment without notice, I will be responsible for the $ XXX hourly fee. I agree to pay this fee if I do not provide 24 h notice to Dr. Doe before cancelling. I can contact the office at (555) 555-5555 if I need to cancel or reschedule.

Voluntary

I am aware that my participation in therapy with Dr. Doe is completely voluntary. I understand that I can end services at any time without penalty and that Dr. Doe will work with me to provide another referral, if desired.

Client Consent to Services

[If the person consenting is the person receiving services]: I, (*insert patient name*), have read this entire document and have had the opportunity to ask any questions. I

acknowledge all content in this document. I understand the limits of confidentiality when using CV and when required to report by law. I agree to pay my $ 20 copay at each therapy session, at the time of services. I agree that I may end therapy at any time and may refuse to participate in any portions of the therapy.

[If the person consenting is a PROXY]: I have signed this consent agreement on behalf of a person who may be temporarily or permanently incompetent, unable to sign, or a minor, I represent that I have the authority to sign this consent agreement on behalf of this person. This use of the first person in this consent agreement shall include me, and the person for whom I am representing.

I have read and understand the information provided above regarding treatment, have discussed it with my physician or such assistants as may be designated, and all of my questions have been answered to my satisfaction. I hereby give my informed consent for the participation in this treatment.

_____

Signature of Patient   **Date**

If patient is unable to sign, secure consent of Next of Kin or Legal Agent and Indicate Reason:

☐ **Minor**   ☐ **Disoriented**   ☐ **Medically Unstable**   ☐ **Incompetent**

_____

Signature of or Next of Kin, Legal Agent/guardian or Relationship to patient

Appendix 7.B: In-Home Clinical Videoconferencing Informed Consent Template

[Note: This is a modified version of the in-office template. This version includes specific language that is unique to in-home CV.]

Jane Doe, PhD
Center for the Treatment of Psychological Disorders
100 Sunshine Drive
San Diego, CA 92013

Informed Consent for Treatment

Overview of Services

I understand that the purpose of the treatment that Dr. Doe will be providing to me is to help reduce my posttraumatic stress disorder (PTSD) symptoms. Dr. Doe will be using cognitive processing therapy (CPT), a treatment that has been shown to be effective at reducing PTSD symptoms. The purpose of CPT is to help identify negative thoughts that I am having about myself, the world, and others after experiencing the traumatic event. I understand that Dr. Doe and I will be working together on evaluating thoughts related to my traumatic event. I understand that I may experience an increase in anxiety and other symptoms at the beginning of treatment but that Dr. Doe will work through these symptoms with me. I understand that I will be responsible for completing weekly practice assignments that I will discuss via clinical video (CV) with Dr. Doe. I understand that Dr. Doe will assist me with managing any distress that I may have and will work with me to try to improve my PTSD symptoms. I understand that I am expected to actively engage in the therapy in order to receive the most benefit.

I understand that I will be meeting with Dr. Doe over the next *12 weeks on Mondays at 3 pm* via CV software. CV includes the use of videoconferencing technology over a computer screen to meet with Dr. Doe. I understand that I will be responsible for providing the CV equipment (e.g., webcam, microphone and speakers), installing the CV equipment onto my home computer prior to my first therapy session. If for some reason the CV technology does not work or I have problems, I will call the clinic staff for help over the phone. However, I understand that the staff is unable to provide me help in person. I acknowledge that I may encounter technological difficulties when trying to install the software when using CV throughout therapy and I agree to work with Dr. Doe to fix any problems that arise (e.g., dropped calls, frozen images). I understand that Dr. Doe will be at the Center for Treatment of Psychological Disorders, so we will be meeting via CV and not in-person.

I have agreed to treat therapy via CV the same way that I would treat in-person therapy. This agreement includes but is not limited to: appropriate dress (e.g., as if I were being seen in a public clinic), 24 h cancellation notice, active engagement in therapy (e.g., not checking emails or surfing the web during session), etc. I have agreed that I will place any pets that I have in a separate room prior to the start of each session so that I am not distracted during therapy. I confirm that I will be in a private room during therapy and that I have asked for my family and friends to not enter the room while I am in session. I agree to work with Dr. Doe in ensuring that my privacy is protected both via CV and in my home because of the sensitive topics that we may discuss during therapy sessions.

I understand that I can reach Dr. Doe at her office between the hours of 9 am. and 5 pm., Monday through Friday at (555) 555-5555. Also, I understand that I can call Dr. Doe on her cell phone for non-emergencies (e.g., scheduling issues) after these hours and on weekends at (444) 444-4444. I acknowledge that Dr. Doe prefers to communicate over the phone and does not use personal e-mail with clients. Additionally, I understand that I should call 911 in the case of emergency, such as if I am having thoughts of harming myself or others.

Risks and Benefits

I understand that when engaging in psychological treatment, there may not be benefits to me. However, I may end up experiencing an increase in my mental health and overall well-being. I understand that CPT could help decrease my PTSD symptoms and I could feel better. I understand that I may initially experience greater distress because I am talking about my traumatic event. However, I understand that Dr. Doe will help me work through this distress.

I understand that the use of CV for psychological treatment may have some limits of confidentiality. Also, I acknowledge that third parties could access information shared via CV without Dr. Doe or I knowing (e.g., if someone hacks into the computer system or server). However, Dr. Doe, Center for the Treatment of Psychological Disorders and I have all installed encryption (i.e., software that allows only the intended recipient to view information) to help protect information that is shared via CV. All software complies with national and state laws (including HIPAA compliance) to protect information shared via CV.

I understand that CV can result in technological difficulties, such as dropped calls, frozen images, pixilated images, lack of sound, or distorted sound. Dr. Doe and I have agreed that if the CV equipment fails during therapy sessions and cannot be fixed in less than 5 min, she will call me on my cell phone and we will finish the session over the phone. Dr. Doe and I have also agreed that if the CV equipment fails more than twice, we will meet in person so that I can have the best care possible. I understand that I am responsible for fixing any problems that my internet, computer, or CV equipment is having and that staff will not be able to assist me in person.

Confidentiality

I understand that Dr. Doe will keep all of our conversations confidential, but that she must follow mandatory reported laws. I understand that if I reveal any information about child or elder abuse, Dr. Doe will need to report it. I understand that if I reveal any information that I am going to harm myself or others, Dr. Doe will need to report it.

I understand that only Dr. Doe and authorized staff members will have access to my files. Dr. Doe will keep all of my files stored in a locked cabinet in the office so that only she and authorized staff can access them. I am aware that I can request to see Dr. Doe's clinical progress notes about me at any time.

Transmission of Patient Information

I understand that I am not to e-mail any personal information to Dr. Doe or any other staff, but instead I will fill out electronic versions of any questionnaires that Dr. Doe may have for me. I understand that these electronic files are located and saved on a secure portal that only the staff at the Center for the Treatment of Psychological Disorders can access. I recognize that Dr. Doe will not be audio- or video recording any of my sessions. I agree to tell Dr. Doe if I would like to audio or video record my therapy sessions. However, I agree to not share these audio or video recordings online or with the public. Dr. Doe will be documenting weekly clinical progress notes and I understand that I may ask to see these at any time. I understand that clinical progress notes will include a summary of my treatment sessions, mental status information, diagnoses, and treatment plans.

Emergency Plans and Safety

Dr. Doe and I have agreed that if I am in an emergency (e.g., feel like harming myself or others) in-between sessions that I will call 911. I recognize that because I am in my own home and not in a mental health clinic, Dr. Doe and staff will not be able to readily assist me in-person if I become particularly distressed during a session. Therefore, I understand that if I am engaging in a CV therapy session and I feel particularly distressed, I will tell Dr. Doe so that she can contact local emergency personnel, if needed. I have given Dr. Doe my most recent address so that she can identify the local emergency staff and I understand that she will have this information readily available at all times during sessions. I agree to tell Dr. Doe if my address should change so that she can update the information and identify different emergency resources, if needed. I understand that if there is a technological emergency (e.g., CV equipment failing) that Dr. Doe will call me my cell phone where I am located.

Termination or Changes in Care

I understand that all participation in services is voluntary and that I may decide to end care at any time without penalty (or the decision affecting future services). I also understand that once I have completed the 12 weeks of CPT, Dr. Doe may decide to end therapy if my PTSD symptoms have improved. However, if she believes that I need additional sessions, we will continue to meet weekly via CV. I understand that if Dr. Doe believes that more intensive services are needed (e.g., inpatient) that we will stop therapy via CV and will make other arrangements. Dr. Doe will end care if she believes it is in my best interest (e.g., my symptoms are getting worse or the treatment is harmful). Also, I understand that if I skip more than four therapy sessions without notice, Dr. Doe may not provide therapy to me any longer and will give me a referral to another provider.

Billing and Insurance

Dr. Doe accepts Blue Cross Blue Shield and United Healthcare insurance. I have already confirmed that Dr. Doe is an approved provider within my insurance network and I realize that I am responsible for paying the copay of $ 20 at each therapy session. If Dr. Doe is not an approved provider through my insurance company, I do not have insurance, or I am choosing not to use insurance to cover these services, I agree to pay the full cost for these services out of pocket at each session at $ XXX per session. I will pay at the end of each therapy session via the secure online portal (the same one that is used to fill out questionnaires). If for some reason I cannot process the transaction online, I agree to send a check via postal mail to the office. I recognize that the online portal will provide me with a printable receipt of payment for my records. I recognize that Dr. Doe may use a sliding fee scale for individuals who have low-income or extenuating circumstances. If I think that I may be eligible for the sliding fee scale, I should discuss this with Dr. Doe prior to my first therapy appointment. Individuals who earn less than $ XXXX per year (before taxes) or are currently experiencing financial hardship (e.g., chronic illness, medical bills, temporary unemployment) may be eligible for the sliding fee scale.

Other Information

I agree to give Dr. Doe 24 h notice if I need to cancel or reschedule an appointment. Dr. Doe agrees to waive the fee for the first missed appointment without notice. However, if I miss a second appointment without notice, I will be responsible for the $ XXX hourly fee. I agree to pay this fee if I do not provide 24 h notice to Dr. Doe before cancelling. I can contact the office at (555) 555-5555 if I need to cancel or reschedule. If I miss more than four appointments without notice, Dr. Doe may discontinue therapy with me.

Voluntary

I am aware that my participation in therapy with Dr. Doe is completely voluntary. I understand that I can end services at any time without penalty and that Dr. Doe will work with me to provide another referral, if desired.

Client Consent to Services

[If the person consenting is the person receiving services]: I, (insert patient name), have read this entire document and have had the opportunity to ask any questions. I acknowledge all content in this document. I understand the limits of confidentiality when using CV and when required to report by law. I recognize that I am responsible for installing the CV software onto my computer and fixing any problems that come up. I agree to pay my $ 20 copay at the end of each therapy session via the online portal and will mail a check if needed. I acknowledge that I may end therapy at any time and may refuse to participate in any portions of the therapy.

[If the person consenting is a PROXY]: I have signed this consent agreement on behalf of a person who may be temporarily or permanently incompetent, unable to sign, or a minor, I represent that I have the authority to sign this consent agreement on behalf of this person. This use of the first person in this consent agreement shall include me, and the person for whom I am representing.

I have read and understand the information provided above regarding treatment for PTSD, have discussed it with my physician or such assistants as may be designated, and all of my questions have been answered to my satisfaction. I hereby give my informed consent for the participation in this study.

_____

Signature of Patient   Date

If patient is unable to sign, secure consent of Next of Kin or Legal Agent and Indicate Reason:

　　　🔲 Minor   🔲 Disoriented   🔲 Medically Unstable   🔲 Incompetent

_____

Signature of or Next of Kin, Legal Agent/guardian or Relationship to patient

Appendix 7.C: Issues to Address During Initial Contact with Patients Regarding Clinical Videoconferencing Services (Prior to the Informed Consent Process)

The informed consent process will include a more in-depth review of issues related to clinic videoconferencing but potential patients should be primed regarding the relevant issues relating to CV during the initial contact. The person initiating contact with the patient should:

A. Describe CV.

It should be clear that patients will communicate in real-time with the therapist via videoconferencing.

B. Describe where CV will be conducted.

1. Provider-side settings often include clinic office or home.
2. Patient-side settings often include clinic office, home, work, or other community setting.

C. Describe how CV might be integrated into care.

1. For example:

   a. Staged care beginning with in-person services and transitioning to CV, 100 % CV services.
   b. CV as an occasional or planned supplement to face-to-face care.

D. Provide risks and benefits of CV.

　　1. Commonly identified benefits include:

　　　　c. Patient convenience, cost-savings, privacy, and flexibility of scheduling.

　　2. Commonly identified risks include:

　　　　a. Potential threats to data privacy, potential disruptions in the signal and communication, and getting use to a new way of interacting.

　　3. For home-based CV risks also include:

　　　　a. Lack of available on-site emergency personnel, and a potential to collude with existing patient avoidance or isolation.

E. Describe the eligibility requirements and assess suitability for CV services.

　　1. Potential considerations include:

　　　　b. Significant cognitive deficits (dementia, developmental deficits).
　　　　c. High-risk behaviors (imminently suicidal/homicidal, i.e., more than ideation).
　　　　d. History of intoxication during treatment sessions.
　　　　e. Acute psychosis or mania.
　　　　f. History of delusions regarding thought broadcasting via technology.
　　　　g. Sensory deficits that would preclude ability to initiate or communicate via CV.

Appendix 7.D: Checklist: Content to Include in Informed Consent Forms for Clinical Videoconferencing

[Note: The items below should be written in language that is easily understood and consistent with legal requirements and accepted professional standards.]

A. Define what CV consists of and how it differs from in-person care
B. Provide the structure of services
C. Provider and patient expectations

　　1. Role of provider and patient in services
　　2. Boundaries
　　3. State when and how provider will respond to routine electronic messages
　　4. In-between session contact

D. Acknowledge potential risks and benefits of care provided through CV

　　1. Explain potential technological problems (e.g., unpredictable disruption of services)
　　2. Identify alternative means of re-establishing communication in the event services are disrupted (e.g., another form of electronic communication; telephone)

3. Note whether CV programs and services are fully HIPAA-compliant

E. Inform the client about confidentiality and limits to confidentiality

1. Advise client about mandatory reporting laws
2. Clarify who else may have access to communications between provider and client
3. Detail safeguards used to protect against risk related to CV

   a. Methods utilized to ensure that only intended recipients (e.g., provider) have access to client information (e.g., encryption, portals)

F. Communicate how data will be transmitted and stored

1. Indicate whether or not sessions will be recorded
2. Describe how client information will be documented (e.g., clinical notes)
3. Convey how provider stores electronic communications exchanged with the client

G. Instruct the client regarding emergency contact information

1. Present emergency plans
2. Establish alternative means of communication under emergency circumstances

H. Discuss possible changes in care

1. Outline conditions of care delivered through CV
2. List alternative services in the event CV is no longer an appropriate delivery of care
3. Notify the client that they have the right to end treatment without penalty of care

I. Billing and Insurance

1. Overview how all billing and insurance will be handled

J. Voluntary

1. Inform patient that all care is voluntary and that the patient has the right to end care without penalty

K. Define what CV consists of and how it differs from in-person care
L. Provide the structure of services
M. Provider and patient expectations

1. Role of provider and patient in services
2. Boundaries
3. State when and how provider will respond to routine electronic messages
4. In-between session contact

N. Acknowledge potential risks and benefits of care provided through CV

1. Explain potential technological problems (e.g., disruption of services)

2. Identify alternative means of re-establishing communication in the event services are disrupted (e.g., another form of electronic communication; telephone)
3. Note whether CV programs and services are fully HIPAA-compliant

O. Inform the client about confidentiality and limits to confidentiality

1. Advise client about mandatory reporting laws
2. Clarify who else may have access to communications between provider and client
3. Detail safeguards used to protect against risk related to CV

   a. Methods utilized to ensure that only intended recipients (e.g., provider) have access to client information (e.g., encryption, portals)

P. Communicate how data will be transmitted and stored

1. Indicate whether or not sessions will be recorded
2. Describe how client information will be documented (e.g., clinical notes)
3. Convey how provider stores electronic communications exchanged with the client

Q. Instruct the client regarding emergency contact information

1. Present emergency plans
2. Establish alternative means of communication under emergency circumstances

R. Discuss possible changes in care

1. Outline conditions of care delivered through CV
2. List alternative services in the event CV is no longer an appropriate delivery of care
3. Notify the client that they have the right to end treatment without penalty of care

S. Billing and Insurance

1. Overview how all billing and insurance will be handled

T. Voluntary

1. Inform patient that all care is voluntary and that the patient has the right to end care without penalty

Appendix 7.E: Telemedicine Informed Consent Laws

Many US states do not have statutes and regulations specific to CV. However, several states do have statutes and regulations for telemedicine provision, including those involving informed consent. In states without specific CV statues and regulations, providers offering these services can ensure that their practices are HIPAA-compliant and may consult APA ethical guidelines for further guidance. For providers who practice in states with legal statutes guiding telemedicine provision, they should be aware of relevant statues and adhere to them when providing care through videoconferencing. With regard to informed consent, it is important to be aware of any requirements for this process. For example, whether written, verbal, or both forms of consent are required prior to beginning services delivered via CV. Furthermore, determining if electronic signatures are permitted to provide informed consent is also a consideration.

The resources provided here offer a brief overview of CV laws by state; however, due to the evolving nature of CV and related laws, this resource should not be used as a definitive source. Providers should independently verify information, contact their respective state licensing board, and/or contact legal counsel to access the most up-to-date statutes and regulations. For more information about telemedicine laws please visit:

APA—State laws for telemedicine and teleconferencing

http://www.apapracticecentral.org/advocacy/state/telehealth-slides.pdf

Accessed: 29 Oct. 2013

Appendix 7.F: Clinical Note Template for Documenting Initiation of CV Services

[Note: The following is an example of a clinical progress note written by a Veteran's Affairs (VA) provider. The note documents services that were provided via office-to-office CV.]

Clinical Video (CV) from Therapist's Office to Community Based Outpatient Clinic (CBOC):

Appointment was conducted via CV. Veteran was located at *[FILL IN LOCATION]*, where in-person clinicians were available to join the appointment in case of emergency. The provider was located at *[FILL IN LOCATION]*.

At the outset of this appointment, Veteran was provided with the following information:

1. The nature of CV health and its benefits and risks
2. Confidentiality and its limits
3. The emergency plan, which has been established and agreed upon with the CBOC
4. Time-limited, evidence based therapy options available via CV
5. Alternative, non CV, therapy options
6. The importance of consistent therapy attendance and homework completion

The Veteran provided verbal consent to the above items.

Appendix 7.G: Lessons Learned

The purpose of this section is to provide useful examples of "lessons learned" from the authors' use of CV in research trials and clinical care.

Computer Equipment Knowledge and Resources

Patients who are interested in CV treatment are often concerned about obtaining the equipment necessary for in-home CV. More specifically, patients tend to express concern regarding their ability to obtain a computer and their level of computer knowledge. Therefore, providers should be aware that for home-based CV, some patients may not be able to engage in treatment due to a lack of resources (e.g., webcam, computer, fast internet). For example, a patient dropped out of one research study because the study could not provide CV equipment. If the patient is unable to provide the necessary resources for in-home CV, then the provider and patient should come up with an alternative plan for treatment.

Technological Issues

It is important for therapists to properly orient themselves to CV equipment (monitor, camera, and remote) and to have technical and administrative support at each site to help facilitate the process for both providers and patients. Monitoring the call quality and dropped calls can be useful in case the bandwidth needs to be adjusted at each site. When all else fails, re-booting the equipment often solves problems. Technological issues are one of the main risks of CV.

Privacy

Prior to engaging in in-home CV services, the provider will discuss with the patient the importance of a quiet, private place to set up for sessions as well as what type of internet connection is necessary. For example, one patient agreed to find a quiet, private place for in-home CV sessions but when he connected with provider he was in his car. The car was parked, but the patient was using free Wi-Fi from a nearby restaurant. This session was discontinued and the provider discussed with the patient the limitations of public internet connections and the lack of privacy. Another patient connected to CV from a booth in a restaurant and told the provider, "I have on a headset and no one can see the screen, so I am ok with it." Needless to say, the provider discontinued the session and re-visited the informed consent and importance of privacy.

In-Home CV

During the third session with a patient, the patient logged into CV to connect with the provider and was wearing only a bathrobe and had disheveled hair. The provider requested the patient disconnect and dress appropriately prior to engaging in session. When patients call in from the comfort of their home, they may be more casually dressed. It is important for the provider to set expectations about appropriate dress prior to engaging in session. Additionally, when conducting a session with a patient using in-home CV, unexpected visitors may show up or enter the room that the patient is in. Similarly, clinicians have started videoconferencing sessions only to discover later that young children who need supervision are in the room and that no other form of childcare is available, or that family members are nearby and are unwilling or unable to leave. The provider and patient should discuss a plan about how to handle possible interruptions, privacy, and the presence of other family members prior to beginning services. It may be helpful to tell clients that they should be alone in a room for the duration of the service unless special circumstances warrant another person in the room (e.g., couples therapy, exposure treatments that involve other people).

Sometimes interruptions are unavoidable even when they are discussed. During one session, as we noted earlier in this chapter, a patient's dog ran into the room and jumped on the computer keyboard, disconnecting the session. The situation was resolved when the patient reconnected to the provider and plans were made to have the dog in another room during session. Another provider had a different experience with a pet. During an early Exposure and Response Prevention treatment session delivered via in-home CV, a patient diagnosed with obsessive-compulsive disorder was engaging in a challenging exposure. During the course of the exposure, it became clear that the patient was distracted by something in the room. When the clinician asked the patient what she was looking at, the patient turned her screen to show her dog standing at her feet. The patient reported that she had been petting the dog through all previous exposures because it was more comforting and eased the anxiety caused by the exposure. As the clinician had a limited view of the room, she was unable to see that the client was engaging in this new compulsion. It is important for providers to educate patients about how the presence of animals in the room can impact the services. As noted in Backhaus et al. (2012), the limited scope of the camera with CV (usually the head and shoulders of each person) can also block views of wheelchairs or fidgeting.

It is important to have a conversation about expectations for the patient during in-home CV sessions. For example, one patient was editing unrelated documents on the computer during a session, a different patient was texting during the session, and another would prepare his lunch at the beginning of the session. Similar situations and other unexpected events are bound to happen and add to the clinical richness of the situation. In an effort to minimize some of these events, the informed consent process and in depth discussion of appropriate treatment boundaries are necessary prior to the start of services.

The ease of in-home CV also has drawbacks. Patients sometimes display a reduced commitment to treatment or are more apt to cancel a session last minute, as there is often less planning needed to attend a CV session (in comparison to having to visit a local clinic or office). It may be helpful to include a clause in the consent that encourages clients to regard each session as though it were an in-person office visit (e.g., requiring 24 h notice for cancellations) and to emphasize the importance of treating these sessions as though they were occurring in an external environment. Given these experiences, it may be helpful to add a short section in the informed consent that provides guidelines for an appropriate therapeutic environment during sessions (as we have described in our templates, above).

References

1. American Psychological Association. Ethical principles of psychologists and code of conduct. Am Psychol. 2002;57:1060–73.
2. American Psychological Association Practice Organization. Telehealth: legal basics for psychologists. Good Pract. 2010;41:2–7.
3. American Telemedicine Association. What is telemedicine? http://www.americantelemed. org/learn. 2014. Accessed 5 Jan 2014.
4. Backhaus A, Agha Z, Maglione ML, Repp A, Ross B, Zuest D, Rice-Thorp NM, Lohr J, Thorp SR. Videoconferencing psychotherapy: a systematic review. Psychol Serv. 2012;9:111–31.
5. Baker DC, Bufka LF. Preparing for the telehealth world: navigating legal, regulatory, reimbursement and ethical issues in an electronic age. Prof Psychol Res Pract. 2011;42:405–11. doi:10.1037/a0025037.
6. Herbert PB, Young KA. Tarasoff at twenty-five. J Am Acad Psychiatry Law Online. 2002;30:27581.
7. Kramer G, Ayers T, Mishkind M, Norem A. DoD telemental health guidebook; 2011. http:// t2health.dcoe.mil/sites/default/files/cth/guidebook/tmh-guidebook_06-11.pdf. Assessed 1 May 2014.
8. Kumekawa J. Health information privacy protection: crisis or common sense? Online Journal of Issues in Nursing, 6. http://www.nursingworld.org/MainMenuCategories/ANAMarketplace/ANAPeriodicals/OJIN/TableOfContents/Volume62001/No3Sept01/PrivacyProtection-Crisis.aspx. 2001. Accessed 29 April 2014.
9. Manhal-Baugus M. E-therapy: practical, ethical, and legal issues. Cyberpsychol Behav. 2001;4:551–63.
10. Mathews B, Kenny MC. Mandatory reporting legislation in the United States, Canada, and Australia: a cross-jurisdictional review of key features, differences, and issues. Child Maltreat. 2008;13(1):50–63.
11. McCarty D, Clancy C. Telehealth: implications for social work practice. Soc Work. 2002;47:153–61. doi:10.1093/sw/47.2.153.
12. Shore JH. Telepsychiatry: videoconferencing in the delivery of psychiatric care. Am J Psychiatry. 2013;170:256–62.
13. Turvey C, Coleman M, Dennison O, Drude K, Goldenson M, Hirsch P, Bernard P. ATA practice guidelines for video-based online mental health services. Telemed e-Health. 2013;19:722–30. doi:10.1089/tmj.2013.9989.
14. Thorp SR, Fidler J, Moreno L, Floto E, Agha Z. Lessons learned from studies of psychotherapy for PTSD via video teleconferencing. Psychol Serv. 2012;9:197–9.

15. Welfel ER, Danzinger PR, Santoro S. Mandated reporting of abuse/maltreatment of older adults: a primer for counselors. J Couns Dev. 2000;78(3):284–92.
16. Werth JL. US involuntary mental health commitment statutes: requirements for persons perceived to be a potential harm to self. Suicide Life Threat Behav. 2001;31(3):348–57.
17. Yuen EK, Goetter EM, Herbert JD, Forman EM. Challenges and opportunities in internet-mediated telemental health. Prof Psychol Res Pract. 2012;43:1–8. doi:10.1037/a0025524.

Chapter 8
Patient Safety Planning and Emergency Management

Peter Shore and Mary Lu

> *The experience of separateness arouses anxiety; it is indeed,*
> *the source of all anxiety… the deepest need of man, then is the*
> *need to overcome his separateness, to leave the prison of his*
> *aloneness.*
>
> Erich Fromm (1956) [1]

Chapter Summary

Purpose This chapter provides practice guidelines and resources for patient risk evaluation and emergency response when providing clinical videoconferencing (CV) services to clinic-based and nonclinic-based settings. It contains information regarding provider preparation for both behavioral and medical emergencies. Additionally, this chapter provides information regarding the identification of suitable patients for CV services.

Context This chapter is useful for clinicians because although behavioral and medical emergencies in mental health settings have been addressed in the literature for decades, guidelines for handling emergencies via CV are somewhat new. Providers offering or preparing to offer CV services must necessarily attend to the specifics of risk evaluation and emergency response protocols in CV settings.

Tools This chapter provides an overview of available recommendations regarding emergency planning and response in CV settings, identifies

P. Shore (✉) · M. Lu
Department of Psychiatry, Oregon Health & Science University,
Portland, OR, USA
e-mail: shore@ohsu.edu

P. Shore
VA Northwest Health Network (VISN 20), Department of Veterans Affairs,
Portland, OR, USA

M. Lu
Portland VA Medical Center, Department of Veterans Affairs,
Portland, OR, USA

© Springer International Publishing Switzerland 2015
P. W. Tuerk, P. Shore (eds.), *Clinical Videoconferencing in Telehealth,*
Behavioral Telehealth, DOI 10.1007/978-3-319-08765-8_8

specific procedures for selecting suitable patients and for conducting emergency planning prior to and during treatment for both clinic-based and nonclinic-based settings. This chapter also includes the following tools in the appendices: Pre-treatment checklists, pre-session checklists, emergency planning templates, clinical note template for documenting emergency plans, the Assessment for Suitability Home-Based Telemental Health (ASH-25)—a suicide risk assessment tool, and a list of additional resources related to chapter topics.

8.1   Introduction: Current Practice Guidelines for Telehealth and Rapidly Evolving Practice Models

This chapter describes the current standards and recommendations for clinical considerations and planning relevant to patient safety and emergency situations that may arise during the course of treatment via CV. It does not address the uses of clinical video to assist local providers to conduct emergency evaluations or as a means of providing evaluations for involuntary admission or other legal proceedings [2]. The treatment model being addressed is that of real-time videoconferencing via a dedicated videoconferencing unit, personal computer, or a mobile device, with the patient being in either a supervised (i.e., clinic-based or hospital) or unsupervised (i.e., home or other nonclinic-based) setting. Current American Telemedicine Association (ATA) practice guidelines have followed the model set forth by Shore et al. in describing administrative, legal/ethical and clinical concerns relevant to telemental health emergency management[2–4]. This chapter will address these areas, with special consideration given to how to translate guidelines into clinical practice.

Several published practice guidelines (2008–2013) address emergency management in the context of telehealth. For a complete list of practice guidelines, please see the Appendix G in this chapter. Software, devices and administrative structures of care delivery are multiplying and changing at a rapid pace, necessitating careful attention to unique clinical considerations of these care environments, as well as safety issues and their management [2]. Nonclinic-based settings for CV are a relatively new area with regard to the development of standards and protocols. A systematic review of known safety issues has been published [3] and further research studies, including randomized controlled trials, are pending [5]. This chapter will highlight key differences between settings with regard to emergency management protocols.

Existing practice guidelines for clinic-based settings contain some consistent themes on the topic of managing emergencies and containing safety risks [2–4, 6–8]. Three of the most common themes are: (1) Have a clear emergency protocol agreed upon in advance between the provider and the patient's clinical site, or the provider and the patient; (2) Know the local laws (where the patient is receiving care) regarding involuntary care and commitment; (3) Emergency planning should involve some predetermined means of coordination and communication with local resources as appropriate, including on-site staff for clinic-based settings, local emergency numbers and resources, personal emergency contacts designated by the patient, and the patient's local mental health or other medical providers.

In addition to these clinic-based guidelines, a systematic review of the safety of telemental health care delivered to nonclinic-based settings, where no professional staff are available, reported that the use of safety plans to prevent adverse effects was helpful in both emergent (i.e., reported suicidal ideation) and nonemergent (increase in depression, failure to enter data into a monitoring system) situations [5]. Also, a standard operating procedure (SOP) for a Home-Based Telemental Health (HBTMH) Pilot program was developed in 2009 at the Portland VAMC. The SOP detailed emergency management protocols and practice guidelines for nonclinic-based settings for the veteran population [8].

8.2 Emergency Management Protocol Design

This section will cover three main areas that are integral to establishing a sound emergency plan: (1) suicide risk assessment; (2) legal considerations and (3) clinical considerations. The final section, clinical considerations, provides practical information to help determine whether a particular patient is suitable to receive mental health services via technology and at a distance.

Prior to beginning treatment with any patient via clinical video, it is recommended that clinicians understand the fundamentals of suicide risk assessment, legal considerations for delivering services via clinical video and clinical consideration. Additionally, prior to initiating telemental health patient care, clinicians are urged to also maintain a basic level of technical skill as users of the software and hardware utilized to deliver their mental health care [2].

8.2.1 Suicide Risk Assessment

Prior to addressing operational procedures and emergency preparations, it is important to assess the suitability of patients who will be receiving mental health services via technology. A major component of this is a thorough suicide risk assessment. Before clinicians begin seeing patients via telehealth, they must complete basic education and training in suicide prevention [2] and should be able to manage a behavioral emergency with a certain degree of confidence. The depth of training and definition of basic training is at the clinician's discretion [2], although usually mental health clinics, private or public, will have established their own requirements. Table 8.1 identifies basic factors that should be included in the assessment of risk for suicide.

In addition to the factors identified in Table 8.1, the focus for consideration should be the patient's means and lethality of the active suicidal or homicidal ideation. For patients who have a gun, knife, poison, or other weapon readily available and a specific plan on how to convert the ideation into action, the focus is on safety.

Table 8.1 Factors to consider when evaluating for risk of suicide

1. Sociodemographic risk factors
2. Stressors, including an overall assessment of health, financial, marital, family, legal, and occupational factors
3. Depression, anxiety, agitation, and irritability
4. Alcohol abuse
5. Suicidal ideation and past attempts, including further evaluation for plans and lethality of attempts
6. Family history of suicide
7. Identification/clarification of focal problems
8. Assessment of strengths and resources
9. Mobilization of existing resources (patients'/others')

Addressing suicidal ideation in language specific to the means and lethality reduces ambiguity for assessment and treatment planning purposes [8]. For additional Suicide Risk Assessment resources please refer to Appendix F in this chapter.

8.2.2 Legal Considerations

Each state has different laws outlining criteria and conditions for an involuntary psychiatric commitment and voluntary psychiatric hospitalizations. Clinicians and administrators should familiarize themselves with the laws where the patient is receiving care. *When in doubt, consult with an attorney.* As a general rule, patients who are deemed a danger to themselves or others can be detained and/or committed to hospitalization involuntarily if they meet the criteria determined by the state in which they are located. Clinicians should be mindful of the following questions: does the clinician have the authority to write detention orders? If not, whom should the clinician contact to obtain detention orders? What restrictions does the treating clinician have in ordering a psychiatric hold?

Some state laws may appear counterintuitive at face value. For example, in Maryland any individual may request another individual to be evaluated against their will. The hold requires an Emergency Evaluation form, approval from a judge and a police escort to the hospital. Two licensed mental health professionals would then determine whether the individual meets Maryland criteria for an involuntary psychiatric admission of up to 10 days [9].

If a patient acknowledges a need for psychiatric hospitalization and agrees to a voluntary admission, the clinician should be familiar with procedures at local emergency (hospital or psychiatric) facilities. If the patient elects to receive care at a local medical center, the clinician may coordinate this by contacting the identified medical center via telephone, identifying the patient and communicating the nature of the emergency. Transportation should be arranged accordingly.

In order to better understand state laws regarding telehealth statutes, clinicians may (1) contact the state governing health board of their specific health discipline; (2) conduct a search via the internet using "telehealth state statutes," or (3) search the ATA web site (http://www.americantelemed.org) for updated information. As a

Table 8.2 Inclusion criteria for clinical video conferencing services

1. The patient has an identified need to receive mental health treatment
2. The patient consents and expresses an interest in receiving mental health care via telehealth technologies
3. The patient agrees to appropriate emergency management protocols

matter of terminology, most laws define the location of the patient as the originating site [10].

While providing mental health care via telehealth, clinicians are bound by the same duty of reasonable care provision that face-to-face appointments adhere to [11]. There are two main areas of concern in providing care at a distance via telehealth technologies: abandonment and negligence. Regarding abandonment, the clinician may mitigate risk by having a contingency plan for technology failures. The other area of concern is negligence. Clinicians have a duty to protect patients from danger to self or others, and a clinician's failure to provide medical attention to a suicidal patient may be considered negligent.

Legally, the use of videoteleconferencing (clinical video) equipment has been determined to be equal to a face-to-face evaluation (US v. Baker 1993) [12]. Baker, an inmate under involuntary psychiatric commitment at a correctional facility in North Carolina, argued that the quality of the videoteleconferencing equipment used during his evaluation was limited and increased the "risk of erroneous result," and that his due process rights were therefore violated under the fifth amendment. The district court upheld the ruling that videoconferencing for legal evaluation was appropriate, and the decision was affirmed on appeal, by the fourth Circuit Court (US v. Baker 1995) [13].

8.2.3   Clinical Considerations

There are several factors involved in determining who may or may not be clinically appropriate for CV services. Based on information provided in this chapter and other resources, administrators and clinicians may elect to develop their own set of criteria for inclusion and exclusion, and they may vary by setting; i.e. some patients may be appropriate for clinic-based CV but not appropriate for nonclinic-based CV. Table 8.2 provides *Inclusion Criteria* [8] and Table 8.3 provides *Exclusion Criteria* as examples.

It is important for clinicians and/or administrators to determine under what clinical circumstances the clinician (or clinic) will not feel comfortable treating patients via telehealth technologies. Table 8.3 identifies common exclusion criteria for remote services. It should be noted that each clinical situation is unique and if in a clinician's best judgment he or she deems that the necessity to treat an individual outweighs the potential risk of treatment via CV, then services can be delivered, although the clinician should clearly document the thought process in the patient's clinical record.

Table 8.3 Exclusion criteria for clinical video conferencing services

1. Patients who reject telehealth during the informed consent process
2. News that may be more appropriately delivered in person. For example, a new diagnosis of a terminal illness, significant findings on a lab result, etc.
3. Untreated substance abuse/dependence that interferes with treatment compliance
4. History of intoxication during treatment
5. Acutely violent or unstable
6. Active suicidal or homicidal ideation
7. Severely decompensated
8. Needs acute hospitalization
9. Psychotic conditions, particularly those that may be exacerbated by telehealth technologies, including schizophrenia and paranoid states; that is, thoughts of being broadcast
10. Acute psychosis
11. Dementia, confusion or cognitive decline in individuals requiring caregiver support who are without such support
12. Patient who require involuntary commitment
13. Significant sensory deficits that can impair the ability to interact over CV
14. Patients with multiple medical problems that may significantly affect cognitive/behavioral states

Table 8.4 Exclusion criteria for CV specific to nonclinic-based settings

1. Patients who lack access to appropriate technology (DSL, cable, 3 g or 4 g internet connection/computer)
2. Patient Support Person (PSP) or other alternative is clinically indicated, but the patient is unable to identify anyone
3. Needs consist of medical monitoring that is unavailable at home
4. Lack of privacy (i.e., family members are interrupting sessions on a consistent basis)

In order to address the added component of services delivered to clinically un-supervised settings, where there is less control over the environment of care, additional exclusion criteria are often applied. Table 8.4 identifies common exclusion criteria specific to nonclinic-based settings.

8.2.4 Patient Evaluation: A Risk Mitigation Assessment Approach

Evaluating patient suitability for telehealth treatment is a dynamic process, and in some cases, can be very challenging. Clinician expectations, comfort level and per-ceived efficacy of the safety planning process factor into judgments of whether telehealth is appropriate in any given situation [10].

In general, having a risk mitigation perspective toward emergency management can be an effective approach in evaluating a patient. The first step is to identify any risk factors for suicide, homicide, and/or medical emergencies. Once the initial risk assessment is complete, clinicians should routinely monitor risk factor symptoms and circumstances throughout treatment.

In the event a patient is located in their home or other nonclinic-based setting via technology, there are additional things to consider. Geographic distance and time to emergency services are significant factors, as is the local emergency system's average response time [2]. It is important to determine whether the patient's current medical status and presenting psychiatric disorder are appropriate for a nonclinic-based setting, or whether it would be more appropriate to see the patient, if possible, at a clinic-based setting via telehealth or in person. For example, many of the psychotic spectrum disorders are typically not recommended for nonclinic-based settings, nor are individuals with complex and severe medical conditions who are geographically distant from emergency medical personnel. If the current local mental health and medical support is limited, clinicians should make efforts to determine whether more community-based resources should be involved in the patient's care.

The ASH-25 (A Structured Guide for the Assessment of Suitability for Home-Based Telemental Health) is a 25-item clinician-completed questionnaire that uses objective and subjective clinical observations to evaluate whether a patient is suitable to receive behavioral health care in a nonclinic-based setting (typically the patient's home) [14]. The ASH-25 considers five domains: (1) mental health, (2) medical considerations, (3) access to care, (4) systems (family, community), and (5) patient support system. ASH-25 norms have not yet been defined, but scores may suggest what level of emergency management planning is warranted. A high score on the ASH-25 may suggest a higher level of complexity across the five factors. For example, an individual who is currently suffering from serious mental illness, has a complicated medical condition, lives far from a medical facility, lives alone and is socially isolated would have a higher score suggesting the clinician should, with the patient's assistance, identify a Patient Support Person, (PSP, see below) [15]. For a complete version of the ASH-25, please see Appendix D.

In cases with patients who are particularly at high risk (more complex, significant distance to emergency services) clinicians may benefit from gathering a detailed social history, including the patient's perception of his or her overall health, financial, marital, family, legal, and occupational status. Such information can be helpful in emergency planning. A thorough assessment creates a foundation to help mitigate dynamic or situational risk factors, either before or during a crisis. Another particularly important part of the initial assessment, in a telehealth context, is better understanding the patient's strengths and existing resources and supports. Exploring attitudes and beliefs about their resources and the role(s) the individuals or systems have played in the patient's life can aid the clinician in understanding how they may affect the overall risk or be used in safety planning. Taking a risk mitigation approach, conducting a thorough initial clinical assessment, evaluating for dynamic and static risk factors, determining the patient's access to emergency services, and acquiring information from the patient's perspective will all contribute to developing a sound emergency plan that is rooted in the patient's context.

8.2.5   Patient Support Person (PSP) for Nonclinic-Based Settings

The role of a PSP was initially defined as someone chosen by the patient who could be asked to assist the clinician in case of a behavioral and/or medical emergency [8].

Table 8.5 Patient support person (PSP) basics [8]

Identified PSP	PSP expectations	Clinician duties
An individual chosen by the patient	PSP is the "eyes and ears" for the clinician	Deliver brief behavioral emergency education to minimize potential risk
May be a family member, caregiver, neighbor, or any adult	Contacted by clinician to assist in the event of an emergency	Discuss PSP role and expectations prior to initiation of treatment
Does not have to be at the patient's home during sessions or live with the patient	Should ideally be at home or within 5–7 min of the patient's location during sessions	Document a release of information allowing PSP to be involved during crisis

The most recent ATA guidelines [3] for video-based online mental health services suggest that a PSP may be used to assist the clinician in evaluating any emergencies and/or calling 911 [3]. At minimum, the expectation is for them to be accessible during a crisis. The PSP can be a significant other, neighbor, friend, or relative—anyone who would be easily accessible during the patient's appointment. In some cases in the HBTMH pilot, the PSP has also been utilized to assist the patient with technical issues [8]. Rural patients enrolled in the HBTMH pilot have commented that, in addition to being a "safety net" the PSPs provide valuable social support [8].

Prior to beginning treatment with the patient, the clinician should provide the PSP with brief education on suicide prevention and their role as PSP. It is at the clinician's discretion how much education to offer beyond a basic understanding of emergency management. If the clinician and patient engage in extended treatment (i.e., beyond 90 days) the clinician may provide the PSP with a booster session of psychoeducation as needed [8].

The primary function of the PSP is to assist the clinician with evaluating the severity and nature of an emergency situation [8]. Clinicians should be prepared, however, for the possibility that the PSP may not or cannot cooperate in certain situations [2]. If there is a safety risk to the PSP, the clinician may rely directly on local 911 responders or local police [8, 10]. As will be discussed in further detail later in this chapter, it is important for clinicians to have direct telephone numbers for the local emergency service(s) where the patient is located. Clinicians or support staff should always keep in mind that dialing 911 from their office will likely not result in being connected to emergency services in the patient's community, unless they are in the same community.

The role of family or friends, particularly in rural or small communities, may be magnified and clinicians should to be attentive to circumstances when choosing a PSP [4]. For example, if a family member is identified as the PSP, clinicians should be sensitive to the potential for exacerbating family tensions due to the patient's psychiatric disorder, course of treatment and/or involvement with emergency assistance [4]. In some cases, the patient will not be able to identify an adequate PSP or the clinician elects not to enroll a PSP. If the patient is located in a highly rural setting, clinicians should identify another individual as a secondary contact, for example, a "family support person," if an adequate PSP cannot be identified [8] (Table 8.5).

Table 8.6 Issues to address at the initiation of clinical videoconferencing (CV) services

1. Informed consent and authentication
2. Emergency management plan
3. Distant side location
4. Local emergency personnel
5. Contingency plans for related issues
6. Technology disruption/failure
7. Pre-session procedures
8. Imminent risk

8.3 Patient Enrollment, Emergency Planning, and Pre-session Procedures

Once a clinician has evaluated the patient and the patient and provider have mutually agreed to engage in treatment, there are additional steps the clinician should take prior to initiating behavioral health services via clinical video. Table 8.6 outlines those steps and information to cover. This following section will highlight the specific details of each factor.

8.3.1 Informed Consent and Authentication

The clinician should verify the identity of the patient prior to commencing care. With most new referrals the clinician will have had an opportunity to verify the identity of the patient. In nonclinic-based settings, such as the patient's home, this may be difficult. An ideal referral is a patient who has previously enrolled in a known health care system whereby identities have been authenticated. For those in private practice, an ideal referral would be someone already known to the clinician during the course of previous visits or during a face-to-face intake.

Informed consent is covered in detail in Chap. 7 of this book. It is important to communicate the limits of confidentiality to the patient and for the clinician to fully understand the patient's expectations prior to commencing treatment. In both clinic-based and nonclinic-based settings, the informed consent should be modified to include receiving care via clinical video technologies. Modifications to the informed consent include disclosure of additional risks to the patient, such as the patient's potential need to seek emergency care off-site. Along with informed consent, the clinician may want to obtain the patient's consent to communicate about any clinical emergency to a designated PSP or family support contact [8].

The clinician should describe what circumstances would require initiating contact with local emergency personnel directly or via the PSP or another designated emergency contact. The patient should be informed that under emergency circumstances they would either have to be transported and/or evaluated by emergency personnel who would be called to their location. The clinician should explain that in an emergency he or she may need to reveal the patient's identity and any other pertinent, potentially sensitive, clinical information to local emergency personnel, and/or personnel situated at the nearest emergency center. The clinician should also communicate mandatory reporting requirements consistent with state law where the patient resides. In cases where the clinician suspects the patient may use a firearm for harming self or others, the clinician should inform the patient that in an emergency they would need to inform emergency personnel that the patient is armed, and that the clinician would be unable to directly assist if a situation escalates. As noted in next section, if firearms are in the home or present in other settings, it is important to mutually agree to plan for securing the firearms during the session.

Once emergency and other contingency plans are determined (see below), the clinician should communicate what those plans are during the informed consent process and ensure the patient understands and is in agreement before proceeding.

8.3.2   Emergency Management Planning

Developing a sound emergency management plan involves several key areas: firearms, telephone contacts, technology, and contingencies for various issues may differ depending on the setting. No matter where the patient is seen, it is vital to establish a mutually agreeable plan. Safety planning should take into consideration the protection of individuals involved in the patient's care, including on-site staff, and other involved individuals such as PSPs [8, 10]. In general, patient cooperation is crucial for managing safety issues, particularly in nonclinic-based settings [2, 8].

As an integral part of the planning, the clinician should first discuss with the patient whether they have access to firearms and/or weapons, particularly in home/nonclinic settings [8] or rural areas [4]. If so, the clinician should negotiate a mutually agreeable disposition of the firearms and/or weapons during the period of each appointment [2]. As a part of the discussion, the clinician should attempt to understand the meaning of firearms to the patient and may consider involving family members to assist (as appropriate) for proper disposition [2, 8]. In some cases, individuals will have a gun-locker which has a lock and is in another location in the property; this can be an appropriate way to secure a weapon [8]. The use of trigger safety lock devices may be useful to decrease risk [10]. If the patient does not agree with the plan, it is advised that treatment should not commence.

It is important for clinicians to have current phone numbers for the patient, emergency response system, any clinic-based staff, and relevant community contacts. Direct emergency dispatch numbers can often be requested by calling the non-emergency number closest to the patient's address [10]. These contacts should be verified on a routine basis to ensure they remain current (Table 8.7).

For an Emergency Contact Sheet (clinic-based and nonclinic-based) template, please refer to Appendices 8.B and 8.C in this chapter.

For patients who are located in nonclinic-based settings, it is recommended they use a consistent location, due to a potential impact the change in location may have on emergency management [3]. If a patient elects to travel and have sessions in a different location, it is important to notify the clinician well in advance. The provid-

Table 8.7 Telephone contacts to identify prior to initiating clinical video services

Clinic-based settings	Nonclinic-based settings
Technical support staff where clinician is located	Patient's cell phone and home phone lines
Technical support staff where patient is located	Local fire, paramedics, police and/sheriff. (internet search for the community where patient is located, including local direct 911 dispatch number, if available)
Front desk staff where patient is located	Patient support person/family members' cell phones, home phone, and/or work phone numbers
Local fire, paramedics, police and/sheriff. (internet search for the community where patient is located)	Clinician's cell phone or office phone
Patient's primary care doctor or other healthcare provider known to patient	National Suicide Crisis Line
	Medication prescriber in patient's community

er should then acquire new direct phone numbers as outlined above in the nonclinic-based setting column.

If the clinician cannot or has not contacted the patient as expected, or in the rare event the clinician experiences an emergency and is unable to seek help, the patient should have direct phone numbers of the clinician and/or the main phone number of the office or clinic where the clinician is located. If the provider is engaged in tele-work from home or another off-site office location, the patient should have appropriate contact numbers for those settings. For needs arising between sessions, the clinician should provide parameters when voice mails are checked and responded to, phone numbers for any coverage available after hours, any applicable crisis hotline numbers, and discuss use of 911 in emergencies.

Clinicians may provide their patient with contact information for the clinician's office, as well as the main number of the clinician's hospital or clinic. In addition to identifying emergency personnel, the clinician may collaborate with the patient's preexisting medical and/or mental health treatment team [3, 16]. For example, it may be helpful to seek the patient's permission to speak with other members of their treatment team to inform them that the patient will be receiving care in a nonclinic-based setting. Determining the distance between local emergency personnel in the patient's community and the patient's location can also help shape the clinician's decision process in determining appropriate actions, particularly in nonclinic-based settings where professional staff are not available.

Prior to each session:

Clinicians should have all local emergency and patient-specific telephone contacts readily available.

During each session:

For nonclinic-based settings, clinicians should verify the patient's current location and determine whether there have been any changes to the patient's personal support system or the emergency management protocol.

If the clinician works in a healthcare system that utilizes an electronic medical record system, it may be helpful to incorporate emergency information templates into these record systems. For a Pretreatment and Pre-session checklist, please refer to Appendix 8.A in this chapter.

8.3.3 Technology Disruptions

Clinicians should consider various methods to decrease the likelihood of technology disruption. If the patient is using their own equipment in a nonclinic setting, it is advised they hard line their router to their computer using an Ethernet cable, as WI-FI connections are typically less reliable. For more information on technologies for CV, please see Chap. 1.

Despite all precautions, there will inevitably be disruptions and/or outright failure in technologies, leading to degradation or loss of connectivity. Issues of abandonment may occur if a session is disrupted and connectivity cannot be reestablished. Clinicians should understand the essential features of the technology they're using and have some basic troubleshooting skills they can use in session. The clinician should identify in advance the threshold at which they would contact technical support for further assistance. It is necessary to have a backup plan in place for alternative means of contact and communicate this to the patient prior to treatment [3]. The plan may include calling the patient first via telephone and attempting to troubleshoot the issue together [3]. If after three troubleshooting attempts (or 15 min), the issue cannot be resolved, the clinician could complete the session by telephone and seek additional technical support as needed. The plan may also include providing the patient with access to other mental health care [3], either in the clinic or in the community, if reliable connectivity cannot be established. Such a backup plan for alternate care should be communicated to the patient prior to commencing treatment. The clinician may review the technology backup plan on a routine basis.

Elderly, disabled and/or individuals who have sensory impairments may need additional support. For example, if the patient has visual or hearing impairments extra steps should be taken to ensure they can see and hear the clinician [2]. Elderly patients, who may be less comfortable with the technology, may need assistance in navigating the equipment [8]. In all cases, the telephone should be used for backup communications.

8.3.4 Contingency Plans for Other Issues

There are various other nonemergency contingencies that may arise and that should be addressed for emergency planning purposes. In situations where the patient is located in a nonclinic-based setting, such as a church, hotel room, truck stop, homeless shelter or group home, it is important to identify any unique emergency management planning issues. If the patient is located in a clinic-based setting, consult the clinic's emergency policies for contingency planning. The following are examples of areas to consider for contingency planning:

8.3.4.1 Transportation

Who will transport the patient located in a nonclinic-based setting? As clinical video-based telemental health has developed, in part, to increase access to patients in geographically remote areas, it is expected that there may be barriers to transportation to the nearest emergency mental health services. These limitations should be discussed and addressed prior to starting treatment for patients in nonclinic-based settings where professional staff and/or access to services are not readily available [3]. In the event of a behavioral and/or medical emergency, the patient's clinician and/or PSP should discuss with emergency personnel whether they should transport the patient.

8.3.4.2 Natural Disasters, Weather Alerts, Fire Alarms

If the patient is located in a clinic-based setting, the clinician should be familiar with the clinic's evacuation protocols.

8.3.4.3 Unnatural Disasters, Bomb Threats, Acts of Violence

If the patient is located in a clinic-based setting, the clinician should be familiar with the clinic's protocols. In nonclinic-based settings, the clinician should first ensure the patient could seek safety. Secondly, the clinician should notify law enforcement in the community where the patient is located.

8.3.4.4 Referral for Additional Services

The clinician should be familiar with any available local mental health resources in the event these additional services are needed [3, 16]. Information on community referral resources and their availability should be current and accessible.

8.3.4.5 Medical Side Effects

If prescribing, the clinician should be aware of any constraints on availability of specific medications in the patient's health system or location [3]. The clinician should be familiar with how to access the patient's medical team or be able to refer the patient for laboratory procedures. The contact information should be readily available to the treating clinician.

8.3.4.6 Medical Emergencies

In the event of a medical emergency, that is, stroke, heart attack, etc., the clinician should contact local emergency personnel directly. The clinician may not need to contact the PSP, but should use good clinical judgment as to the severity and nature of the medical emergency and decide accordingly. For example, if the patient is complaining of chest pain, but can communicate, it may be appropriate to contact the PSP for assistance. In any case where a patient becomes unconscious, the clinician should contact local emergency personnel directly. For care coordination, the clinician should be familiar with how to contact the patient's primary care provider and any relevant specialty care providers [3].

Once the emergency management plan and contingency plans have been finalized, it is important to put it in writing. If the clinician is in private practice and the patient is seen at a distant side clinic it is recommended that a memoranda of understanding (MOU) between the two parties includes the emergency management plan.

8.4 Pre-session Procedures

Ideally, by the time the clinician is ready to see the patient for the first session, the clinician has a mutually agreed upon emergency plan, and has completed the informed consent, though in many settings the consent process is conducted over the clinical video link but prior to initiation of treatment. Prior to any clinical video contact, the provider should know the state laws regarding involuntary commitment where the patient will be located during the session and have the competence to manage emergencies (Table 8.8).

For a Pretreatment and Pre-session checklist, please refer to Appendix 8.A in this chapter.

8.5 Imminent Risk, Handling an Emergency, and Post-crisis Follow-up

According to the National Suicide Prevention Lifeline, imminent risk is present when "based on information gathered during the exchange from the person at risk or someone calling on his/her behalf, there is a close temporal connection between the person's current risk status and actions that could lead to his/her suicide" [17].

Table 8.8 Procedures to conduct at the beginning of each session to address safety

1. Evaluate whether there have been any significant changes to their mental health/medical status that would affect receipt of care via technology
2. Have all local or other relevant emergency numbers and patient support phone numbers readily available
3. Verify that the patient understands the emergency management plan previously agreed to and offer the patient an opportunity to review the plan
4. Verify the patient's current physical location
a. If they are not at their usual location, the clinician should clarify the current location
b. If the patient doesn't disclose the new location until the session has begun, it shall be the clinician's discretion to decide whether to continue the session
c. If the clinician and patient elect to conduct the session at the new location, then the session should be temporarily delayed so that the clinician may acquire the appropriate telephone contact information for emergency personnel services in community where the patient is located
5. For nonclinic-based settings, verify whether the PSP is accessible during the session
6. Verify the status of the patient's firearms/weapons
7. The patient has the clinician's office or cell phone number

The definition further suggests that the staff member interprets the present risk to create an obligation or "immediate pressure" for the staff member to take action, and without immediate action, the staff member may believe serious self-harm or suicide is inevitable [17].

8.5.1 Across All Settings

By the time a crisis situation emerges in a telehealth appointment, it is assumed that the clinician has an established emergency management plan and has communicated this plan to the patient prior to treatment. The clinician should have the appropriate emergency contacts on hand during any telehealth visit. The clinician should plan on remaining connected to the patient throughout the emergency until it is resolved [8]. Clinicians may need to be aware of the impact of their perception of diminished control over a clinical interaction via telehealth, and how this might increase their own levels of anxiety [2, 4]. On the other hand, clinician perceptions of their own safety may be increased when assessing potentially dangerous patients [10], which may increase tolerance of strong affect [4]. Clinicians should note a patient's affect and behavioral state at the end of the session and may want to communicate with local staff about potential effects on subsequent interactions [2, 4] (Table 8.9).

If a clinician has designated a PSP and/or another emergency contact, they should not necessarily rely on these individuals in every scenario. In the event a PSP cannot be contacted during an emergency, the clinician should contact the local emergency personnel.

Table 8.9 Procedures to follow in the event of a behavioral emergency in nonclinic-based settings

1. If the assessment of the patient indicates that they are at imminent risk of self-harm or harm to others, do not leave the patient alone or disconnect from CV

2. Tell the patient that you will enact the emergency safety plan previously agreed to

3. Make an initial decision whether to contact 911 services directly or the PSP or other family support contact. If calling the PSP or family member, indicate the nature of the emergency, and request they assist with helping patient remain calm

4. Once the PSP arrives, they can assist with evaluation of the emergency

5. If indicated, the clinician can instruct the PSP to initiate contact with local emergency personnel by calling 9-1-1 from the patient's phone. The PSP or family support contact can communicate directly with emergency personnel and follow their instructions while the clinician remains connected via technology

6. The clinician will remain connected via technology or via telephone until emergency personnel arrive

7. The PSP or family support contact should not transport the patient, unless directed by emergency personnel due to a potential delay in arrival or other clinically determined reasons

8. Once the patient has been transported, the clinician may contact the patient's treatment team, and additional family members as necessary to inform them

9. The clinician should document the emergency

10. If the patient becomes unconscious and disappears from the camera view, the provider should contact the PSP to request visual assistance in further evaluation

11. In the event the patient leaves their nonclinic-based location, and is in a state of crisis, contact local emergency personnel immediately to notify them of the location and nature of emergency

Table 8.10 Procedures to follow in the event of a behavioral emergency in a clinic-based setting

1. If the assessment of the patient indicates that they are at imminent risk of self-harm or harm to others, do not leave the patient alone or disconnect from CV

2. Tell the patient that you will enact the emergency safety plan previously agreed to

3. The clinician should contact the on-site staff member to assist or, if appropriate, contact local emergency personnel directly

4. The clinician will remain connected via technology or via telephone until emergency personnel arrive

5. Once the patient has been transported, the clinician may contact the patient's treatment team to inform them of the crisis

6. The clinician should document the emergency

8.5.2 Clinic-Based Settings

Typically, as part of the prearranged plans, professional staff would be available in clinic-based settings to assist during behavioral and/or medical emergencies (Table 8.10).

For an Emergency Safety Plan for clinic-based settings, please refer to Appendix 8.E in this chapter.

8.6   Postcrisis Follow-Up

What is the clinician's role after the patient has been transported to a hospital or other facility? Of significant importance on the continuum of care is the postcrisis phase. Clinicians should remain connected to their patient following an emergency. Follow-up care should be approached in a similar manner as if the patient were being seen in person. While the patient is admitted to a hospital, the clinician may decide what level of contact is appropriate.

8.7   Summary

Providing behavioral health care via clinical video into clinic-based and nonclinic-based settings creates unprecedented access to care. In general, a wide variety of psychiatric diagnoses are appropriate to treat via CV. Typically it's the clinician's discretion and sound clinical judgment that ultimately determine what factors should be exclusionary or inclusionary for treatment. Patients who are acutely suicidal, homicidal and/or are suffering from a medical condition that requires immediate attention, are generally not recommended to receive care via CV.

Think for a moment. You're a clinician and you're educated in behavioral and medical emergency protocols, and you've identified a suitable patient to receive care via clinical video in a clinic-based setting. You're familiar with all of the emergency management protocols at the setting and you've conducted several sessions without incident. Now your patient is in a crisis. We're hoping this chapter has provided you with enough information to have the confidence to know what to do. For additional resources, not covered in detail in this chapter, please refer to Appendix 8.G.

In summary, it is critical to develop a sound emergency management plan and to communicate this plan to the patient. The plan should include telephone contact numbers for various resources; emergency personnel, on-site staff, PSP, and family support contact or community resources as needed. The plan should be evaluated periodically and modified to include change of telephone contact numbers. In addition, it is important that clinicians and administrators alike become familiar with state laws regarding involuntary commitment and welfare checks where the patient is located during the session.

Appendix 8.A

Pre-treatment and Pre-session Checklist

Pre-treatment	Recommended steps	Complete
Education and training	Complete basic training in suicide prevention as outlined by local guidance	
State laws: involuntary psychiatric hospitalization	Be familiar with state law where patient is located	
Evaluating patients/dangerousness		
Firearms and weapons		
Patient Support Person		
Local Emergency Personnel		
National Crisis Line	Be familiar with procedures to engage with National Crisis Line	
Distant side clinic		
Technology breakdown	Clinician to have contingency plan. Use telephone in interim	
Medical emergencies	Clinician to contact local emergency personnel directly	
Transportation	Be familiar with patient's transportation limitations, access	
Pharmacy		
Laboratory		
Referral resources		
Informed consent and authentication		
Pre-session		
Contact Info: Local Emergency Personnel		
Contact info: Crisis Line		
Verify patient's physical location		
Verify PSP/Family Support		
Status of firearms/weapons		
Review emergency plan with patient		
Clinician contact info to patient		

Appendix 8.B

Emergency Contact Sheet for Clinic-Based CV Service [15]

Please keep this form accessible during all telehealth sessions.
   Clinic address:
   Hours:
   Telemental health patient rooms (and any other room location information)

1. Alert the XX CLINIC front desk clerk: (555)555-5555
2. Alert JOHN DOE Clinic Coordinator (555) 555-5555-
3. If needed, contact the on-call Psychiatrist/CLINICAL BACKUP for the day/ week. See below for names and contact numbers:

	Monday	Tuesday	Wednesday	Thursday	Friday
8 A.M.–12 P.M.	JOHN DOE	JANE DOE	CAPTAIN AMERICA	WONDER WOMAN	BATMAN
12 P.M.–4 P.M.	CAPTAIN HOOK	TINKERBELL	SUPERMAN	JAMES BROWN	ARETHA FRANKLIN

Name	Extension	XX Office #	Pager
HOOK	X5551	Rm 1	
WONDER WOMAN	X5552	Rm 2	
ARETHA FRANKLIN	X5553	Rm 3	None listed
JAMES BROWN	X5554	Rm 4	None listed
SUPERMAN	X5556	Rm 5	
TINKERBELL	X5558	Rm 6	
BATMAN	X5561	Rm 7	
CAPTAIN AMERICAN	X5562	Rm 8	

4. MUDDY WATERS can also be contacted at XX CLINIC ext: (555) 555-5555 or cell: (555) 555-5555

For safety emergencies call Security: (555) 555-5555
For technical disruptions call the front desk clerk or technical support (444) 444-4444.

Appendix 8.C

Emergency Contact Sheet—Nonclinic-Based [18]

Keep accessible during all nonclinic-based visits

(Patient Name)	
[Address where the patient will be routinely located during the sessions]	
Contact information	Home: Cell:
Detailed contact information from the patient with particular attention to whom could be contacted in the event of an emergency Nearby relatives or significant individuals that the patient deems appropriate for contact (e.g., other relatives, friends, and neighbors), their contact information should be documented in the medical record Any additional means of contact should be obtained and should be documented in the medical record or patient notes (e.g., in the initial video into the Home note and/or on the top of each visit note)	
Identify the local emergency response contact for the patient It is recommended to test the number and confirm whether it would be appropriate to use for reporting emergency situation at the patient's physical address	
Other providers (primary care, mental health) or community resources (social work, home nurses, caregivers, etc.)	

Appendix 8.D

ASH-25, A Structured Guide for the Assessment of Suitability for Home-Based Telemental Health [8]

Each question should be viewed as a variable in determining the level of risk the patient may pose in terms of a psychiatric and/or medical emergency.

EXAMINER: _____   DATE: _____

NAME: _____

There are several variables that comprise a goodness of fit between a patient seeking care and the treating clinician. Please fill out spaces according to your direct knowledge, either by way of medical records review, interview with patient, their previous and/or current and/or former providers.

Background

1) REFERRAL SOURCE: Primary Care ( )   Mental Health Clinic ( )   Examiner ( )
2) AGE _____
3) DISABILITY _____% _____
4) Miles to nearest clinic_____
5) Miles to nearest Medical Center _____
6) Would patient have received your services if otherwise not offered in the home or non-clinical setting? YES ( ) NO ( )
7) Does patient have ac cess to additional resources for treatment in their community? YES ( ) NO ( )
8) If yes to # 7, please list: _____
9) What is the patient's primary reason for seeking services in the home or non-clinical settin g? _____
10) In patient's own words, describe any perceived stigma associated with receiving health care.
_____

Please circle the response that best represents your interpretation and objective information pertaining to each variable. Please note: active substance abuse/dependence, active suicidal ideation with intent and untreated thought disorders are exclusion factors.

Factor I: Mental Health

1.   PRIMARY MENTAL HEALTH DIAGNOSIS: _____
0   Thought disorder (untreated or difficult to manage). Substance use/abuse dependence (current, recent), PTSD (chronic, MST, untreated/or minimal tx hx).

1   Axis II disorder and/or traits; PTSD (moderate); Substance use dependence (non-alcohol); Bipolar disorder (untreated, not well-treated); Serious Mental Illness (untreated, not well-treated)
2   PTSD (not chronic); substance use disorders (in remission).
3   Depressive disorders / Anxiety disorders.

If substance use present, please describe type, frequency, etc:

_____

2.   PSYCHIATRIC HOSPITALIZATIONS
0   Hospitalization within last 30 days.
1   Hospitalization 31 days to previous 6 months.
2   Remote history of hospitalization.
3   No history

3.   MOTIVATION FOR MENTAL HEALTH TREATMENT (CURRENT)
0   Ambivalent.
1   Pre-contemplative.
2   Contemplative (provider recommended treatment and home based program).
3   Action (Veteran requested treatment).
4   Maintenance (transfer from current MH provider).

4.   PREVIOUS MENTAL HEALTH TREATMENT COMPLIANCE
0   Multiple cancellations / no-shows.
1   Variable no-shows / cancellations (difficult to determine pattern).
2   Relatively compliant (pattern consistent with good compliance, but occasional).
3   Compliant.

5.   PREVIOUS MENTAL HEALTH TREATMENT SUCCESS / FAILURE
0   Multiple drop outs of time limited treatments.
1   Majority of failures/incomplete treatments.
2   Variable successes/failures to complete.
3   Majority of successes/completion of treatments.

6.   PATIENT'S SUBJECTIVE PERSPECTIVE ON STIGMA
0   Perceived stigmas correlated with no interest in receiving MH treatment.
1   Perceived stigma, but Veteran would only receive MH treatment in home.
2   Perceived stigma, but Veteran comfortable with receiving MH treatment at VA facility.
3   No perceived stigma.

7.   MOOD INVENTORY SCORES: MOST RECENT PCL/DATE: _____ MOST RECENT BDI/DATE: _____
0   BDI, PCL or other measures significantly elevated within last 30 days.
1   BDI, PCL or other measures significantly elevated 31-days to 6 months.

2   BDI, PCL or other measures mild to moderately elevated within last 30 days.
3   BDI, PCL or other measures within normal range.

8.   COGNITIVE FUNCTIONING
0   Significant deficits.
1   Moderate deficits.
2   Mild deficits.
3   Within normal range.

9.   SUICIDE HISTORY
0   Recent active ideation / attempt. High risk: YES / NO
1   Remote ideation / attempt.
2   Passive ideation / low lethality.
3   Denies ideation (remote).
4   Denies ideation (current, recent).

10.   DISRUPTIVE BEHAVIOR HISTORY (aggressive behavior, drug-seeking behavior, or behaviors interfering with the receipt or delivery of health care)

0   Recent history (within 60 days). Legal involved.
1   Recent history (within 61 days to a year). No legal.
2   Remote history (over a year). Legal involved.
3   No history.

11.   NEW MENTAL HEALTH DIAGNOSIS (within 60 days): _____

12.   INITIAL MENTAL HEALTH TREATMENT PLAN: _____

Factor II: Medical

13.   CURRENT MEDICAL STATUS
0   Medically compromised, requires assistance with daily functioning.
1   Medically compromised, requires partial assistance with daily functioning.
2   Medical conditions well treated/managed; patient independent.
3   Medically clear, no secondary interventions.

14.   PREVIOUS MEDICATION COMPLIANCE
0   Multiple records of non-compliance.
1   Variable compliance (due to extraneous factors such as complicated medical).
2   Relatively compliant (pattern consistent with good compliance, but occasional miss).
3   Compliant.

15.   MEDICAL COMPLICATIONS (within 60 days): _____

Factor III: Access to Care

16. BARRIERS TO CARE
0   Financial limitations (can't afford gasoline).
1   Without transportation, limited resources for childcare.
2   Geographic hardship (Approximately 60+ miles to closest clinic, difficult travel terrain).
3   Physical limitations, chronic medical and/or psychiatric conditions.
4   Home bound.

17. COMFORT WITH PERSONAL COMPUTER / TECHNOLOGY
0   Doesn't feel comfortable.
1   Rarely uses computer/technology.
2   Some comfort level with computer/technology, but relies on others.
3   Checks email regularly, surfs internet, working knowledge of personal computer.
4   Sophisticated understanding of computer / technology; uses it daily and integrates into
     routine.

Factor IV: Systems

18. FAMILY
0   No family contact.
1   Family geographically diverse, not physically close.
2   Family located locally.
3   Lives with family.

19. SOCIAL NETWORK
0   Avoidant, isolates, unemployed.
1   No current relationship.
2   Some friends, passive relationships
3   Friends, deeper/meaningful relationships.
4   Friends, wide network, active in community.

20. CURRENT LIVING SITUATION
0   Alone.
1   Roommate (non-relationship, family member in negative standing).
2   Roommate (non-sexual relationship, family member in positive standing).
3   Significant other (relatively unstable).
4   Partnered, married (stable relationship).

21. STABILITY OF SYSTEM
0   Family and/or social network unreliable; fractured
1   Individual family member and/or social network moderately reliable/stable.
2   Multiple family members and/or social network moderately reliable/stable.
3   Individual family member and/or social network reliable/stable.
4   Multiple family members and/or social network reliable/stable.

22. MILES TO EMERGENCY PERSONNEL
     (Fire, Paramedic, Police, Sheriff) _____   0-1-2-3

Factor V: Patient Support Person (PSP)

23. PSP RELATIONSHIP STATUS
0   Acquaintance.
1   Neighbor (not regular social contact).
2   Friends/Family (stable relationship).
3   Significant other (stable relationship).

24. PSP DISTANCE IN MILES/TIME TO PATIENT ___/____   0-1-2-3

25. PSP EXPERIENCE WITH CRISIS
0   No experience.
1   Some experience (non life-threatening).
2   Some experience (life-threatening).
3   Numerous experiences (life-threatening).

EXAMINER COMMENTS:

_____

FINDINGS:

Total Score: _____

Approved ____

Approved (conditional) ____
   Conditions of approval_____

Temporary Denial_____

Denial _____

Date: _____

Appendix 8.E

Emergency Safety Plan for Clinic-Based Telemental Health [15]

Purpose. To establish emergency guidelines for the remote patient location during a Telemental Health (TMH) encounter.

1. Objective. In the event of a medical or psychiatric emergency of a patient being seen by videoconferencing, the immediate response goals are to:
   – Bring an onsite provider into the patient room.
   – Activate the existing on-site emergency protocol.

- Ensure the appropriate level of medical, psychiatric and/or security response for the situation.

2. Preparation

   a. Screening. TMH patients must be screened in advance to minimize the risk of an emergency. Patients who are at high risk due to suicidal ideation, a history of violence or a preexisting, potentially life-threatening emergent medical condition could be disqualified from participation in TMH.
   b. Every TMH provider will have emergency contact information readily available for the sites to which they will deliver care remotely. This information must be printed out and posted at the provider location. The following contact information must be included:

      - Phone numbers for on-site security:
        • ANYWHERE CLINIC: (555) 555-5555
        • OVER THERE CLINIC: (555) 555-5555
        • RURAL CLINIC Front Desk (No on-site security): (555) 555-5555
      - Any on-site clinician pagers/cell phone numbers
      - All patient room extensions in case an on-site provider cannot be reached
      - All email or instant messaging addresses necessary for emergency response (e.g., clinic providers, support staff, police, etc.). Emails should only be used to contact those who have been prepared in advance to monitor and respond to an email alert.
      - Suicide Prevention Information: FOR THE XYZ HEALTHCARE SYSTEM:
        • (INSERT APPROPRIATE CONTACT INFO)
      - In crisis situations the clinician should call 911 or the local emergency dispatch number at the patient site (this needs to be confirmed before initiation of services).

3. Initiating an On-site Intervention in the Patient Room

   a. Third Party Intervention Support. The TMH provider must coordinate in advance for two third-party personnel to assist at both the provider and patient locations in case of an emergency. These support staff may include clerks and administrative personnel:
      - Stand-by Intervention Support, TMH Provider Site. Coordinates with the remote Patient Site clinic staff (Primarily with the Stand-by Intervention Support, Patient Site), paramedic or police response in the event of an emergency intervention.
      - Stand-by Intervention Support, Patient Site. Coordinates for on-site clinician, security, paramedic or police response in the event of an emergency intervention.
   b. Informing the Patient. Ideally, the patient can be told directly by the TMH Provider that the assistance of on-site staff is needed to ensure that the patient receives the best care. The TMH provider may choose to explain that they

will be phoning or emailing an on-site clinician to ask that they enter the room with the patient to continue the treatment session together via video. The TMH provider is responsible for determining how much the patient needs to know about an imminent on-site intervention.

c. Not Informing the Patient. If the clinical situation warrants bringing an on-site provider into the room without the patient being told (e.g., concern that the patient may leave if told), this will be coordinated by the provider via one of the preselected third-party intervention support staff. The on-line communication with the patient should be muted at the provider end and the TMH provider should then proceed to contact the predetermined third party to initiate an intervention at the patient site.

   - Email or electronic messaging: Alerts to on-site clinicians can be done with or without the patient's awareness, asking that an on-site clinician enter the patient room emergently. Electronic communications should only be used with individuals who are prepared in advance to monitor and respond to such emails immediately.
   - Phone: The TMH provider can alert the predetermined intervention support staff at their site to phone the patient site to ask that an on-site provider intervene in the patient room.

4. Methods of Activating the On-Site Emergency Protocol

   a. Each clinic should have emergency protocols in place. The TMH provider facilitates the on-site plan rather than creating any new protocol. The TMH provider or a designated representative will coordinate with the Stand-by Intervention Support, Patient Site, in advance to ensure that correct protocols are followed.
   b. Once an on-site clinician is in the room with the patient and can assess the situation, the on-site clinician is responsible for initiating the on-site emergency protocols. The TMH provider supports the on-site clinician as requested.

5. Police/Security Intervention.

   a. The TMH provider must be aware of the basic security protocols at the remote site (e.g., Do they contact hospital police? Do they contact local police? Is there a security guard on site?). The predetermined Stand-by Intervention Support Staff, Patient Site, can assist the TMH provider in this regard.
   b. The Telemental Health Program Specialist provides the LOCAL SECURITY/ Police at the parent facility with details of an upcoming TMH appointment, if the patient is assessed to be at high risk for self-harm or disruptive behavior.
   c. If the TMH provider believes the clinical situation warrants immediate police involvement without waiting for the on-site staff to initiate their emergency protocol, the TMH provider or a third party should contact the local or hospital police. The police can then assess the situation while the TMH provider remains on the videoconference.

6. Legal Detainment

    a. Many sites have a protocol in place for legal detainment of patients (e.g., "5150"). Clinic site supervisors must contact the CLINIC Police and the CLINIC Psychiatry Service for assistance in developing appropriate procedures in compliance with State and Federal laws.

    b. If there is no clinician on-site who can initiate a legal detention order, then each site will establish a site-specific procedure to support participation in Telemental Health. In such a case, the recommended intervention procedure would be for the TMH provider to contact the patient site clerical staff or police and direct them to contact the local police to detain the patient.

    c. When in doubt, contact local law enforcement.

7. Questions concerning these procedures should be directed to the Director of Telehealth, ext. 5555.

Appendix 8.F

Suicide Risk Assessment Resources

Why does someone want to kill themselves? Much is known and has been described in the literature on the basic tenets of suicidal and self-harming behaviors, which may precipitate an act toward a finite response to thwart their distorted thinking. Leopold Bellak discusses this thinking with an analogy similar to tunnel vision [19], while Edwin Shneidman refers to it as constriction [20]. In most cases there is a diminished capacity to problem-solve. The clinician's role, as Bruce Bongar affectionately cites in a New Yorker magazine cartoon, "we are the lifeguards at the sea of despair [21]." The job of a clinician is to throw a life raft to a drowning patient and to help them to safety. According to Shneidman et al. [20] there are three prominent aspects of suicidal thinking: crisis, ambivalence and communication. He describes that the clinician's effect on communication is important to the patient. Excess anxiety within the clinician may cause loss of confidence in being helped.

    Among current best practices for suicide risk assessment and prevention, there are several elements clinicians should consider.

Risk Factors

In 2010, there were 295 completed service member suicides. As noted in the DoD Suicide Event Report 9 DoDSER [22], some of the risk factors in this population are financial stress, administrative or legal issues, relationship distress, divorced, lower education level, and lower rank. Among service members who had attempted suicide, approximately 66% indicated they did not talk to anyone about their potential for self-harm prior to their suicide attempt [22].

According to Shneidman et al. [20] there are three prominent aspects of suicidal thinking: crisis, ambivalence and communication. He describes that the clinician's effect on communication is important to the patient. Excess anxiety within the clinician may cause loss of confidence in being helped.

Factors for increased suicide risk include [20]:

- Age/sex
- Symptoms
- Stress from patient POV
- Suicide plan
- Lack of resources
- Prior suicide attempt
- Medical status
- Communication
- Reactions of others
- Older males
- Depression
- Psychosis
- Agitation, including agitated depression
- Isolated and alone

Patients with chronic substance use disorders, psychotic disorders, and/or chronic depression are also at elevated risk for suicide. Individuals who have sustained a traumatic brain injury (TBI) have an increased risk of suicide attempts and completed suicide [23]. Warning signs include family and/or social relationship problems, isolation, arguments, poor communication, work, and school or community-based issues, such as frequent absences, conflicts or poor performance. Frequent or severe depressed or angry moods and other significant and disruptive physical, cognitive, emotional and behavioral symptoms such as erratic driving, keeping a firearm under the pillow, or withdrawing into a "shut down" or uncommunicative state are also concerning for suicide risk.

Individuals with a history of TBI are at increased risk for suicidal ideation. There are several demographic, psychiatric and sociological factors that are common among individuals who have sustained a TBI and increase suicide risk: older age, male gender, substance use, psychiatric disorders, and aggressive behavior [23]. Not surprisingly, individuals who have sustained a TBI have an increased risk of suicide attempts and completed suicide, compared to the general population [23].

National Suicide Prevention Lifeline

The National Suicide Prevention Lifeline (NSPL), at 1-800-273-TALK (8255), is a national suicide prevention network of over 150 call centers that are independently operated and interconnected through multiple toll-free telephone lines. In 2007, NSPL established a partnership in 2007 with the Department of Veterans Affairs that serves as the Veterans Crisis Line. Veterans, active military, and their families can

be connected, through an automated prompt, to a veterans suicide prevention hotline specialist [17]. NSPL published policies pertaining to Emergency Intervention;
a recent 2007 draft is available at http://www.crisiscentersblog.com/wp-content/
uploads/2007/11/emergency_intervention_policy_nspl_draft_11-07-07.pdf [17].

For a comprehensive review of suicide assessment measures, a useful resource
is A Review of Suicide Assessment Measures for Intervention Research with Adults
and Older Adults by Gregory K. Brown [24].

Publically Available Resources Through the Department of Veterans Affairs

The Department of Veterans Affairs (VA) has extensive resources that are publically
available. For example, there are numerous Department of VA suicide prevention
education and training resources throughout the VA and available in the literature,
many of which are listed at http://www.mentalhealth.va.gov/suicide_prevention
[25].

1. The VA ACE (Ask, Care, Escort) [25] is a brochure and a small card VA staff
   members can use themselves and give to Veterans and family members for educational purposes. The mnemonic is intended to remind users of an "ACE in their
   pocket" in dealing with a crisis. The following information is provided on the
   ACE card:

   a. *"Ask the Veteran*: Are you thinking about killing yourself? Do you think you
      might try to hurt yourself? Ask directly.
   b. *Care for the Veteran.* Remove any means that could be used for self-injury.
      Stay calm. Actively listen to show understanding and produce relief.
   c. *Escort the Veteran.* Never leave the Veteran alone. Escort to emergency room
      or medical clinic. Call VA Suicide Prevention Hotline." (Retrieved 16 Jan.
      2012 from http://www.mentalhealth.va.gov/suicide_prevention/index.asp)

2. *Suicide Risk Assessment Guide.* This brochure contains information on looking for warning signs, assessing for specific factors that may increase or
   decrease risk for suicide, asking the relevant questions, and responding to suicide risk [25]. (Retrieved 16 Jan. 2012 from http://www.mentalhealth.va.gov/
   suicide_prevention/index.asp)

3. *Safety Plan Quick Guide For Clinicians.* This brief guide to developing a safety
   plan for a suicidal patient, typically a joint effort between the patient and the
   clinician, is a product of the Department of Veterans Affairs' Suicide Prevention
   Program [25]. Constructing the safety plan comprises six parts, each of which
   provides explicit instruction for the clinician's use: (1) Warning signs; (2) Internal coping strategies; (3) Social contacts who may distract from the crisis; (4)
   Family members or friends who may offer help; (5) Professionals and agencies
   to contact for help; (6) Making the environment safe. (Retrieved 16 Jan 2012
   from http://www.mentalhealth.va.gov/docs/VASafetyPlanColor.pdf)

4. The VA VISN 19 Mental Illness Research, Education and Clinical Center (MIRECC) has published extensively on the relationship between TBI and suicide (http://www.mirecc.va.gov/visn19/specialties/tbi.asp) [26]. Readers are encouraged to also review *Traumatic Brain Injury and Suicide: An information and resources guide for clinicians* [23]. In addition to the resources of suicide prevention research, there are available public resources providing suicide prevention training. Although lacking definitive evidence for efficacy, a structured approach to safety planning may be a reasonable strategy to mitigate suicide risk factors.

5. *Self-Directed Violence Classification System.* The Department of Veterans Affairs VISN 19 MIRECC in collaboration with the Center for Disease Control and Prevention developed and published a *Self-Directed Violence Classification System* (VA, MIRECC 19) [26]. The classification system provides an overview and distinct definitions for various aspects of suicidal thoughts and behaviors. For clinicians, this may provide a useful tool in determining where a patient may be on the risk spectrum.

6. For veterans and service members, the VA Veterans Crisis line (800-273-8255) is an option for emergency help. While we recommend that the treating clinician maintain contact with the patient throughout the emergency, a warm handoff to crisis line staff may be appropriate in some cases. The treating clinician should receive verbal permission from the Veteran to initiate contact with the crisis line, then place the call and identify themselves as a VA provider currently in contact with a Veteran in crisis.

Appendix 8.G

Additional Patient Safety Resources

Suicide Prevention/Self-Directed Violence/Crisis Intervention

1. Self-Directed Violence Surveillance: Uniformed Definitions and Recommended Data Elements, Version 1.0. National Center for Injury Prevention and Control, Division of Violence Prevention, Centers for Disease Control and Prevention
2. National Suicide Prevention Lifeline Emergency Intervention Values, Policies and Standards, Draft 11/7/07. National Suicide Prevention Lifeline. (http://www.suicidepreventionlifeline.org/)

Department of Veterans Affairs

1. Suicide Prevention website: http://www.mentalhealth.va.gov/suicide_prevention/
2. MIRECC VISN 19 Rocky Mountain Network, Centers for Disease Control and Prevention, *Self-Directed Violence Classification System.*

3. Veterans Health Administration—Office of Telehealth Services (2011). Telemental Health Emergency and Contingency Guidelines
4. Veterans Health Administration—Office of Care Coordination Services (2011). Telemental Health Suicide Prevention and Emergency Care
5. Veterans Health Administration—Office of Telehealth Services (2011). Clinical Video Telehealth Emergency Procedures and Planning. Rocky Mountain Telehealth Training Center
6. Veteran's Crisis Line/National Suicide Prevention Lifeline (800-273-8255)
7. Veterans Health Administration-Employee Education System *Telemental Health Suicide Prevention and Emergency Care.*
8. Information and Support After a Suicide Attempt: A Department of Veterans Affairs Resource Guide for Family Members of Veterans Who are Coping with Suicidality. VISN 19 Mental Illness Research, Education and Clinical Center, Office of Mental Health Services, VA Central Office.

Department of Defense

1. Real Warriors. http://www.realwarriors.net
2. In Transition. http://www.health.mil/inTransition
3. Reserve Component Suicide Postvention Plan: A Toolkit for Commanders: http://www.suicideoutreach.org/Docs/PostventionPlan.ReserveComponents.pdf

Telemental Health Practice Guidelines

1. Agence d'Evaluation des Technologies et des Modes d'Intervention en Sante. (2006) Telehealth: Clinical Guidelines and Technical Standards for Telepsychiatry. Downloaded 19 Jan 2014 at http://www.inesss.qc.ca/fileadmin/doc/AETMIS/Rapports/Telesante/ETMIS2006_Vol2_No1.pdf
2. American Psychological Association. (2012, July). Guidelines for the practice of Telepsychology
3. New Zealand Psychologists Board. Information related to emergency management can be found on
4. Telepsychology Guidelines. Ohio Psychological Association, Communications & Technology Committee. Ohio Psychological Association (2009). [NEED URL ADDRESS]
5. National Center for Telehealth & Technology (T2), Defense Centers of Excellence for Psychological Health & TBI (DCoE). DoD Telemental Health Guidebook, Version 1. (2011).
6. Evidence-based practice for telemental health. American Telemedicine Association (2009).

7. Practice guidelines for videoconferencing-based telemental health. American Telemedicine Association (2009).
8. Practice guidelines for video-based online mental health services. American Telemedicine Association (2013).
9. VISN 20 Home Based Telemental Health Pilot Standard Operating Procedure Manual, Department of Veterans Affairs.
10. Telemental Health Suicide Prevention and Emergency Care, U.S. Department of Veterans Affairs, Employee Education System, revision October 2012
11. Draft Guidelines: Psychology services delivered via the internet and other electronic media. New Zealand Psychologists Board. November 2011

Laws Related to Telemental Health

1. Maryland Department of Health and Mental Hygeine, DHMH, (2002). Rights of Persons in Maryland's Psychiatric Facilities
2. APA—State laws for telemedicine and teleconferencing: http://www.apapracticecentral.org/advocacy/state/telehealth-slides.pdf. Accessed: 29 Oct. 2013)

Books

1. Handbook of Intensive Brief and Emergency Psychotherapy, 2nd and Revised Edition; 1992. Leopold Bellak MD with Abrams DM, PhD and Ruby Ackermann-Engel MA C.P.S. Inc. Box 83 Larchmont, NY 10538.
2. The suicidal patient: clinical and legal standards of care; 1991. Bruce Bongar. Washington, DC: American Psychological Association.
3. The psychology of suicide: a clinician's guide to evaluation and treatment; 1994. Shneidman E, Faberow NL, Litman R, editors. Northvale: Jason Aronson.

References

1. Fromm E. The art of loving. New York: Harper and Row; 1956. p. 8–9.
2. American Telemedicine Association. Evidence-based practice for telemental health. http://www.americantelemed.org/docs/default-source/standards/evidence-based-practice-for-telemental-health.pdf. 2009.
3. American Telemedicine Association. Practice guidelines for video-based online mental health services. http://www.americantelemed.org/docs/default-source/standards/practice-guidelines-for-video-based-online-mental-health-services.pdf. Accessed 1 July 2013.
4. Shore JH, Hilty DM, Yellowlees P. Emergency management guidelines for telepsychiatry. Gen Hosp Psychiatry. 2007;29:199–206.

5. Luxton DD, Sirotin BA, Mishkind MC. Safety of telemental healthcare delivered to clinically unsupervised settings: a systematic telemedicine and e-Health. Mary Ann Liebert. 2010;16(6).

6. National Center for Telehealth & Technology (T2), Defense Centers of Excellence for Psychological Health & TBI (DCoE). DoD Telemental Health Guidebook, Version 1. 2011.

7. New Zealand Psychological Association: Draft Guidelines. Psychology services delivered via internet and other electronic media. 2011. http://psychologistsboard.org.nz/cms_show_download.php?id=141. Accessed 1 May 2014.

8. Shore P. VISN 20 Home-Based Telemental Health (HBTMH) pilot standard operating procedure manual. Department of Veterans Affairs. 2011.

9. Maryland Department of Health and Mental Hygiene, DHMH. Rights of Persons in Maryland's Psychiatric Facilities. 2002.

10. Luxton DD, O'Brien K, McCann RA, Mishkind MC. Home-based telemental healthcare safety planning: what you need to know. Telemed e-Health. 2012;18(8):625–633.

11. Veterans Health Administration—Office of Telehealth Services. Emergency and Contigency Guidelines. http://vaww.telehealth.va.gov/telehealth/cvt/tmh/emergency.asp. 2011. Accessed 10 Oct 2011.

12. US v. Baker. United States of America, Petitioner-Appellee v. Leroy Baker, Respondent-Appellant; No. 93-7139. United States Court of Appeals, Fourth Circuit. Argued 13 July 1994. Decided 25 Jan. 1995. http://openjurist.org/45/f3d/837/united-states-v-baker. 1993. Accessed 1 May 2014.

13. US v. Baker. United States of America, Petitioner-Appellee v. Leroy Baker, Respondent-Appellant; No. 93-7139. United States Court of Appeals, Fourth Circuit. Argued 13 July 1994. Decided 25 Jan. 1995. http://openjurist.org/45/f3d/837/united-states-v-baker. 1995. Accessed 1 May 2014.

14. Shore P. The Assessment of Suitability for Home Based Telemental Health, ASH-25. 25 item questionnaire. 2011.

15. Wells SY, Williams K, Walter K, Moreno L, Butler E, Glassman L, Thorp SR. Establishing informed consent for therapeutic communication in clinical videoconferencing. In: Tuerk P, Shore P, editors. Behavioral telehealth series volume 1—clinical video conferencing: program development and practice. Springer International. In Press.

16. Gros DF, Veronee K, Strachan M, Ruggiero KJ, Acierno R. Managing suicidality in home-based telehealth. J Telemed Telecare. 2011;17:332–5.

17. National Suicide Prevention Lifeline (NSPL). http://www.suicidepreventionlifeline.org. Accessed 1 May 2014.

18. Department of veterans affairs, clinical video into home—addendum, clinical video operations manual. Telehealth Services.

19. Bellak L, Abrams DM, Ackermann-Engel R. Handbook of intensive brief and emergency psychotherapy. 2nd ed. (Revised). Westchester: C.P.S.; 1992.

20. Shneidman E, Faberow N, Litman R, editors. The psychology of suicide. Lanham: Jason Aronson; 1994.

21. Pompili M. A lifeguard at the sea of despair: reflections on a professional career in suicidology/Bruce Bongar. Suicide in the words of suicidologists. Hauppauge: Nova Science; 2010.

22. Kinn J, Luxton DD, Reger MA, Skopp NA, Bush N, Gahm GA. Department of defense suicide event report: calendar year 2010 annual report. National Center for Telehealth & Technology (T2), Defense Centers of Excellence for Psychological Health & TBI (DCoE). 2011.

23. Kemp J, Brenner LA, Homaifar B, Olson-Madden J. Traumatic brain injury and suicide: information and resources for clinicians. http://www.sprc.org/sites/sprc.org/files/library/TBI_Suicide.pdf. (n.d.).

24. Brown GK. A review of suicide assessment measures for intervention research with adults and older adults. Technical report submitted to NIMH under Contract No. 263-MH914950.

Bethesda: National Institute of Mental Health; 2000. http://www.suicidology.org/c/document_library/get_file?folderId=235&name=DLFE-113.pdf. Accessed 16 Mar 2014.

25. Department Veterans Affairs, Mental Health Services. www.mentalhealth.va.gov/suicide_prevention. Accessed 1 May 2014.

26. Department Veterans Affairs, MIRECC 19. http://www.mirecc.va.gov/visn19. Accessed 1 May 2014.

Chapter 9
Clinical Assessment in Clinical Videoconferencing

David D. Luxton, Larry D. Pruitt and Michael A. Jenkins-Guarnieri

Purpose   This chapter addresses the barriers, solutions, and best practices for conducting patient assessments with clinical videoconferencing (CV) technologies. Specific attention is given to the benefits of CV assessment and recommendations for preparing, optimizing, and conducting clinical assessments over CV. Practical concerns such as the exchange of assessment materials, data security, processes for determining the appropriateness of CV-based assessments, and recommendations for assuring the integrity of assessment instruments are also covered.

Context   The information is relevant to clinicians and clinical managers because unfamiliarity with best practices and technical capabilities can threaten the practice of competent, ethical, and effective clinical assessment services, even when replicating well-known and familiar in-person assessment practices via CV.

Tools   The chapter provides useful information for selecting compatible assessment measures and procedures, a table of psychological and neurocognitive measures previously used in CV settings, a list of common methods and best practices for the exchange of assessment materials to and from remote treatment sites, guidelines for conducting informed consent for CV assessment, and a working knowledge of the technological aspects of CV-based clinical assessments.

The views, opinions, and/or findings contained in this article are those of the author and should not be construed as an official Department of Defense position, policy or decision unless so designated by other official documentation

---

D. D. Luxton (✉) · L. D. Pruitt · M. A. Jenkins-Guarnieri
National Center for Telehealth & Technology, Joint Base Lewis-McChord, WA, USA
e-mail: david.d.luxton.civ@mail.mil

Department of Psychiatry and Behavioral Sciences, University of Washington School of Medicine, Seattle, USA

© Springer International Publishing Switzerland 2015
P. W. Tuerk, P. Shore (eds.), *Clinical Videoconferencing in Telehealth,*
Behavioral Telehealth, DOI 10.1007/978-3-319-08765-8_9

9.1   Introduction

Behavioral, psychological, and neurocognitive assessment via clinical videoconferencing (CV) is becoming more commonplace. Insurers have begun to reimburse for CV-delivered assessments and federal legal precedent recognizes CV as an acceptable means to provide important clinical assessments such as suicide risk evaluation in involuntary commitment contexts [1]. This chapter addresses best practices for conducting clinical assessments with CV technologies. As with in-person clinical assessments, CV-based assessments can be used for diagnostics, screening, symptom monitoring, evaluations of treatment progress and outcomes, and to provide further understanding of client contextual factors and needs. Clinical assessments can be conducted with various CV platforms that are available today including professional videoconferencing systems, webcams, and camera enabled mobile devices (i.e., smartphones and tablets devices). It is critical for clinicians and clinical managers to be familiar with the best-practices for CV-based assessments in order to assure that they are conducted appropriately and are optimally useful. Practitioners also should be aware of whether a particular measure or assessment technique is appropriate for use with CV and aware of proper CV administration procedures to assure competent and ethical practice.

9.2   Determining the appropriateness
of CV-based assessment

The appropriateness of CV-based clinical assessment must be determined across contexts. As with in-person assessment, this process should be guided by evidence-based practice that, as described by the American Psychological Association (APA), involves "the integration of best available research and clinical expertise in the context of patient characteristics, culture, and preferences" [2]. While the decision-making process is similar to clinical assessments conducted in conventional office settings, there are specific issues associated with CV-based assessments that need to be considered. Of course, issues related to privacy, safety, and patient attitude regarding the experience with technology are important factors [3]. Chapters 7–9 provide recommendations related to establishing an informed consent for services, promoting patient safety, and supporting productive communication in CV contexts, and lessons from these chapters are centrally relevant to assessment services as well. Moreover, it is important to note that recommended procedures for CV safety, data security, and enhanced communication protocols related to in-depth clinical services via CV are equally applicable to even the most routine and brief clinical assessment encounters. Yet the assessment context, especially in unsupervised CV settings, like the home, can create additional concerns requiring special consideration for assessors. For example, the involvement of a Patient Support Person (PSP) [4, 5] to bolster patient safety protocols can present additional threats to privacy in assessment settings, especially during initial or comprehensive assessments regarding social or environmental functioning. Moreover, the familiar context and ease related to receiving services in a patient's home may provide a benefit to therapeutic protocols but may negatively impact effort or attentiveness on assessment measures normed in institutional settings. We believe that most complicating issues related to CV-based assessment can be overcome with forethought and intentionality and offer this chapter as a starting place or guide to assist in the initiation of CV-based assessments.

In each of the following sections, the issues associated with determining the appropriateness of CV-based assessment are reviewed in greater detail. While several of these issues are discussed in other chapters, they are presented here in the specific context of CV-based clinical assessment. It is important to note that while these issues should be considered prior to initiating CV-based clinical assessments, they are also essential to incorporate and re-evaluate throughout the assessment process.

9.2.1 Clinical Appropriateness

Patient clinical presentations (e.g., diagnosis, symptoms etc.) are necessary for practitioners to take into account as these may influence whether CV-based assessment procedures are appropriate or feasible. For example, it may not be appropriate to conduct an assessment via CV with a person who is experiencing delusional beliefs that involve technology because of potential iatrogenic effects. Clinical assessment via CV may also not be the best option if the safety of the patient or that of collaterals (i.e., family members at home) is a concern due to a known history of suicidal or violent behavior. It is therefore necessary to evaluate and assess whether CV-based assessments are appropriate via review of treatment records or other patient data (if available). It may also be appropriate to consult with other practitioners who have been directly involved with treatment of the patient. Risk of violence assessments may be incorporated into prescreening procedures along with assessment of other patient characteristics such as vision or hearing limitations.

Clinical contraindications may also be discovered during the course of the assessment process. For example, it may be discovered that a patient has a cognitive deficit or problems with vision, not previously identified, that may influence the validity of assessment results. In those cases, clinicians should consider the pros and cons of continuing the assessment, and as with any conventional in-person assessment, document and disclose how those factors may have influenced assessment results.

9.2.2 Culture and Acceptability

Acceptability of assessment procedures can influence assessment accuracy as well as patient compliance and motivation [6]. Just as a patient's cultural background is relevant to the procedures and interpretations of a given assessment tool [7], a patient's culture is also relevant to their acceptability and level of comfort with remote assessment and the CV medium [8].

Similarly, expectations and accepted norms for specific aspects of interpersonal interactions can vary considerably in different cultures. In Native cultures, for example, direct eye contact may be considered disrespectful and rude [9]. Thus, clinicians need to consider cultural expectations associated with eye gaze when using CV technologies as this is important for both establishing rapport, and preventing misinterpretation of behaviors during a clinical assessment (e.g., mistaking a consistently downward eye gaze as a symptom of depression). Although such cultural competency is also a requirement of in-person services as well, CV technologies enable assessment services to be conducted in highly rural areas and between individuals separated by great distances, both of which increase the risk of cultural miscues between parties. Accordingly, cultural competence or incompetence may play a larger role in the delivery of CV assessments as compared to traditional assessments.

Although familiarity with CV technology has become more commonplace due to the popularity of media services and videoconferencing software (e.g., Facetime, Skype), significant portions of the population are still unfamiliar with these technologies. In particular, older adults represent a growing population of mental health consumers [10] who may particularly benefit from increased access to clinical assessment services delivered via CV [11, 12]. However, this population may be less familiar with CV technologies and may prefer traditional in-person interactions [13], especially if not offered a clear rationale for why CV is being used or suggested.

Important for the initial decision making process is the practitioner's own comfort level and experience with technology and its use during clinical assessments. While it is likely not necessary for the clinician to be an expert regarding how the technology works, it is important for the clinician to be adequately competent with using it and confident that he or she can effectively troubleshoot technical issues if they occur during an assessment session. Access to troubleshooting guides and a plan to involve external technical support or in some cases a PSP to assist with technical issues is recommended and should be considered before initiating CV based assessments.

9.2.3 Balancing the Specific Needs of CV-Based Assessment with the Literature Base

It is natural for practitioners planning assessments via CV for the first time to focus planning efforts on the exchange of materials. Procedures for the exchange of materials are of primary importance and will be addressed later in this chapter; however, the planning stages of CV-mediated assessment should first clearly focus on the specific reason or need for assessment and the validity and reliability of proposed measures to meet that need, this step is even more important if the proposed measures were normed in face-to-face settings. Just because the validity and reliability of a particular instrument or procedure has been established for in-person administration, it does not mean that those qualities will hold when it is administered over CV [14]. Indeed, researchers have highlighted a gap in the literature base regarding CV-based assessments [15]. Some have pointed out the need to establish separate psychometric norms [16] whereas, others have recommended the development of assessments specifically designed for use with CV technologies [11]. The decision to administer any particular measure via CV must therefore be based on available psychometric data as well as information regarding the modification of measures and procedures for remote administration.

It is important to note that assessment objectives and the client's needs may require a particular type of assessment that lacks an established evidence-base for the use of CV administration or that has not been demonstrated as feasible for remote administration [14, 17]. In some cases, remote assessment via CV may be the only option and therefore the best option for a particular patient. This may be true for populations that live in remote areas, such as parts of Alaska, which become inaccessible or very treacherous to travel through during substantial portions of the year. A home-bound elder that risks a life threatening fall by traveling to a clinic is another example of a situation in which CV assessments may be the best choice. A more common situation where some assessment may be deemed better than no assessment is when self-report measures are used to track or guide progress over the course of a CV-mediated treatment. In all of these cases, it may be advisable to administer CV-mediated assessments but to narrow the interpretation of results.

Accordingly, if no norms or information are available regarding CV administration of specific desired measures, then it is appropriate to apply a pragmatic framework that considers the minimally relevant information necessary in order to justify the collection of potentially imperfect data. In weighing assessment decisions it is helpful to recognize that the value or logic of a some-is-better-than-none approach may diminish as the stakes of a potential assessment increase. For example, assessments tied to disability claims or to a patient's candidacy for an organ transplant most likely require a much more conservative approach. Accordingly, as the field and knowledge base develop, practitioners are encouraged to consider a value vs. risk spectrum and to make context-specific decisions in the best interests of their particular clients or patients.

9.3 Clinical and Behavioral Assessment Measures

Several available published reviews provide useful information regarding the validity and reliability of clinical assessments conducted via telehealth technologies. For example, Hyler and colleagues conducted a review and meta-analysis of 14 studies that compared face-to-face with CV psychiatric assessments [18]. Five of the studies used clinical assessment measures (e.g., Y-BOCS, MMSE, SCID-III-R), two studies used satisfaction measures (i.e., clinician or patient satisfaction), and seven studies used the combination of clinical assessment and satisfaction measures. The meta-analytic results indicated that clinical measures administered via CV were comparable to in-person assessments in regard to diagnosis or symptoms assessment. The Telemental Health Standards and Guidelines Working Group [19] also reviewed and reported data regarding the psychometric properties of remote telehealth-based assessments. These authors highlighted evidence that supported the use of standard objective measures via CV, such as the Hamilton Depression Rating Scale, with some caveats about the negative effects of low bandwidth on reliability for symptom rating scales [20, 21].

Evidence of the reliability and comparability to in-person assessments for structured clinical interviews and psychiatric evaluations via CV has also been reported by multiple research groups [22–24]. A systematic review by Backhaus and colleagues [11] supported these previous individual conclusions and reported that the majority of studies they evaluated (69%) utilized "at least one standardized measure with well-accepted psychometrics" (p. 118). Notably, the review included popular rating scales such as the Beck Depression Inventory-II (BDI-II) [25] and the Structured Clinical Interview for the DSM-IV Axis I Disorders, Research Version, Patient Edition (SCID-I/P) [26]. Some measures commonly used in published CV research, such as the BDI-II [11], also have established evidence for comparability in computer and paper forms [27], which is notable since computer administration of assessment measures is one way to conduct at-distance assessments in combination with CV sessions. See Table 9.1 for a list of common measures that have been employed in a CV context.

Table 9.1 presents clinical assessment measures and tools that have evidence for use during CV practice. It is important to note that the majority of the studies shown in Table 9.1 involved small samples sizes, and few studies have provided strong evidence for the equivalent validity of remote assessment measures compared to their paper-and-pencil versions. Practitioners are encouraged to review the most current relevant research in order to evaluate the evolving evidence on remote assessment with specific measures before implementing them in clinical practice. Even more helpful may be to contact the authors of the studies listed in Table 9.1 directly for instrument-specific guidance or for evolving formats and procedures, as many clinical scientists often continue to work with the same measures and methods they have previously published on.

9.4 Cognitive and Neuropsychological Assessment Measures

CV-delivered neuropsychological assessments have been demonstrated to be feasible [19] and a small number of studies have investigated the agreement between neuropsychological tests conducted in-person and via CV [17, 41]. Generally,

Table 9.1 Clinical assessment measures used via Clinical Videoconferencing (CV)

Clinical/symptom inventories

Assessment instrument	Delivery medium	Example of use
Alcohol Use Disorders Identification Test (AUDIT)	Telephone	Hunkeler et al. [28]
Beck Depression Inventory (BDI-II)	CV via Internet; fax for self-report measures[a]	Luxton et al. [29], Tuerk et al. [30]
Behavioral Assessment System for Children (BASC)	Mailed to parents[a]	Van Allen et al. [31]
Brief Psychiatric Rating Scale (BPRS)	CV via Internet	Grob et al. [32]
Brief Symptom Inventory (BSI)	Mail (self-addressed stamped envelope for return)[a]	O'Reilly et al. [33]
Center for Epidemiological Studies Depression Scale (CES-D)	Telephone	Smith et al. [34]
Child Behavior Checklist (CBCL)	Mailed to parents[a]	Van Allen et al. [31]
Clinically Useful Depression Outcome Scale (CUDOS)	Web-based format	Zimmerman and Martinez [35]
Geriatric Depression Scale (GDS)	VCT via Internet	Grob et al. [32]
Hamilton Anxiety Rating Scale (HAM-A)	VCT via low-bandwidth Internet (128 kb/s) with document camera	Baer et al. [36]
Hamilton Depression Rating Scale (HAM-D)	VCT via low-bandwidth Internet with document camera	Baer et al. [36]
Insomnia Severity Index (ISI)	Telephone	Lichstein et al. [37]
Minnesota Multiphasic Personality Inventory-2 Restructured (MMPI-2-RF)	CV via Intranet network	Turner et al. [38]
Medical Outcomes Study-Short Form 36 Health Survey (SF-36)	Telephone; mail (self-addressed stamped envelope for return)[a]	Hunkeler et al. [28] O'Reilly et al. [33]
Multidimensional Anxiety Scale for Children (MASC)	Secure web site	Myers et al. [39]
Patient Health Questionnaire (PHQ-9)	Interactive voice response technology	Turvey et al. [40]
PTSD Checklist-Military (PCL-M)	VCT via Internet; fax for self-report measures[a]	Luxton et al. [29], Tuerk et al. [30], Turner et al. [38]
Yale-Brown Obsessive Compulsive Scale (Y-BOCS)	VCT via low-bandwidth Internet (128 kb/s) with document camera	Baer et al. [36]

[a] Indicates assessment measures completed in paper-and-pencil format remotely

findings suggest adequate comparability, with some evidence for greater reliability with measures that primarily use verbal instructions [41]. Yet special cautions for neuropsychological measures have been suggested given the underdeveloped protocols for adapting established measures to CV as well as the paucity of research, in general, on delivery through CV, which may influence testing procedures, accuracy of assessments, and the interpretation of results [16, 42]. For example, the established normative performance data for the Halstead-Reitan Neuropsychological Battery were developed well before the advent of the personal computer, thus, it may be inappropriate to use these data to gauge performance on tests if administered

Table 9.2 Cognitive and neuropsychological assessment measures used via Clinical Videoconferencing (CV)

Cognitive/neuropsychological Measure	Method	Example
Boston Diagnostic Aphasia Examination (BDAE)	CV via Intranet	Turner et al. [38]
Boston Naming Test (BNT)	CV via Intranet CV via Internet	Turner et al. [38] Vestal et al. [43]
Clock drawing	CV via Intranet; CV via Internet with document camera	Hildebrand et al. [42] Parikh et al. [41]
California Verbal Learning Test, 2nd edition (CVLT-2)	CV via Intranet	Turner et al. [38]
Conners Adult ADHD (CAARS)	CV via Intranet	Turner et al. [38]
Controlled Oral Word Association Test (COWAT)	CV via Internet with document camera	Hildebrand et al. [44] Turner et al. [38]
Delis–Kaplan Executive Function System (D-KEFS)	CV via Intranet	Turner et al. [38]
Digit span	CV via Intranet	Parikh et al. [41]
Hopkins Verbal Learning Test-Rvsd (HVLT-R)	CV via Intranet	Parikh et al. [41]
Judgment of Line Orientation Test (JOLO)	CV via Intranet	Turner et al. [38]
Neuropsychological Assessment Battery(NAB)	CV via Intranet	Turner et al. [38]
Mini-Mental State Examination (MMSE)	CV via Intranet	Parikh et al. [41]
Mental Status Exam (MSE)	CV via Internet	Grady and Melcer [45]
Paced Auditory Serial Addition Test (PASAT)	CV via Intranet	Turner et al. [38]
Rey–Osterreith Complex Figure Test (RCFT)	CV via Intranet	Turner et al. [38]
Seashore Rhythm Test	CV via Internet	Jacobsen et al. [68]
Structured Interview of Reported Symptoms (SIRS)	CV via Intranet	Turner et al. [38]
Spielberg State/Trait Anxiety Inventory(STAI)	CV via Intranet	Turner et al. [38]
Trail Making Test (TMT)	CV via Intranet	Turner et al. [38]
Test of Memory Malingering (TOMM)	CV via Intranet	Turner et al. [38]
Wisconsin Card Sorting Test	CV via Intranet	Turner et al. [38]
Wechsler Memory Scale, 3rd ed. (WMS-3)	CV via Intranet	Turner et al. [38]
Green Word Memory Test (WMT)	CV via Intranet	Turner et al. [38]
Wender- Utah Rating Scale (WURS)	CV via Intranet	Turner et al. [38]
WMS-Logical Memory 1	CV via Internet	Jacobsen et al. [68]
Videoconference-based Mini-Mental State Examination (VMMSE; Italian version)	CV via Internet	Timpano et al. [46]

remotely via CV. Even though cognitive measures have been administered via CV and patients have generally indicated acceptance of and satisfaction with the assessment process [17, 41], some researchers have suggested that similar caution be applied to cognitive testing as with neuropsychological due to the lack of data regarding the use of standardized measures that are administered electronically [15]. Grady and colleagues noted that research on personality assessment delivered via CV is nonexistent and that "there is no information about projective testing over CV (p. 138)" [19]. As mentioned above, practitioners are encouraged to contemplate the value vs. risk of specific assessments in specific situations (Table 9.2).

In summary, clinicians who are interested in conducting assessment via CV must consider the evidence base supporting specific measures and their use with this medium. Recommendations for appropriate adaptation of measures and administration procedures should also be considered. Recent research reviews support the use of many popular clinical rating scales, structured interviews, neuropsychological measures, and satisfaction measures administered via CV. There are, however, limitations to the available data that will require additional study. The need for separate norms for existing tests as well as measures designed specifically for CV administration has been recommended.

9.5   Informed Consent Process

In addition to completing the procedures related to the standard informed consent process for CV services (see Chap. 7), assessors should also include a discussion of the potential risks and issues relevant to specific assessment instruments [4, 47, 48]. In regards to CV-based clinical assessments, clinicians should discuss the ways that the modality may differ from alternative options as well as the unique risks and benefits [47]. Of particular relevance is disclosure of confidentiality and privacy measures and expectations associated with the electronic storage and transmission of assessment data and results. Practitioners should also discuss with the patient that there is a possibility that the accuracy of the assessment data collected could be influenced by the quality of the CV connection or other disruptions. This is especially important in circumstances where assessment performance will be used to make lasting decisions about a patient's care, entitled benefits, or legal status. Where possible, potential solutions to disruptions and contingency plans should be addressed before initiating measures. Clinicians must also be sure to provide ample time to address any questions that the patient may have regarding CV-based clinical assessment. Given the evolving laws and guidelines, practitioners must also remain current on laws and practice standards that have impact on the overall informed consent process [4, 47].

9.6   Exchange of Materials

Before CV-mediated assessment, practitioners must prepare or oversee preparation of the rooms at both ends of the connection. In addition to assuring that all assessment materials, scoring materials, measurement, and timekeeping tools are in place, practitioners should also verify that patients have adequate materials and space (e.g., writing tools, ample desk surface area, etc.). The clinical space on the provider's side must be adequately lit and the background should provide adequate image clarity [49]. See Chap. 10 for staging of physical and technological details to optimize communication. In situations where CV services are provided to a remote clinic-based setting, support staff may assist with preparation. When clinical support staff are unavailable, such as during home-based assessments, the patient may be asked to prepare the room or a PSP may assist if available.

The exchange of assessment materials is the most common obstacle to overcome when conducting CV-mediated behavioral assessments. Both flexibility and trial and error are often necessary to address specific needs of any given CV situation. Timing, support staff, and available resources may vary across settings and, temporally, within settings. Below is a list of common methods and best practices for the exchange of assessment materials during CV sessions (Table 9.3).

9.7   Optimizing Assessment Conditions

One of the primary factors that may influence the validity and reliability of remote assessments conducted via CV is the fact that the client and practitioner are not physically in the same room. A patient's off camera nonverbal cues can provide useful information about their emotional state, symptom severity, and even risk behaviors. Olfactory data can provide relevant information regarding a patient's alcohol and substance use, as well as hygiene. Clinical impressions and conceptualizations can be influenced by body posture and language (e.g., foot tapping, hand wringing), minute changes to facial expression, and other non-verbal emotional responses such as facial flushing, tearing up, and eye-gaze direction, which may be more difficult to see during CV assessment. Accordingly, clinicians should feel free to provide directive instructions or to gather any information necessary to support accurate assessment. For example, many CV clinicians have become used to asking patients (especially young adults and adolescents) to remove their baseball caps to increase facial visibility. Likewise, when administering assessment measures such as the Brief Psychiatric Rating Scale (BPRS) [50], the practitioner may need to ask additional questions regarding the somatic manifestation of symptoms in order to most accurately determine the rating that best describes a patient's symptoms for domains such as anxiety, tension, mannerisms, posturing, motor retardation, and excitement since observation of the patient's full body may not be possible. In some cases, in-person assessment procedures need to be modified or adapted to allow for accurate CV assessment; practitioners are cautioned to review the instructions or administration manuals of the measures to ensure that the appropriate procedures and environmental conditions for standardized administration are maintained in a way that does not threaten the reliability or validity of a given assessment. Accordingly, creative clinical adaptations need to be weighed against the necessity of standardization for a given instrument.

Psychomotor and other medically relevant symptoms may need to be observed during psychological assessments as well, in which case the practitioner can query them directly (e.g., to assess gait problems, the patient may need to be asked to stand back from the camera and walk across the room). Furthermore, the observation of *how* an examinee approaches a test or measure may be critical for making an accurate assessment. For example, along with measuring the accuracy of an

Table 9.3 Common methods and best practices for the exchange of assessment materials during clinical videoconferencing

Providing assessment materials at the patient-end	Clinicians may fax the appropriate forms to support staff or the patient before the appointment. The use of a fax cover sheet with large font or handwriting is recommended to alert the recipient(s) of what should be expected with the fax as well as its importance. If sending materials directly to a patient, it is critical to assure that the patient has instructions on how to operate the fax machine
	Clinicians may send assessment materials via postal mail to remote clinical facilities or directly to patient's homes. When mailing bulk materials to clinical facilities, it may be helpful to place different measures in easily identified and numbered folders or packets. The use of numbered folders with large-font facilitates ease of distribution of the correct assessments by busy support staff that may not be familiar with assessment names. A sequential numbering system can help identify correct order of instruments to be administered (e.g., neuropsychological assessment batteries that have a large number of sequential instruments)
	Assessment materials can be made available for download from web sites or to be completed directly on-line. The use of passwords is recommended in order to protect the integrity of the instruments from unauthorized access
	Assessment materials may be sent via email. While this method may be technically feasible and convenient, clinician must also consider the appropriateness of this method. Clinicians should consider the privacy risks due to the potential for patients to reply to email with protected health information (PHI). Relying on patients to download and print materials may also be susceptible to technical issues, such as when printing the materials
Receiving assessment materials at the provider-end	If available, support staff at the patient-end can collect the materials and fax them back to the clinician. If using this method and if the provider-side fax machine is not secured in a private area, it may be prudent to use a special cover sheet indicating the transmission is confidential
	Patients may be asked to hold up competed measures directly to the camera so that clinicians can record the relevant responses
	Some CV systems, such as the TANBERG EX-90, have built in document cameras that can capture and enlarge documents sitting on a flat desktop. This not only conveys information about the completed measure but it also provides real-time observation of the assessment (e.g., item endorsement, etc.)
	Patients may be asked to verbally report responses to self-report measures. If using this method, it may be best to wait until the patient has completed the entire measure, rather than reporting as he or she goes. This process may help to limit unintended effects or demand characteristics; almost all self-report measures are normed using an answer-straight-through procedure, thus, breaking it up question by question may influence the validity and reliability of the assessment
	If the assessment measures are to be mailed back to the clinician, a self-addressed stamped envelope may be provided for patients to return the completed measures

examinee's copy and recall drawings of the Rey-Osterrieth Complex Figure [51], it is important to examine the process by which a patient completes their drawing. With a camera capturing only a patient's face, the provider may not have access to this information. In this situation, and other similar situations, if integrated document cameras are not available on the primary CV equipment, the remote location may need multiple cameras so that the practitioner is able to view the patient's desktop surface where they are completing assessment tasks.

Lastly, patients should be asked to paraphrase instructions back to the practitioner to ensure clear receipt of a task's demands. While it is advisable to do this regardless of assessment medium, it may be particularly important to do so when making use of CV as occasional fluctuation in bandwidth may briefly distort audio transmissions.

9.8   Technology Specific Considerations for Assessment via CV

There are several factors associated with the use of technology that may influence the reliability and validity of clinical assessment when videoconferencing. Chapter 10 addresses general communication issues and solutions regarding CV but it is worthwhile to outline a few issues here that are particularly relevant to providing assessments. Eye gaze angle (the angle between the eye and the camera, and the eye and the center of the display) is one issue that has been discussed in depth [52]. Users of CV tend to make eye contact with the image on the screen rather than with the camera [53]. This tendency may lead the person on the other end of the connection to the impression that the person is avoiding eye contact. Eye contact during assessments is important because it provides visual cues the participants can respond to and is also a marker for interpersonal skill and social ability 52, 53, 54]. Eye contact is also an important source of clinical information for determining the presence of psychological states (e.g., delirium) or particular disorders (e.g., Autism Spectrum Disorder). Improved eye contact can be realized by increasing the distance of participants from the videoconferencing unit and zooming in the lens [52]. Chapters 10 and 11 offer additional solutions to ensure appropriate eye contact during CV.

Patients and providers should be centered on the viewing monitors. Patients may shift position or the video camera may accidently be shifted from the optimal angle during the course of an assessment. It may therefore be necessary to make adjustments to the camera position or to the patient's physical location in relation to the camera. Practitioners should feel comfortable asking the patient to make adjustments to camera angle or their physical position. Some CV camera systems include remote tilt, zoom, and panning features that may make sense to use during assessments, yet if patients can detect the camera movement it is important to discuss why you are moving the camera so as to limit feelings of alienation or the sense that they are an object of study. It is also recommended to use the "picture in picture" function, available on many CV devices, to provide the clinician with visual verification of proper framing. As noted by Luxton and colleagues [14], it is also advised to check-in with patients throughout the assessment process to make sure that they can see and hear clearly. It is important to consistently remember that technological limitations may influence how well the patient understands the practitioner (not just how well the practitioner understands the patient).

Audio quality is another important factor. Low microphone input volume or speaker output volume may make it difficult to understand questions, responses, and instructions. Jones and colleagues [55] found that inadequate audio quality can influence the ability to accurately gather information from the patient. Moreover, it is important to note that lower quality audio/visual during CV assessment has been found to be acceptable to both patients and practitioners even when that lower quality negatively impacts the degree of reliability between assessments [56]. Accordingly, practitioners themselves are not always the best judge of what qualifies as a strong enough audio/visual signal to maximize assessment validity. Volume levels should therefore be established and tested at the outset of the interaction, and must be weighed against the possibility that the audio could be overheard by others or uncomfortably too loud. As with conventional office settings, the use of a white-noise machine outside the assessment room door may make sense.

It is also possible that the use of technology (e.g., web cam, personal computer, microphone) may distract or require extra attention that may influence the assessment session. For example, when conducting a clinical interview over a web cam, the patient may become distracted by inconsistent connections or other technical anomalies [57]. Shifts in a patient's attention may influence testing or assessment scores, potentially decreasing performance in domains requiring sustained attention and concentration. When engaged in home-based CV via the web, it is particularly important to ask patients to close out of their email or social networking sites that might be running in the background as new message alerts may interfere with attention.

Lengthy or complex assessment procedures can be quite demanding on patients. While longer and more in-depth assessments generally provide the greatest reliability, participant dropout is also much more likely [58]. Overly long assessments may be particularly problematic during CV assessment [59]. Exposure to a new medium of interaction (CV) for persons who are not experienced with it may add additional stress or frustration, especially if technical problems occur [60, 61]. Given this, clinicians must remain mindful of the patient's degree of frustration and how likely it is that providing a given assessment in a novel manner may affect a patient's performance or patterns of responding.

While it may seem difficult initially to manage all of the various components of CV-administered assessments, with practice, the preparation necessary for a high-quality CV interaction can become seamless and routine. It is important for clinicians and clinic managers who plan to use CV to obtain experience with the technology prior to offering these services. Practice sessions are highly encouraged, including the simulation of common technical difficulties and the use of backup plans.

9.9   Providing Assessment Results

As with conventional in-person assessment, assessment results can be provided verbally over CV. Written feedback can also be provided using technologies. Some CV software provides a display of digital documents, and other technologies such as "screen share," encrypted e-mail, or a log-in to a secure web-portal may also be used to convey text or graphical post-assessment feedback. See Chap. 1 for various system functionality.

Practitioners must utilize clinical judgment and incorporate available scientific knowledge regarding the appropriateness of providing assessment feedback via CV [47], a process which may vary significantly for different tests, patients, and practice guidelines. Interpretation and explanation of results in CV contexts must incorporate such factors as possible adaptations to administration protocols, interference from technology and hardware functioning, and distracters in the patient's physical environment [47]. Just as practitioners can note in written reports the potential limitations of adapting tests for CV that were originally developed for in-person administration [47], verbal feedback provided via CV should also specify these same limitations where appropriate.

9.10   Insurance

The expansion of telehealth in general can be expected to advance insurance coverage for TMH-related CV services. Insurance coverage for general telehealth services varies from state to state and not all states have specific provisions for CV services. As of 2014, telehealth services can be billed for via Medicaid in 42 US states. Seventeen states require that privately held insurance allow remote services to be billed, while five states do not require Medicaid or private insurance to cover telehealth services [62]. For example, regulations in Vermont mandate that telemedicine services delivered to a patient in a health care facility be covered to the same extent that those services would be covered if they were provided through in-person consultation [63]. However, these state specific laws and regulations can be a barrier for providing remote care. Providers must not only be licensed to practice in, but also be aware of the legal mandates and reimbursement policies of the patient's state of residence. For example, Colorado, whose state medical assistance program recognizes telehealth as a valid mode of treatment delivery, does not require in-person contact between a patient and provider for program-approved mental health services [64–66], whereas Tennessee reimburses for remote mental health care in the provision of crisis services only [67]. A state-by-state breakdown of laws pertaining to insurance coverage of telehealth services can be found on-line, via the National Conference of State Legislatures, at http://www.ncsl.org/research/health/state-coverage-for-telehealth-services.aspx.

Conclusions

Clinical assessment via CV or other telehealth technologies provides many benefits to both patients and clinicians. CV-based assessments can help overcome barriers to care by providing access to clinical services in rural or underserved areas, increasing the availability of practitioners familiar with the nuances of a particular culture or population, and allowing access to providers who specialize in particular areas of assessment. Clinical assessment via CV can also be a solution to language barriers by connecting patients with practitioners who are familiar with the patient's language or by connecting hearing impaired patients to clinicians who are capable of conducting clinical assessment via American Sign Language. Clinical assessment via CV also allows clinicians to expand their practice and provide services that they otherwise could not provide due to their geographical location.

The use of CV for conducting clinical assessment can be expected to become more common in parallel with the overall growth and expansion of CV practice. The increasing availability of CV technologies and the budding evidence-base in support of their use for remote clinical assessment will continue to advance capabilities. As outlined in this chapter, there are many factors that clinicians and clinic managers need to consider in order to assure optimal CV-based clinical assessments. All of these issues can be effectively addressed given attention to available best-practices and appropriate training.

References

1. U.S. v Baker, 836 F. Supp. 1237 (NC 1993), aff'd 45 F3d 837 (4th Cir 1995).
2. APA Presidential Task Force on Evidence-Based Practice. Evidence-based practice in psychology. Am Psychol. 2006;61:271–85.
3. Shore J, Kaufmann L, Brooks E, Bair B, Dailey N, Richardson W, Manson S. Review of American Indian veteran telemental health. Telemed J E Health. 2012;18:87–94.
4. American Telemedicine Association's Practice Guidelines for Videoconferencing-based Telemental Health. http://www.americantelemed.org/practice/standards/ata-standards-guidelines. Accessed: 5 Sept 2013.
5. Luxton DD, O'Brien K, McCann RA, Mishkind MC. Home-based telemental healthcare safety planning: what you need to know. Telemed J E Health. 2012;18:629–33.
6. Rogers R. Handbook of diagnostic and structured interviewing. New York: Guilford; 2001.
7. Verney SP, Granholm E, Marshall SP, Malcarne VL, Saccuzzo DP. Culture-fair cognitive ability assessment: information processing and psychological approaches. Assessment. 2005;12:303–19.
8. Shore JH, Manson SM. Telepsychiatric care of American Indian veterans with post-traumatic stress disorder: bridging gaps in geography, organizations, and culture. Telemed J E Health. 2004;10:64–9.
9. Shore JH, Savin D, Novins D, Manson SM. Cultural aspects of telepsychiatry. J Telemed Telecare. 2006;12:116–21.
10. Palinkas LA, Criado V, Fuentes D, Shepherd S, Milian H, Folsom D, Jeste D. Unmet needs for services for older adults with mental illness: comparison of views of different stakeholder groups. Am J Geriatr Psychiatry. 2007;15:530–40.

11. Backhaus A, Agha Z, Maglione ML, Repp A, Ross B, Zuest D, Thorp SR. Videoconferencing psychotherapy: a systematic review. Psychol Serv. 2012;9:111–31.
12. Richardson LK, Frueh B, Grubaugh AL, Egede L, Elhai JD. Current directions in videoconferencing tele-mental health research. Clin Psychol Sci Pract. 2009;16:323–38.
13. McMurtrey ME, Downey JP, Zeltmann SM, McGaughey RE. Seniors and technology: results from a field study. J Comput Inform Syst. 2011;51:22–30.
14. Luxton DD, Pruitt LD, Osenbach JE. Best practices for remote psychological assessment via telehealth technologies. Prof Psychol Res Pract. 2013; 45:27–35.
15. Colbow AJ. Looking to the future: integrating telemental health therapy into psychologist training. Train Edu Prof Psychol. 2013;7:155–65.
16. Grosch MC, Gottlieb MC, Cullum C. Initial practice recommendations for teleneuropsychology. Clin Neuropsychol. 2011;25:1119–33.
17. Cullum C, Weiner MF, Gehrmann, HR, Hynan LS. Feasibility of telecognitive assessment in dementia. Assessment. 2006;13:385–90.
18. Hyler SE, Gangure DP, Batchelder ST. Can telepsychiatry replace in-person psychiatric assessments? A review and meta-analysis of comparison studies. CNS Spectr. 2005;10:403–13.
19. Grady B, Myers K, Nelson E, Belz N, Bennett L, Carnahan L, Voyles D. Evidence-based practice for telemental health. Telemed J E Health. 2011;17:131–48.
20. Kobak KA. A comparison of face-to-face and videoconference administration of the Hamilton Depression Rating Scale. J Telemed Telecare. 2004;10:231–5.
21. Kobak KA, Williams JBW, Engelhardt N. A comparison of face-to-face and remote assessment of inter-rater reliability on the Hamilton Depression Rating Scale via videoconferencing. Psychiatry Res. 2008;158:99–103.
22. Ruskin PE, Reed S, Kumar R, Kling MA, Siegel E, Rosen M, Hauser P. Reliability and acceptability of psychiatric diagnosis via telecommunication and audiovisual technology. Psychiatr Serv. 1998;49:1086–8.
23. Shore JH, Savin D, Orton H, Beals J, Manson SM. Diagnostic reliability of telepsychiatry in American Indian veterans. Am J Psychiatry. 2007;164:115–8.
24. Singh SP, Arya D, Peters T. Accuracy of telepsychiatric assessment of new routine outpatient referrals. BMC Psychiatry. 2007;7:55.
25. Beck AT, Steer RA, Brown GK. Manual for beck depression inventory-II. San Antonio: Psychological Corporation.
26. First MB, Spitzer RL, Gibbon M, Williams JBW. Structured clinical interview for DSM-IV-TR Axis I disorders, Research Version, Patient Edition. (SCID-I/P). New York: State Psychiatric Institute; 2002.
27. Naus MJ, Philipp LM, Samsi M. From paper to pixels: a comparison of paper and computer formats in psychological assessment. Comput Hum Behav. 2009;25:1–7.
28. Hunkeler EM, Hargreaves WA, Fireman B, Terdiman J, Meresman JF, Porterfield Y, Lee J, Dea R, Simon GE, Bauer MS, Unutzer J, Taylor CB. A web-delivered care management and patient self-management program for recurrent depression: a randomized trial. Psychiatr Serv. 2012;63:1063–71.
29. Luxton DD, Pruitt LD, O'Brien K, Kramer G. A pilot study of in-home telehealth-based behavioral activation for PTSD. 2014; manuscript submitted for publication.
30. Tuerk PW, Yoder M, Ruggiero KJ, Gros DF, Acierno R. A pilot study of prolonged exposure therapy for posttraumatic stress disorder delivered via telehealth technology. J Traum Stress. 2010;23(1):116–23. doi:10.1002/jts.20494.
31. Van Allen J, Davis AM, Lassen S. The use of telemedicine in pediatric psychology: research review and current applications. Child Adolesc Psychiatr Clin N Am. 2011;20:55–66.
32. Grob P, Weintraub D, Sayles D, Raskin A, Ruskin P. Psychiatric assessment of a nursing home population using audiovisual telecommunication. J Geriatr Psychiatry Neurol. 2001;14:63–5.
33. O'Reilly R, Bishop J, Maddox K, Hutchinson L, Fisman M, Takhar J. Is telepsychiatry equivalent to face-to-face psychiatry? Results from a randomized controlled equivalence trial. Psychiatr Serv. 2007. doi:10.1176/appi.ps.58.6.836.

34. Smith GC, Egbert N, Dellman-Jenkins M, Nanna K, Palmieri PA. Reducing depression in stroke survivors and their informal caregivers: a randomized clinical trial of a web-based intervention. Rehab Psychol. 2012;57:196–206.
35. Zimmerman M, Martinez JH. Web-based assessment of depression in patients treated in clinical practice: reliability, validity, and patient acceptance. J Clin Psychiatry. 2012;73:333–8.
36. Baer L, Cukor P, Jenike MA, Leahy L, O'Laughlen J, Coyle JT. Pilot studies of telemedicine for patients with obsessive-compulsive disorder. Am J Psychiatry. 1995;152:1383–5.
37. Lichstein KL, Scogin F, Thomas SJ, DiNapoli EA, Dillon HR, McFadden A. Telehealth cognitive behavior therapy for co-occurring insomnia and depression symptoms in older adults. J Clin Psychol. 2013;69:1056–65.
38. Turner TH, Horner MD, VanKirk KK, Myrick DH, Tuerk PW. A pilot trial of neuropsychological evaluations conducted via telemedicine in the veterans health administration. Telemed J E Health. 2012;18(9):662–7.
39. Myers K, Stoep AV, Lobdell C. Feasibility of conducting a randomized controlled trial of telemental health with children diagnosed with attention-deficit/hyperactivity disorder in underserved communities. J Child Adolesc Psychopharm. 2013;23:372–8.
40. Turvey C, Sheeran T, Dindo L, Wakefield B, Klein D. Validity of the Patient Health Questionnaire, PHQ-9, administered through interactive-voice-response technology. J Telemed Telecare. 2012 Sept;18(6):348–51. doi:10.1258/jtt.2012.120220.
41. Parikh M, Grosch MC, Graham LL, Hynan LS, Weiner M, Shore JH, Cullum C. Consumer acceptability of brief videoconference-based neuropsychological assessment in older individuals with and without cognitive impairment. Clin Neuropsychol. 2013;27:808–17.
42. Hildebrand R, Chow H, Williams C, Nelson M, Wass P. Feasibility of neuropsychological testing of older adults via videoconference: implications for assessing the capacity for independent living. J Telemed Telecare. 2004;10:130–4.
43. Vestal L, Smith-Olinde L, Hutton T, Hart J. Efficacy of language assessment in Alzheimer's disease: comparing in-person examination and telemedicine. Clin Interv Aging. 2006;1(4):467–71.
44. Hildebrand R, Chow H, Williams C, Nelson M, Wass P. Feasibility of neuropsychological testing of older adults via videoconference: implications for assessing the capacity for independent living. Telemed J E Health. 2009 June;15(5):476–8.
45. Grady BJ, Melcer T. A retrospective evaluation of TeleMental Healthcare services for remote military populations. Telemed J E Health. 2005;11:551–8.
46. Timpano F, Pirrotta F, Bonanno L, Marino S, Marra A, Bramanti P, Lanzafame P. Videoconference-based Mini Mental State Examination: a validation study. Telemed J E Health. 2013;19:931–7.
47. American Psychological Association's Guidelines for the practice of Telepsychology. http://www.apapracticecentral.org/ce/guidelines/telepsychology-guidelines.pdf. Accessed: 31 July 2013.
48. Baker DC, Bufka LF. Preparing for the telehealth world: navigating legal, regulatory, reimbursement, and ethical issues in an electronic age. Prof Psychol Res Pract. 2011;42:405–11.
49. Kramer G, Ayers TS, Mishkind M, Norem A. DoD telemental health guidebook. http://t2health.org/sites/default/files/cth/guidebook/tmh-guidebook_06-11.pdf. Accessed: 9 June 2013.
50. Overall JE, Gorham DR. The brief psychiatric rating scale. Psychol Rep. 1962;10:799–812.
51. Rey A. The psychological examination in cases of traumatic encepholopathy. Arch Psychol. 1941;28:215–85.
52. Tam T, Cafazzo JA, Seto E, Salenieks ME, Rossos PG. Perception of eye contact in video teleconsultation. J Telemed Telecare. 2007;13:35–9.
53. Chen M. Leveraging the asymmetric sensitivity of eye contact for videoconferencing. In: Terveen L, editor. Proceedings of the SIGCHI Conference on Human Factors in Computing Systems. Minneapolis: ACM; 2002. pp. 49–56.
54. Grayson DM, Monk AF. Are you looking at me? Eye contact and desktop video conferencing. ACM Trans Comput Hum Interact. 2003;10:221–43.

55. Jones BN, Johnston D, Reboussin B, McCall WV. Reliability of telepsychiatry assessments: subjective versus observational ratings. J Geriatr Psychiatry Neurol. 2001;14:66–71.
56. Zarate CA, Weinstock L, Cukor P, Morabito C, Leahy L, Burns C, Lee B. Applicability of telemedicine for assessing patients with schizophrenia: acceptance and reliability. J Clin Psychiatry. 1997;58:22–5.
57. Germain V, Marchand A, Bouchard S, Drouin MS, Guay S. Effectiveness of cognitive behavioural therapy administered by videoconference for posttraumatic stress disorder. Cogn Behav Ther. 2009;38:42–53.
58. Buchanan T. Internet-based questionnaire assessment: appropriate use in clinical contexts. Cogn Behav Ther. 2003;32:100–9.
59. Yoshino A, Shigemura J, Kobayashi Y, Nomura S, Shishikura K, Den R, Ashida H. Telepsychiatry: assessment of televideo psychiatric interview reliability with present- and next-generation internet infrastructures. Acta Psychiatr Scand. 2001;104:223–6.
60. Cowain T. Cognitive-behavioural therapy via videoconferencing to a rural area. Aust N Z J Psychiatry. 2001;35:62–4.
61. Folen RA, James LC, Earles JE, Andrasik F. Biofeedback via telehealth: a new frontier for applied psychophysiology. Appl Psychophysiol Biofeedback. 2001;26:195–204.
62. National Conference of State Legislatures' State Coverage for Telehealth Services. http://www.ncsl.org/research/health/state-coverage-for-telehealth-services.aspx. Accessed: 9 Dec 2013.
63. Vermont Statutes Annotated; Title 8, Chapter 107, §4100k. http://www.leg.state.vt.us/statutes/fullsection.cfm?Title=08&Chapter=107&Section=04100k. Accessed: 9 Dec 2013.
64. Colorado Revised Statute §10-16-102. http://www.state.co.us/gov_dir/leg_dir/olls/sl2011a/sl_133.htm. Accessed: 9 Dec 2013.
65. Colorado Revised Statute §10-16-123. http://www.state.co.us/gov_dir/leg_dir/olls/sl2001/sl_300.htm. Accessed: 9 Dec 2013.
66. Colorado Revised Statute §25.5-5-320. http://www.state.co.us/gov_dir/leg_dir/olls/sl2008a/sl_46.htm. Accessed: 9 Dec 2013.
67. Tennessee Department of Mental Health and Substance Abuse Services' Telecommunication Guidelines for Tennessee Department of Mental Health and Substance Abuse Services Designated Crisis Services. http://www.state.tn.us/mental/recovery/crisis_serv_docs/TelemedicineGuidelines.pdf. Accessed: 9 Dec. 2013.
68. Jacobsen SE, Sprenger T, Andersson S, Krogstad J. Neuropsychological assessment and telemedicine: a preliminary study examining the reliability of neuropsychology services performed via telecommunication. Journal of the International Neuropsychological Society 2003;9(3):472–478.

Chapter 10
Therapeutic Alliance in Clinical Videoconferencing: Optimizing the Communication Context

Brian E. Lozano, Anna Hynes Birks, Karen Kloezeman, Nancy Cha, Leslie A. Morland and Peter W. Tuerk

Chapter Summary

Purpose   This chapter addresses methods to establish or bolster therapeutic alliance with patients engaged in clinical videoconferencing (CV). The chapter will present a brief summary of the existing literature on therapeutic alliance to support a discussion of how therapeutic alliance may be impacted when conducting CV services. The chapter will also denote modifications to standard clinical behaviors which have been linked to strong therapeutic alliance in CV settings.

Context   The information is helpful for clinicians and managers because alliance has been demonstrated to be related to clinical outcomes for behavioral treatments. Stakeholders and clinicians new to CV contexts often question the ability of CV services to facilitate appropriate levels of alliance; accordingly, it is helpful to have access to a quick-reference summary in order to provide support for programming. Moreover, though the scientific literature base regarding CV provides broad evidence that appropriate alliance is most often achieved via CV, it is still important to convey specialized nuances of alliance in CV contexts. The authors have logged over 10,000 clinical hours via CV and have amassed a significant amount of highly-specific procedural knowledge regarding at-

B. E. Lozano (✉) · P. W. Tuerk
Department of Psychiatry and Behavioral Sciences, Medical University of South Carolina;
Mental Health Service, Ralph H. Johnson VA Medical Center, Veterans Health Administration,
Charleston, SC, USA
e-mail: Lozano@musc.edu

A. H. Birks
Mental Health Service, Ralph H. Johnson VA Medical Center,
Veterans Health Administration, Charleston, SC, USA
e-mail: anna.birks@va.gov

K. Kloezeman · N. Cha · L. A. Morland
National Center for PTSD—Pacific Islands Division, Department of Veterans
Affairs Pacific Islands Healthcare System, Honolulu, HI, USA

© Springer International Publishing Switzerland 2015   221
P. W. Tuerk, P. Shore (eds.), *Clinical Videoconferencing in Telehealth,*
Behavioral Telehealth, DOI 10.1007/978-3-319-08765-8_10

distance relationship building through practical experience and trial and error. Accordingly, the information is helpful in preventing those new to CV from starting from scratch or recreating the wheel when considering alliance in CV contexts.

Tools   The chapter provides the following tools: a brief review of the literature regarding therapeutic alliance and the effects of alliance on clinical outcomes in CV contexts, a list of psychotherapy contexts in which CV treatment has been associated with strong or adequate patient-provider alliance, a separate list of more general health care domains in which CV treatment has been associated with strong or adequate patient-provider satisfaction, a list of clinical techniques and clinician attributes that have been empirically associated with alliance, a more targeted list of suggestions to bolster alliance in CV contexts, a provider-oriented checklist of tasks to complete before initial CV sessions to safeguard alliance, a provider-oriented checklist of tasks to complete during initial CV sessions to safeguard alliance, and a checklist of procedures for when patients express concerns regarding receiving treatment via CV modalities. Finally, links to resources documenting technical and physical configurations to support alliance in CV contexts are provided, as are sample videos of provider/patient interactions over the modality.

10.1   History and Theory of Therapeutic Alliance

The concept of alliance in the patient-provider relationship is one of the most central and highly studied constructs in psychotherapy research. Teamwork and alliance are cornerstones of many current evidence-based psychotherapies. Historically, emphasis on the therapeutic dynamics between patients and providers has its origins in early psychodynamic approaches to therapy. The significance of a positive therapeutic relationship is conceptualized in Freud's notion of positive transference [1, 2], in which the patient's positive associations with the provider facilitate continued collaboration in treatment despite challenges and distress inherent to the treatment process. Conceptualizations of alliance have since evolved from these early formulations in psychodynamic therapy to current perspectives, which emphasize elements of conscious and active collaboration in all helping relationships. Most current conceptualizations of therapeutic alliance are based, at least in part, on Bordin's definition [3], which asserts that alliance is achieved through collaboration in treatment and consists of three elements: agreement on treatment goals, agreement on the tasks that are part of treatment, and patient–provider reciprocal positive regard.

According to Bordin, alliance influences treatment outcome through its effect on patients' openness to engaging in treatment and confidence in the utility of treatment activities. The continued development of behavioral therapies, physical therapies, and health behavior-related interventions have also led to theories that therapeutic alliance may additionally influence outcomes through its effect on patients' confidence in themselves to complete the proposed treatment activities and attain a target state of being [4].

10.2 Beyond Theory: Empirical Moderators of the Effect of Alliance on Outcome

Continued interest in alliance over the past 20 years stems from empirical findings that diverse psychotherapies often result in similar outcomes, thus, compelling researchers to identify nonspecific factors common to all forms of patient–provider relationships [5]. Meta-analyses investigating associations between therapeutic alliance and psychotherapy outcomes have consistently identified the quality of alliance as being moderately- to highly-related to outcomes in individual psychotherapy for a range of problem areas (e.g., anxiety disorders, depression, disruptive behaviors or delinquency, bereavement, eating disorders, and addiction/substance abuse) for adults [5–8] as well as for children and adolescents [9].

Given the relatively robust association between alliance and treatment outcome, researchers have sought to understand this association more fully by investigating variables that might moderate the alliance–outcome relationship. In general, it appears that the association between alliance and outcome is not influenced by the type or duration of treatment provided, the way in which alliance is measured, or type of treatment outcome used in the study [5–7].

There is less consensus regarding the dynamic measured effects of alliance throughout the course of treatment (i.e., early-, mid-, and late-treatment) especially related to the source of alliance measurement (e.g., patient, provider, or observer). In studies with adult samples, there is evidence suggesting that patients' and observers' reports of alliance are more correlated with outcomes than are those reported by providers [6, 8] and that alliance earlier in treatment (i.e., between sessions 1–5) and late in treatment are slightly better predictors of outcome than alliance measured at mid-treatment [8]. However, others have failed to identify such differences in adult populations [5, 7]. Moreover, studies with child and adolescent samples suggest an opposite trend, with providers' alliance ratings being more strongly associated with outcomes than reports from child and adolescent patients [9] and that measures of alliance late in therapy are generally more strongly associated with outcomes than those obtained early in treatment. Observed differences between adult and child/adolescent samples may be due to developmental differences in social cognitive skills used to accurately evaluate alliance, tendency for child/adolescent patients' report of alliance to be more positively biased, or slower rate of relationship formation among child/adolescent patients [9]. There is, however, an under-identified methodological concern that in both adult and child/adolescent samples, alliance ratings late in therapy may be confounded with treatment outcome.

We believe a helpful focus in understanding the alliance-outcome association can be attained by investigating the relative impact of patient vs. provider factors in alliance. While some studies indicate that patient variables such as problem se-

Table 10.1 Provider behaviors positively related to therapeutic alliance

1. Accurate reflections and interpretation
2. Attending to patient's experience
3. Communicating acceptance and respect
4. Communicating interest
5. Communicating positive expectancy of encounter
6. Communicating sense of hope to meet goals
7. Communicating trust in patient's ability to use skills learned in treatment
8. Conveying a sense of collaboration
9. Conveying genuine interest in treatment process with patient
10. Demonstrating clinical competence
11. Ensuring that patient understands and is comfortable with treatment
12. Expressing ideas coherently
13. Facilitating expression of emotion
14. Facilitating use of patient's healthy coping behaviors and supportive activities
15. Identification and clarification of patient problems
16. Identifying treatment tasks that accurately reflect the patient's goals
17. Making efforts to understand patient
18. Non-defensive response to criticism
19. Noting patient progress toward goals

Given an adequate audiovisual signal, reasonable CV-related threats to these specific provider behaviors are difficult to identify.

verity, type of impairment, and quality of attachment style may impact therapeutic alliance [10–12], there is increasing evidence that suggests therapist variables have greater impact on the alliance–outcome correlation than do patient variables [13–15]. A review of the literature on therapist attributes and techniques that positively impact alliance suggests therapist characteristics such as flexibility, honesty, warmth, openness, and being interested, respectful and trustworthy are important in the development and maintenance of strong therapeutic alliance [16]. Therapist techniques including exploration, accurate reflection and interpretation, affirming, and facilitating expression of emotion are also found to positively impact alliance. In the context of group/family treatment, therapist attributes such as having a calm demeanor, being nonjudgmental, attentive, and unhurried are positively related to the development of strong therapeutic alliance [17]. Interestingly, findings regarding the effect of therapist level of experience on the formation of alliance are equivocal (which may call into question our assertion at the beginning of the chapter that we are uniquely qualified to discuss alliance due to our amassed therapeutic experience!); however, some findings suggest that patients with difficult presentations may achieve stronger alliances with more experienced therapists, whereas, patients with less problematic presentations do not respond differentially based on the therapist's experience [8, 10].

Taken together, the literature indicates that strong alliance in the patient-provider relationship positively impacts treatment outcome across numerous contexts, treatment modalities, patient populations, and problem areas. Moreover, mounting evidence suggests that therapist attributes and particular techniques impact the development of alliance more than patient attributes. This view highlights the importance of fostering specific provider behaviors to support development of strong patient–provider alliance. Table 10.1 provides a list of specific provider behaviors that have been empirically associated with alliance and/or clinical outcomes in behavioral contexts (see for Ackerman and Hilsenroth 2003 [16] for review). Note that it is difficult to identify reasonable CV-related threats to the behaviors listed in Table 10.1, given an adequate audiovisual signal.

10.3 Alliance in Treatment via Clinical Videoconferencing

Thus far, our review and description of literature on therapeutic alliance has been based in the context of in-person patient–provider exchanges. Advances in telecommunication technology have enabled providers of mental health services as well as those in many other health care settings (e.g., primary care, correctional centers) and fields (e.g., dermatology, ophthalmology, oncology, pediatrics, etc.) to effectively meet with patients remotely rather than in-person. The use of CV, which permits patients and providers to see and hear each other in real time across geographical distances, is one example of technology being used by providers in an effort to expand and improve access to treatment services. An area of concern and uncertainty among many providers as they consider initiating CV services is how the modality might alter or interfere with the capacity to effectively develop alliance with patients. Specifically, some psychologists have expressed concern that CV may impede communication of therapist qualities such as warmth, empathy, and understanding during therapy with patients [18]. Accordingly, we now turn to evidence regarding therapeutic alliance as it has been investigated in CV contexts.

Recent reviews of the literature on psychotherapy via CV [19] and CV-based interventions for long-term conditions [20] indicate that treatment delivered via the modality is feasible and typically associated with good user satisfaction. Moreover, the literature demonstrates comparable outcomes to traditional in-person treatment using various treatment approaches with diverse populations and problem areas (e.g., depression, anxiety, eating disorders, physical health problems, and addiction/substance abuse). A randomized controlled trial of 495 patients referred for psychiatric services found similar levels of satisfaction and clinical outcomes for patients assigned to CV or in-person modalities [21]. Moreover, many studies have specifically examined and documented that both patients and providers perceive strong alliance using CV modalities [22–25], as well as comparable alliance to that achieved via in-person treatment [24, 26, 27]. Table 10.2 provides a list of health care domains in which CV treatment has been associated with strong or adequate patient–provider alliance. The table is not exhaustive of all published CV studies assessing alliance; entries were selected to demonstrate wide heterogeneity in services provided.

Beyond demonstrating similarly adequate levels of alliance as in in-person settings, research indicates that CV modalities may be associated with some unique benefits regarding alliance under certain circumstances or with specific patients. Day and Schneider [26] conducted one of the few randomized controlled trials of CV treatment in which patient–provider alliance was examined. They randomly

Table 10.2 Health care domains in which clinical videoconferencing (CV) has been associated with strong or adequate patient–provider alliance

Health care domains	Author
Behavioral family counseling	Bischoff et al. [28]
TBI-specific behavior management for children with TBI	Wade et al. [29]
Family counseling for rural teenagers with epilepsy	Glueckauf et al. [30]
Home-based family counseling for teens with epilepsy	Hufford et al. [31]
Cognitive-behavioral therapy for panic and agoraphobia	Bouchard et al. [23]
Cognitive-behavioral therapy to community sample	Day and Schneider [26]
Cognitive-behavioral therapy for post-traumatic stress disorder (PTSD)	Frueh et al. [32]
Cognitive-behavioral therapy for PTSD	Germain et al. [27]
Cognitive-behavioral therapy for OCD	Himle et al. 2006 [33]
Group therapy for anger with veterans	Greene et al. [34]
General psychiatry & psychology with inmates	Morgan et al. [24]
Assessment of PTSD	Porcari et al. 2009 [35]
General psychology to remote islands from mainland	Simpson [25]
CBT for bulimia to remote islands from mainland	Simpson et al. [36]

assigned patients to receive five sessions of individual cognitive-behavioral therapy (CBT) for various mental health problems delivered in-person, through CV, or by two-way audio. Trained observers' ratings of alliance specifically assessed therapists' exploration, client participation, and client hostility during the fourth session of therapy. Results indicated no significant differences in alliance variables, except that compared to in-person patients, those in the CV and two-way radio conditions were rated higher in participation. The authors speculated that higher ratings of participation among patients in the CV and two-way radio conditions may be due to these patients taking greater responsibility in the patient–provider interaction or that physical distance associated with these modalities made openness in treatment seem safer. Limited support for these hypotheses has been provided by separate findings indicting that some patients report feeling more comfortable communicating by videoconference [37] and that treatment by CV is associated with an increased sense of personal space, perceived control, and that it is less intimidating for some than meeting with providers for in-person treatment [36, 38]. For these reasons it has been suggested that treatment by videoconference may be particularly well suited for patients who experience high levels of shame, self-consciousness, or who have greater need for sense of control; however, there has yet to be empirical examination of these specific patient variable as they relate to treatment by CV.

While the balance of data seems to indicate that CV modalities do not pose additional threats to therapeutic alliance in general, there are reports from rigorous studies that do highlight attenuated alliance in CV conditions when treating *groups* of people. In two randomized controlled trials, one in a group therapy setting [34] and one in a family therapy setting [30], patients who received treatment by CV reported lower alliance with providers than those who received treatment in-person. Yet, it is difficult to interpret the meaning of these differences because both studies note generally high alliance in each condition with no differences between conditions in clinical outcomes. One might conclude that these CV group treatments may be associated with lower alliance compared to the in-person group treatments, but that a critical level of alliance was still maintained so as to not negatively impact outcomes. Indeed, other studies of CV group indicate adequate alliance. An investigation of a home-based CV intervention for adolescents with epilepsy and their families [31] found that reported distraction in using videoconferencing media was low and that alliance and comfort ratings were universally high across CV modalities. Similarly, strong therapeutic alliance was achieved with a web-based CV problem-solving intervention for children with traumatic brain injury and their parents [29]. While children with traumatic brain injury and their siblings rated therapists highly in terms of caring, younger children and those with brain injury noted difficulty attending to and comprehending the therapist through videoconferencing. When employing CV in group formats, it is recommended that a group be no larger than approximately 5–7 members to ensure that the provider can view all of the group members within the camera's field of vision.

Findings from less stringent nonrandomized and noncontrolled studies regarding alliance in CV modalities are generally consistent with the results from randomized controlled trials in demonstrating adequate levels of alliance and satisfaction with treatment through CV. Table 10.2 lists a number of diverse domains where alliance was measured. As an example, let us consider an investigation of alliance with patients engaged in CV or in-person CBT for posttraumatic stress disorder (PTSD) [27]. Patients reported high ratings of alliance in both conditions. Development of alliance was not differentially related to patients' report of initial perception of videoconference meetings or initial comfort with remote communication. This suggests that effective alliance can be established even when patients are initially reticent. Therapist attitudes toward videoconferencing were not assessed even though none of the providers in the study had any prior experience with CV. Nonuniformity in methods and measures used to investigate alliance in CV contexts is a concern for scientific efficiency in discovering potentially nuanced relationships and understandings; however, such nonuniformity in methods and measures also lends weight and credibility to the general main finding that alliance is most often adequate or high in CV contexts. In other words, no matter how, when, or where we ask the question, the answer is generally the same.

10.4   Patient Satisfaction with Clinical Videoconferencing

CV technologies are utilized in a number of health-care domains other than psychotherapy, including primary care, specialized medical treatment, and follow-up services. Studies investigating treatment through videoconferencing in these domains do not often include assessment of patient–provider alliance per se, however, many report on broader patient/provider satisfaction with treatment delivered via videoconferencing. Satisfaction is perceived to be a necessary first step for the development of good therapist–client relationships [62]. These studies offer additional

Table 10.3 Health care domains in which clinical videoconferencing (CV) has been associated with strong or adequate patient satisfaction

Health care domains	Author
Medical checkups for older adults	Bratton and Short [39]
CBT for depression in cancer patients	Cluver et al. [40]
Intervention for speech—language impairments	Constantinescu et al. [41, 42]
Biofeedback for the treatment of pain	Earles et al. [43]
Group therapy for alcohol use disorders	Frueh et al. [44]
Specialty medical services	Gustke et al. [45]
Behavioral treatment for weight-control	Harvey-Berino [46]
Urinary incontinence in older women	Hui [47]
Management of chronic cardiovascular diseases	Karagiannis et al. [48]
Methadone maintenance	King et al. [49]
Pediatric anxiety and pain	Lingley-Pottie and McGrath [50]
Dermatology	Loane et al. [51]
Dermatology	Lowitt et al. [52]
Voice therapy	Mashima et al. [53]
Psychiatric care for migrants and refugees	Mucic [54]
Adult psychiatry	O'Reilly et al. [21]
Occupational therapy and physiotherapy	Sanford [55]
CBT for anxiety in cancer patients	Shepherd et al. [56]
Intervention for speech—language impairments	Sicotte et al. [57]
Home-based mental health care	Shore et al. [58]
Assessment of communication and swallowing postlaryngectomy	Ward et al. [59]
Assessment of chronic fatigue syndrome	Weatherburn et al. [60]
Management of chronic pulmonary disease and heart failure	Whitten and Mickus [61]

information regarding the acceptability of provider–patient interactions through videoconferencing, and might be used as a proxy measure for the concept of alliance in nonpsychotherapeutic health care settings. However, there are limits to equating alliance with satisfaction that are worth noting. Unlike alliance in psychotherapy, satisfaction in broader healthcare settings is not always associated with positive clinical outcomes. Notably, there is a growing literature suggesting that high patient satisfaction with medical services is associated with poorer health outcomes in some contexts, utilization overuse, and even higher mortality rates [63]. Ostensibly, this may be due to decisions regarding prescribed medications and procedures being too influenced by patients' desires and perceptions. Regardless, satisfaction, as measured in the context of CV, most often focuses on the quality of communication and other CV-related factors. Accordingly, we believe that considering the data on CV satisfaction will further the goals of this chapter in a relevant way.

Based on their review of videoconferencing services for individuals with a range of physical disabilities, Kairy and colleagues [64] concluded that treatment via videoconferencing yields clinical outcomes that are at least comparable to conventional interventions and that patient and provider satisfaction with the videoconferencing modality was consistently high, regardless of the patient population, setting, or study design. Similarly, Gustke et al. [45] reported a 98 % satisfaction rate among 495 patients receiving CV-based care from a variety of specialty clinics (e.g., dermatology, allergy, cardiology, psychiatry, and endocrinology). No significant differences in satisfaction were correlated with sociodemographic variables; however, lack of variability in satisfaction ratings may have limited capacity to detect such correlations.

Favorable satisfaction with CV services has been documented by studies with diverse patient populations and in various contexts, including: management of diabetes for reducing hospitalizations [65], methadone maintenance [49], connecting refugees to bilingual providers [54], general medical check-ups with geriatric patients [39], CBT for depression [40] and anxiety [56] in patients with cancer, intervention for speech-language impairments [41, 42, 57], biofeedback in the treatment of pain and other physiological disorders [43], group therapy for alcohol use disorders [44], behavioral weight-control treatment for obesity [46], dermatology treatment [51, 52], management of urinary incontinence [47], treatment for pediatric anxiety or recurrent headache/abdominal pain [50], occupational therapy and physiotherapy [55], assessment of communication and swallowing postlaryngectomy [59], assessment of chronic fatigue syndrome [60], management of chronic obstructive pulmonary disease and/or congestive heart failure [61], and management of severe chronic cardiovascular diseases [48]. Table 10.3 identifies these and a sampling of other domains where satisfaction with CV modalities has been found to be favorable or adequate.

As reported in many of these studies, much of what comprises patient satisfaction with treatment by videoconferencing is captured by patients' affirmative statements reflecting: appreciation of the CV option for increasing accessibility to care, convenience associated with decreased time and money for associated travel, perceived comfort and privacy with videoconferencing, ease of using videoconferencing equipment, minimal interruption due to technical difficulties, being able to clearly see and hear providers with adequate audio/video quality, feeling present with provider during sessions (i.e., forgetting that they are communicating through videoconference monitor), and perceived similarity in terms of quality of care compared to in-person treatment. In contrast, some patients have noted concern or dissatisfaction with instances of poor audio/visual quality and technical difficulties, confidentiality or privacy, and hesitancy due to unfamiliarity with the videoconferencing equipment. In most cases, however, patients relate overall positive experience and satisfaction with videoconferencing despite these difficulties and appear more receptive to it after some experience with CV treatment delivery.

Findings on satisfaction with treatment through videoconferencing are encouraging and suggest that patient satisfaction with videoconferencing is consistently high, regardless of the patient population, setting, or study design. However, many of these studies suffer from weak methodological design, small sample sizes, and measurement issues such as poor description of measures, lack of standardization, and few comparisons of satisfaction ratings between videoconferencing and control conditions, thereby limiting unequivocal conclusions regarding underlying reasons for satisfaction or dissatisfaction with treatment through videoconferencing [64, 66, 67].

10.5 Providers' Perspectives on Treatment via Clinical Videoconferencing

While the overwhelming majority of studies suggest patients are highly satisfied receiving treatment through videoconferencing, providers often report less favorable perceptions or attitudes of providing services via videoconferencing [20, 68]. In general, clinicians are reported to be less comfortable adopting new technology into their practice than are their patients [69, 70], raising concerns that providers' negative expectations may impede effective use of CV technologies. Provider characteristics reported to negatively impact alliance including being uncertain, critical, or tense [71], which may be factors if providers are uncomfortable with CV [27]. Interestingly, psychologists' ratings of alliance in videoconferencing sessions have been shown to be biased by negative pretreatment expectations regarding the modality [18].

Barriers or challenges in using videoconferencing technology often reported by providers include concerns regarding: negative effects of CV on personal relationships with patients, appropriateness of CV for certain patient populations, acceptance of CV by patients, and being able to effectively intervene during crisis with patients [37, 72, 73]. Additional provider concerns relate to technical and organizational aspects of CV such as additional workload or time associated with CV, quality of audio/video reception, operation of the equipment or managing technical difficulties, and the need for patient/provider education and training on how to use CV equipment. Even when providers perceive CV technology to be useful for treatment delivery, it is their perceptions of ease of use that predict how frequently they utilize the technology with patients [74]. Lack of confidence to manage problems with videoconferencing equipment is cited as a concern among both patients and providers [75, 76] and lack of training in and opportunity to use CV equipment predict low confidence with CV among mental health workers [77]. Providers who receive training in the use of CV technology report finding it easier to use and are more likely to use it with their patients [72]. Others have noted that providers' attitudes regarding videoconferencing shift toward more positive perspectives as they gain more experience delivering treatment through the modality [37]. Furthermore, the organizational culture and perceptions of CV among colleagues greatly influence one's perceptions and openness to the modality. Gagnon et al. [78] surveyed factors that influence the use of telemedicine among physicians and found that the decision to use this technology was greatly influenced by the provider's perception of how their professional peer group views telemedicine. These findings highlight the importance of an organizational culture supportive of the use of CV where providers receive relevant training in the use of CV equipment and are encouraged to gain experience with the modality.

Many providers often convey positive attitudes toward videoconferencing. Studies that assessed providers' perspectives on treatment through videoconferencing reveal perceived benefits or advantages of CV, including: increased access to care, increased frequency of provider–patient contact, increased continuity and consistency in therapeutic relationships, improvement in facilitating timely responses to patient problems, and opportunity to provide care at patients' homes to decrease wait times for services and patient travel time. Providers have also indicated high levels of satisfaction regarding the use of CV to facilitate evidence based treatments in novel settings. Tuerk and colleagues found high approval ratings by psychologists using CV to facilitate international clinical case review and training in evidence based treatments for PTSD in postdisaster settings [79]. Thus, many providers are well aware of potential benefits associated with offering clinical services and clinical case review through CV. As noted previously, evidence suggests that providers' attitudes regarding CV become more favorable with increased experience.

In sum, the majority of evidence to date on alliance in treatment through CV suggests that patients and providers are able to achieve strong alliance using CV and comparable alliance to that achieved with in-person treatment. Moreover, there is some suggestion that some patients may actually prefer communicating via CV due to increased sense of control, privacy, and feeling less intimidated during encounters with providers. The limited data on the use of CV for conducting group therapy or with certain patient populations (e.g., younger children or individuals with brain damage) suggests that good alliance can be established even in these contexts, albeit at lower levels than with in-person treatment. Attention to aspects of the CV equipment and associated features (e.g., image/audio quality; picture-in-picture function) is helpful in fostering more positive experiences with treatment through videoconferencing. While these findings are encouraging, and provide a strong base to support the dissemination of CV-oriented treatment delivery, many of the studies utilize less than rigorous methodological designs, small sample sizes, have not been able to take advantage of standardized measurement of alliance and clinical outcome variables [19], and were conducted by "champions" or advocates of CV dissemination. Accordingly, less is known regarding alliance outcomes for broadly disseminated "at-scale" initiatives or for situations where providers were not given a choice. However, the positive findings are noteworthy and significant given their consistency across a range of treatment approaches with diverse populations and problem areas.

10.6 Methods to Foster Therapeutic Alliance in Clinical Videoconferencing: The Intersection of Technology, Environment, and Provider Behaviors

As the literature on alliance and CV suggests, sustained implementation of successful programs necessitates attention to technology-related, environment-related, and provider-related variables. Many factors should be optimized to facilitate ease of CV communication and alliance. Although studies almost universally evidence high rates of alliance over CV mediums, perhaps conveying a nonchalance about the necessity of even attending to it, it is important to keep in mind that most of the studies were conducted by providers and managers who were specifically interested in CV modalities, and thus paid close attention to relevant clinical details and ongoing program evaluation/improvements. Accordingly, in the sections that follow, we offer suggestions derived from the empirical literature, our own experiences, and the experiences of our extended network of colleagues regarding how to cultivate positive therapeutic relationships with patients through CV.

10.6.1 Technological Functions and Pitfalls

10.6.1.1 Picture-in-Picture (PIP)

The ability of patients and providers to see *themselves* on a monitor during CV treatment represents perhaps a larger departure from in-person communication than the ability of patients and providers to see and hear each other on a monitor. All CV systems provide a self-view function, often called picture-in-picture (PIP). The PIP function allows users to see themselves at all times in a small square located in one corner of the screen. In a study comparing effectiveness of CBT for panic disorder with agoraphobia delivered via CV or in-person, Bouchard et al. [23] reported high ratings of alliance and comparable positive treatment outcomes in both conditions. The authors suggested that providers' use of the PIP function during CV sessions may have assisted with development of high alliance because the feature provides continuous visual feedback to the provider regarding their performance (e.g., nonverbal communication) and fosters attention to more effective communication. However, most of us using social videoconferencing technologies have had the experience of being distracted by our real-time image, either due to vanity, novelty, or just having more to look at and process in front of us. Accordingly, Bouchard's interpretation regarding the usefulness of provider-end PIP must be weighed against the potential for provider distraction. Though the question is still awaiting empirical study, most providers seem to appreciate and use PIP as standard practice for a variety of functions.

A clear distinction should be made between PIP use on the provider side and PIP use on the patient side, which should be avoided as the default CV policy, unless there is an identified clinical reason for it. Self-viewing may be important for patients engaged in a primary care or dermatology appointment, who wish to show their doctor swelling or abnormalities on their body. In such cases, it allows patients to see what the doctor is seeing so that they can position the target clearly. However, in general we do not want patients distracted by their own image while interacting with health professionals. More specifically, it is not ideal to foster in the patient a constant awareness and/or meta-awareness of their own appearance. Use of PIP on the patient end may lead to disruption in communication, exacerbate distress, or make the sharing of intense emotions more difficult. The potential unhelpful effects of constant self-visual feedback may be particularly notable among patients presenting with body-image difficulties, or who are emotionally guarded, or new to therapy [36, 77]. Although this question is far from being resolved empirically, we generally recommend that alliance is best served in clinical settings by only having the provider-end configurations set to PIP. Thus patients will be free to focus on the provider, while the provider will have an extra tool to help gauge patient perception and guide therapeutic communication. Occasionally the PIP feature is enabled at the patient site without the provider being aware; this can often be detected through attention to the patient's eye contact (e.g., eyes repeatedly shifting or gravitating to a certain location on the monitor). Providers can communicate with patients or staff at the patient site to ensure that PIP is turned off.

There are several common exceptions to the default of discouraging the self-view option for patients. In non-office based CV contexts, that is, home-based or mobile device-based CV, the PIP setting may be necessary for patients to appropriately frame the sessions. However, if possible, providers should ask that the PIP be turned off once camera and body positioning are established. In family- or group-based CV interventions, the PIP can be useful to give group members the ability to self-regulate their movements to stay within the monitor frame. Even if the camera and room are adjusted beforehand to fit all the chairs, patients can shift and move out of frame. When this occurs it is important that clinicians notice, and stay in constant verbal communication with the patient until he or she is back in view. Enabling the PIP in group or family contexts can help to minimize such disruptions. Additionally, it should be noted that the potential deleterious effects of patient self-view may be somewhat mitigated in group contexts, as individuals are sitting further away from the camera and will not be getting close-up feedback focused on their faces. Interestingly, it may be entirely possible that PIP in family or groups settings could be found to play a therapeutic role in unification, in so much as it provides constant feedback or meta-awareness that the family or group is together and doing something together (ostensibly) for the positive benefit of all involved. Of course, this notion has not been empirically validated in therapeutic settings.

10.6.1.2   Eye Contact

On a CV unit, unless the clinician is looking directly at the camera, there is no "direct" eye contact. In other words, when the clinician is looking directly at the patient on the monitor, it appears to the patient as if the clinician is looking at the patient's face, but not making direct eye contact.

Eye contact plays an important role in the communication of empathy and respect. Dowell and Berman [80] suggest that therapists with increased eye contact and a forward leaning posture communicate greater empathy and treatment credibility. Achieving good, direct eye contact during CV encounters is a common area of concern among providers starting CV and while challenges exist, minor adjustments can facilitate more direct eye contact and enhance communication. Here it should be noted, as in in-person clinical encounters, that appropriate levels of eye contact can very culturally.

During CV encounters the camera is typically located directly above the monitor and consequently limits the perception of direct eye contact. It has been suggested that to perceive direct eye contact through videoconferencing the camera angle should be 7° [81, 82]. Other factors that influence perception of direct eye contact include the distance from one's eyes to the camera, the distance from one's eyes to the center of the display, and the difference in height between the camera and the center of the display [82]. There are several strategies to assist with improving perceptions of direct eye contact through videoconferencing. Ideally, the image of the person on the monitor should be as close to the camera lens as possible. With most software platforms that support CV the provider can easily move the patient's image to just below the lens and can instruct the patient to do the same. Providers can also alternate their gaze between the monitor and the lens depending on whether they are speaking or listening to the patient. One way to increase the perception of continuous eye contact is for the provider to sit further away from the CV camera and to zoom in. This "zoom method" minimizes subtle distinctions in gaze as the provider toggles attention between the camera and the screen image, and it also encourages a perception of direct eye contact, as the angel of line from the lens to the provider's eye is decreased.

As in all therapeutic encounters and especially so with CV encounters, repeated and prolonged instances of providers averting their gaze away from the patient to take notes or review the medical chart can negatively affect quality of eye contact and perceived attentiveness. Similarly, provider behaviors indicating they are hurried or in a rush can negatively impact alliance in treatment. Providers can ensure better eye contact and unhurried, undivided attention during CV encounters by being well organized and prepared for the patient visit and having all necessary treatment materials at hand. Many practitioners choose to reduce their amount of note taking during CV encounters or otherwise communicate to patients what they are doing when their gaze is averted. Despite challenges to nonverbal communication during CV encounters, providers generally find that they are sufficiently able to observe and reflect facial expression and other nonverbal indicators of affect.

10.6.1.3 Microphones, Volume, and Muting:

The CV equipment loop will often produce an echo effect. This occurs when microphones pick up and transmit back the far-side vocalizations coming through the speakers. Accordingly, the simplest way to address this problem, when it occurs, is to turn down your volume and/or check to see if the patient would care to turn down the volume on the other side. Echoes from the microphone can also be reduced by increasing the distance between the microphone and speakers, using a headset microphone, and sometimes, by unplugging and plugging the microphone back in again. Of these options, inquiring about the volume on the patient end is the best place to start, especially to safeguard alliance and to use our tools optimally. For example, consider a scenario where the patient-side volume is uncomfortably loud for the patient, but she is just tolerating it. An echo ensues, potentially signaling to the provider that the patient volume is too loud. However, reflexively (out of repetition) the provider instructs the patient to pull the microphone away from the speakers. The echo is now solved, but the volume is still too loud for the patient.

Having the volume set too loudly is a common occurrence, especially for providers who are new to CV. Excessive volume threatens the privacy of the encounter, is not conducive to optimal communication, and is not pleasant for nearby providers and patients. Providers should invite colleagues to slip notes under their door during CV sessions if their patients can be heard in the hallway.

CV systems always include a muting option. The muting option is a wonderful means for patients to retain privacy during home-based CV encounters, if a family member unexpectedly interrupts the session with a question or need. Teaching patients how to use their mute options, giving them permission to do so, and affirming their right to privacy is an effective technique to begin building alliance in the first session. Clinicians are also able to mute their microphone at any time. The function is useful for providers to go about their business after they have already logged on to a session, but are waiting for the patient to arrive or be walked back. The mute function can also be used if there is an unexpected knock at the door or if an emergency page requires a response. However, it is suggested that clinicians not only indicate why and when they are muting the patient, but also get confirmation that the patient understands and agrees to being muted. Unfortunately, because the muting option exists, some providers may be tempted to overuse it, answering more phone calls than they should (not just the emergencies calls).

10.6.1.4 Pixilated Images and Dropped Calls:

If neither the provider nor the patient can be seen clearly or smoothly due to low connectivity, establishing alliance or any shared content-related communication will be difficult. Graham et al. [83] reported that alliance, as rated by a single provider, was universally low when using a low-cost analog video-phone link with an 8×8 monitor for assessment and diagnosis of inpatients in a rheumatology clinic. These findings highlight challenges associated with using CV equipment lacking in sufficient audio/video quality. When adequate equipment is not available, or when state-of-the-art equipment is limited by low connectivity, we recommend a relatively low threshold for providers to abandon the CV platform mid-session in favor of telephone communication to preserve therapeutic alliance and protect the integrity of session content. Psychotherapies, even nuanced psychotherapies, such as exposure with response prevention (ERP) for obsessive-compulsive disorder (OCD), have been shown to be effective via telephone communication [84–86], so finishing off a single session over the telephone, in many cases, is not a particularly experimental or risky proposition.

10.6.2   The Physical Environment

10.6.2.1   Lighting and the Communication Context

Lighting in the CV room affects the ability of patients and providers to clearly see one another, to notice nuances of expression, and to not be distracted by stark shadows or bright glares. Lighting issues can be optimized by attention to the types, number, and positioning of lights, and the treatment room configuration. Situating a window in direct view of the camera will likely overexpose the view and should be avoided (images highlighting proper and improper CV room configurations can be accessed online at: http://behavioraltelehealth.org/v1/c10/room).

In order to minimize shadows, it is best to close window blinds and to utilize either diffuse fluorescent lighting or multiple lighting sources. Many providers prefer desk lamps to overhead florescent lighting for aesthetic reasons; accordingly, if desk lamps are used, attention should be given to locate them on both sides of the clinician and preferably behind the camera. Lighting can also cast glares on a white board, framed art work, and medical equipment. In such cases it will be necessary to change either the angle the camera, angle of the object causing glare, or position of the lighting.

10.6.2.2   Patient Room Configuration

As noted, the CV camera should not be directly facing windows, which may have consequences for furniture placement in the CV room. There are other important factors with regard to furniture placement in CV rooms, many are especially relevant for fostering (or at least not hindering) alliance in CV. The patient chair should be directly facing and close to the CV camera. Although body movements may be important to observe in many CV contexts, it is much more important to have a clear and reasonably large view of patients' faces and upper torso. Some CV systems allow the chair to be further away (because of zooming capabilities), and clinicians may prefer to have the option of panning and zooming out for a full body view depending on the circumstances of the conversation. Even so, if the chair is too far away, it may be difficult for the patient to keep their head in the frame of a zoomed-in shot, which would require frequent camera adjustment by the provider. At the same time, frequent panning (which is noticeable at the patient end as the camera moves back and forth) and frequent zooming (which is also noticeable as the lens that patients are staring into dilates and perhaps makes a sound) can be alienating and can unduly objectify patients. Accordingly, forethought, practice, and flexibility with room configurations may be necessary to facilitate alliance while also accommodating provider preference.

At times during treatment, clinicians may want to convey a sense of privacy to allow patients "the space" to feel their emotions, find the right words, or adjust clothing in the case of physical exams. This can be achieved by the clinician slightly turning their head or averting their eyes and is best not conveyed by slanted chair configurations that are more common in in-person settings. Additionally, care should be taken to not to place tables, desks, or other large objects between the patients and camera, such configurations can create a feeling of distance.

In group or family treatment settings, the chairs should be situated in a semi-circle, where patients are able to see one another, as well as the CV screen. Depending on the type of group treatment, a table can be helpful, with the semicircle forming around the table. Once the room is arranged, the clinician may be able to utilize pre-set view functions on the CV system to maximize effective communication in real-time with the push of a button.

Attending to room-related issues will help minimize any real or perceived effect of distance and maximize effective communication/alliance. Even so, CV clinical space is often shared space, which complicates room configuration issues and may place extra burdens on clinical and support staff at the patient end. Multiple chapters in this volume recommend making visits to partner sites before implementing CV services. On these visits, the clinician should check out the designated CV rooms and discuss potential solutions if needed. However, the main purpose of site visits is to build relationships with the partner site providers and administrative support staff—the success of CV programming hinges on their buy-in. Accordingly, configuration issues (especially involving moving furniture or disrupting an established office) should take a back seat to relationship building. If good relationships are established, it will be easier to address room issues later. On the other hand, if provider-side staff come across as overly entitled or demanding upon first impression (and it might not take much for overworked support staff to feel or create that vibe) it may be difficult to get the site to even walk patients back in time, let alone discuss the nuances of chair placement with you. Accordingly, it is necessary to tolerate less than ideal room configurations for the sake of intra-facility relationships, especially at first.

In home-based CV, clinicians and staff have less control over patient-side room configurations. At the same time, there may be more obstacles in home environments that do not present themselves in office settings (e.g., crying children, a knock on the door, land-line phones ringing). Privacy is a primary concern in home-based CV sessions and so options regarding what rooms to use might be limited. Providers must be flexible and creative when helping patients identify or create environments conducive to home-based CV. The process should be viewed as a means to build rapport and alliance in the early stages of treatment. Research suggests that home-based CV can enhance aspects of provider understanding as a result of clinical contact with a patient's actual milieu. Accordingly, depending on the clinical service offered, we suggest reviewing the patient's home layout with him or her (if the patient seems open to this), not only to help identify potentially useful space and configurations for CV treatment, but also as a means to gather relevant alliance-building information, such as the names of family members, or knowledge that there is a trophy room, favorite chair, or absolutely no privacy outside of the bathroom.

Care should be taken in home-based CV to help patients structure their physical environments in a way that will help them adhere to and maximize the usefulness of established home-based CV expectations. Chapter 7, Sect. 7.5.2 discusses provider and patient expectations for home-based CV. The authors recommend having appropriate bandwidth in home settings. This requirement relates to the physical environment in that being physically close to a wireless router promotes faster speeds. Not having other devices (including smart phones and tablets) on the network during CV sessions can be essential in getting the most out of a patient's Wi-Fi system and minimizing disruptions.

10.6.2.3   Keeping the Background in the Back

For years telehealth IT staff have warned against having highly patterned wall hangings or wearing brightly colored clothing when conducting CV. One of the issues is that highly textured or brightly patterned backgrounds and clothing create a higher demand for the amount of information that has to be transmitted, resulting in slower transmission speeds. To some providers, this notion can sound like science-fiction, or otherwise it is easy to assume that the extra burden on a network is negligible. Even so, and against our own expectations, we have witnessed the speed-zapping effect of patterned backgrounds first hand. As slow transmission speeds, pixilation, and choppy audio feeds all threaten clear communication and alliance, we have learned to "keep it tame" on the camera side of our treatment rooms.

A related issue often commented on in the CV literature is that brightly patterned clothing can be a distraction to patients in CV contexts or can lead to patient dizziness, especially if the clinician is given to gesturing when speaking (which is recommended for CV communication and alliance). In general, neutral, solid colors are most easy to view, with the exception of white, which has the tendency to blend into walls, making it difficult for patients to distinguish the outlines of the provider (images available at: http://behavioraltelehealth.org/v1/c10/lighting).

10.6.3   Provider Behaviors to Foster Alliance

10.6.3.1   Verbal Communication

Some providers find that they tend to rely more on vocal strategies to facilitate expression of affect during CV encounters. Additionally, there is some suggestion that patients engaged in CV treatment may participate more, verbally, in the therapeutic encounter or feel more empowered to ask questions than with in-person visits [26, 87]. The flow of conversations during CV encounters may encourage greater back and forth communication and often requires deliberate turn-taking from persons involved. Given that a very slight audio delay may exist, it is helpful for the provider to ensure turn taking to reduce discomfort or hesitation on the patient's part. In response to instances of patients and providers talking over each other, the provider can invite the patient to continue speaking by pausing and gesturing to their ear, or leaning in and slightly turning their ear toward the camera, signifying that the provider is in listening, not talking, mode. Typically, this kind of turn-taking with verbal exchanges develops naturally within the first few encounters, as both patients and providers adjust to any delay in verbal transmission and accommodate to the communication styles of one another. Rather than being a barrier to effective communication, the provider's attention to and collaboration with turn-taking in conversations lends itself to development of positive alliance in that it can convey flexibility, genuine interest, respect, and attentiveness.

Attention to one's volume and tone of voice during CV encounters is an important concern. A common behavior of providers new to CV is to increase the volume of their voice when speaking with patients during CV encounters. This is similar to the experience of increasing the volume of one's voice when speaking through a cellular phone. However, both patients and providers can speak with a normal/moderate volume (just as one would during an in-person visit) and the audio will transmit effectively. Speaking too loudly stilts the tone that most providers typically use for clinical encounters and it also threatens the privacy of the CV encounter. As in the example regarding speaker volume levels, identified in Sect. 10.6.1.3, providers should invite their colleagues to slip notes under their door during CV sessions if they can be heard in the hallway. Catching providers in the act will lead to quicker extinction of the loud-talking behavior (we know from personal experience).

10.6.3.2 Nonverbal Communication

There are challenging aspects of both verbal and nonverbal communication unique to encounters through CV. The ability to directly observe certain aspects of nonverbal communication is reduced slightly with CV due to generally not seeing the patient's arms, hands, or legs during encounters. However, with sufficient bandwidth, subtle changes in facial expression and other nonverbal indicators of affect such as tearfulness, shaking, increased respiration, or a withdrawn demeanor, can be detected. Certain articles of clothing, such as a hat, can obscure and further limit visibility of facial expressions. In these instances, requesting that the patient remove the hat in session and providing him or her with the rationale for this can effectively improve visibility of facial expression. Table 10.4 provides general suggestions to facilitate therapeutic alliance in CV contexts.

It is also important that patients be able to see a clear and adequately large image of their provider in order to facilitate a positive CV encounter. Sharpley et al. [88] found that patients' perception of rapport was positively correlated with providers' communication through facial expression. Thus, a patient's capacity to clearly observe their provider's facial expressions contributes to his/her ability to detect expressions of warmth, genuineness, and empathy from the provider. Many health care providers convey much meaning through body positioning and nonverbal communication. Because body perception is limited in CV contexts, providers may wish to convey more with their facial expressions and hand gestures. This may amount to clinicians slightly exaggerating their normal style, a bit more than they would if actually in the room with the patient. Being slightly more animated does seem to

Table 10.4 General suggestions to facilitate therapeutic alliance in clinical videoconferencing

1. Be well organized and prepared for patient visit
2. Ensure adequate eye contact with patient by
a. Making sure you and patient are seated squarely in front of camera lens
b. Adjusting your view of the patient such that the patient's face on your screen is close to the camera lens. Do the same for patient's view if you have control of remote screen options, otherwise instruct patient
c. Alternate your gaze between the monitor and the lens of the camera when speaking and/or listening to the patient
d. Sit further away from the CV camera and zoom-in to your face. This will minimize subtleties in eye movements
3. Let patient "play with" and learn functions of the remote control on patient-end
4. Consider reducing amount of note taking during CV encounters or otherwise communicate to patients what you are doing when your gaze is averted
5. Be aware of tendency to increase the volume of one's voice when conversing through CV. Try to speak with a normal/moderate volume and assist patients or patient-site staff with adjusting the volume on CV equipment as needed
6. Be informed regarding the patient's environment and culture. Strategies include
a. Research local shopping areas, restaurants, events, and other specific attractions in the patient's local community, make reference to them or show interest
b. Refer to online maps to get a birds-eye view of the patient's community
c. Ask patient about the area
d. Visiting the local area, if possible
e. Do not look up patient's specific address or search it without consent
7. If patient wears clothing such as a hat/cap that obscures visibility of facial expressions, kindly request that the patient remove the hat/cap during CV encounters and provide him/her with the rationale for this request
8. Use every additional piece of information or plan that is necessary for CV encounter as an opportunity to build team work

be an effective strategy of engagement over CV mediums. Of course, care should be taken to (1) remain authentic and not accidentally sound patronizing, (i.e., using exaggerated tones as if talking to a child); and (2) incorporate variability in gestures, that is, avoid overly repetitive movements. For example, head nodding is a common technique to convey active listening, yet repetitive head nodding (when all the patient can see is the provider's head), may be distracting or annoying. In other words, we are suggesting only slightly more animation than usual and incorporating perhaps more variability in nonverbal communication techniques.

10.6.3.3 Understanding the Patient's Community

There are many strategies that can assist in the development of a strong therapeutic alliance with patients over CV. In addition to the actual physical distance between the provider and patient, CV often connects patients in rural areas to providers in urban areas. The differences in these two environments can influence many factors, including patient perceptions of feeling understood and the inclination to trust or be open with their provider. Therefore, it is critical for providers to educate themselves about patients' environments and culture. Strategies include researching the area online, mapping it, becoming familiar with local business and restaurant names, discussing the area with the patient, and even visiting if possible.

Understanding patients' communities is useful in building alliance for variety CV-related clinical contexts. For example, if a primary care provider were to suggest walking as a daily exercise for an older adult who doesn't drive, it might be helpful for her to know that there are no sidewalks in the patient's county, but that the local bus route goes to the mall, where the patient can safely walk and take the bus back home. CBT therapists can also utilize on-line resources to help develop relevant behavioral activation exercises or in-vivo exposure therapy exercises. Being familiar with patients' communities is also an important strategy to avoid negative alliance-threatening interactions. For example consider a therapist who tries to give an in-vivo homework assignment to his patient with PTSD. The therapist might say, "go to a crowded restaurant in town and stay there until your distress comes down." Imagine how the patient might feel about his therapist's ability to understand him, if the only building in "town" was a one-room post office. This is truly an unfortunate case of "same planet, different worlds," and it is entirely the provider's fault for making assumptions and not investigating his patient's community.

Even when behavioral exposures are not part of the treatments being offered via CV, it is generally a good idea to casually refer to or inquire about specific attractions or restaurants in the patient's area over CV. This can relay care, increase connection, and at least demonstrate a good will attempt to understand the patient's environment; it also provides an opportunity for informal alliance-building small-talk or chance for patients to educate providers about their home town.

10.7 Getting Off on the Right Foot: Procedural Protocols to Initiate CV and Address Patient Concerns

10.7.1 Optimizing Alliance Prior to the Initial Clinical Videoconferencing Encounter

The tone and dynamics of patient–provider relationships may be established fairly quickly, even within the first few minutes of an initial encounter. First impressions present opportunities for providers to foster the foundation of a working relationship that promotes trust and collaboration. However, even prior to the first encounter via CV, special care should be made to ensure that patients are aware that appointments will be through the modality. If providers themselves are not scheduling the initial appointment, it is recommended that support staff inform patients that the encounter will occur through CV. Accordingly, it is important that support staff also communicate the merits and benefits associated with treatment services delivered through videoconferencing. Therapists should take the time to discuss or model the communication for support staff. See Chap. 7 for an in-depth discussion of the informed consent process in CV contexts.

Table 10.5 Provider checklist prior to first clinical videoconferencing session

1. Initiate introductions and establish communication with support staff at patient site as well as with support staff at your site
2. If possible, coordinate a visit to patient site in order to meet clinical and support staff, and become more familiar with the surrounding area, layout of the facility, and the rooms used for CV
3. Clarify logistics, including: methods for communicating with support and clinical staff, patient check-in procedures, exchange of patient measures, and identification of point of contact for issues regarding CV equipment (it can be helpful to create a resource guide that includes this information)
4. Review and ensure reliable access to detailed emergency procedures specific to patient-site
5. Become familiar with and practice using CV equipment. Familiarize yourself with the remote control, settings of the device, and camera. Practice initiating and disconnecting calls
6. Experiment with the PIP (i.e., self-view) function on your CV device to determine your own comfort and preference with this feature and also to ensure that the patient's view of you and your office space, including lighting and camera angle, are of sufficient quality
7. Prior to initial encounter with patient through videoconferencing, ensure that patient is aware that the appointment will be conducted through videoconferencing

It is reasonable to anticipate that some providers may feel uneasy about using CV initially, especially if they have limited experience with the technology. Provider anxiety has been associated with less empathic responding and may limit alliance in treatment [89]. Thus, prior to meeting with patients through videoconferencing, it is important that providers take steps to promote comfort and confidence in their use of the equipment. A first step is to become familiar and practice with the videoconferencing equipment. Another important step in facilitating provider comfort with CV is establishing good communication (via phone or in-person) with support staff at the patient-site prior to the scheduled appointment in order to make introductions and forge a positive working relationship.

Good logistical planning and communication is helpful in establishing therapeutic alliance and sending the message that care via CV is not a second rate alternative or afterthought to in-person care. Specifically, at a minimum the following questions should be addressed regarding procedures during CV encounters: How will providers be notified when their patients check-in for appointments? How will exchange of patient self-report measures (if needed) be executed? Who is the point of contact to address problems with videoconferencing equipment? What is the best way to contact support staff if needed? Two concerns most often identified by providers center around their ability to respond to clinical emergencies and technological difficulties. Accordingly, providers should be familiar with and have immediate access to detailed emergency procedures specific to the patient-site, indicating what to do and who to contact in the event of clinical or environmental emergencies at patient-site (see Chap. 8 for in-depth review of safety procedures). Attention to these logistical concerns well in advance of the scheduled CV encounter can assist in alleviating providers' concerns and increase their ability to be present with the patient. Table 10.5 provides provider-oriented checklist of tasks to complete before initial CV sessions.

Lastly, some providers will opt to meet with patients in-person before initiating CV services; however, for many providers and patients this may not be feasible or convenient. While there is no evidence suggesting that an initial in-person encounter is necessary to establish a strong, positive alliance in treatment through CV, providers and patients have shared that when feasible, meeting in-person can help to "break the ice." An initial in-person meeting offers an opportunity for the provider to more directly orient the patient to CV equipment, implement some of the suggestions noted above for promoting positive alliance and openness to CV, and even demonstrate use of the equipment at that time. All available evidence suggests that these objectives can be successfully achieved without meeting with the patients in-person. Accordingly, an initial or periodic in-person meeting may prove beneficial, but it is not necessary, especially if it represents an additional barrier to care.

10.7.2   Optimizing Alliance During Initial Clinical Videoconferencing Encounter

The ways in which providers relate to patients in the initial visit can influence patients' openness to and confidence in the provider, treatment process, and the use of CV. Once the call has been connected, the provider should offer a warm greeting and proceed with introductions much like one would do with a patient seen in person. It can be helpful to inquire about patient's experience with travel to the clinic or with checking in for their appointment. Also, the provider may wish to inquire about the condition of the videoconferencing room (patient's site) and patient's comfort in the room. A statement such as: "How does the room look? You're my eyes and ears there, so please just let me know if it looks like the room is in good condition." These seemingly minor inquiries not only convey a sense of interest, but also set the tone for collaboration in treatment through CV. Moreover, the inquiries may reveal information about the check-in process and condition of the videoconferencing room that warrants attention and provider intervention. The provider should confirm that the patient can see and hear the video signal clearly. Note that relying on the PIP setting to assess the patient-end view is not adequate because providers will be looking at it on their own equipment before the signal travels. Signal troubles on one-end are not necessarily apparent on the other. Providers should also ensure that they can clearly see and hear the patient, even/especially if it means asking the patient to reorient or sit closer to the camera. Attention to other aspects of the physical environment at the patient sight such as background noise, adequate lighting, and room temperature is important in order to ensure that the CV environment is comfortable and conducive to a positive therapeutic encounter. Table 10.6 provides a quick-reference summary of issues to address during first session, especially to build alliance (Note: Chaps. 9 and 10 provide broader clinical procedures and physical/technological configurations for CV services in general). Online provider video vignettes are available to model helpful techniques during a first office-based CV encounter and first home-based CV encounter, as well as to model less-helpful ways to introduce patients to CV (http://behavioraltelehealth.org/v1/c10/clinical).

Inquiring about the patient's comfort and prior experience with videoconferencing technology is important as the patient's attitudes and overall comfort with CV

Table 10.6 Provider checklist for first clinical videoconferencing session with patient

1. At start of CV encounter, offer warm greeting and introduction, as you normally would; that is, the immediate focus is on you and patient, not technology
2. Confirm that patient can adequately see and hear you
3. Describe specific procedures for managing dropped calls, should they arise; convey confidence and flexibility in managing challenges
4. Inquire about patient's experience traveling to the clinic and/or with checking in for their appointment
5. Inquire about the condition of CV room and patient's comfort in the room
6. Inquire if others are present in the CV room at patient-site. If appropriate for others to be present with patient, request that all persons are positioned within view of camera lens on the CV device
7. Inform the patient regarding the presence of anyone other than you in your office during CV encounter
8. Discuss security/privacy, confidentiality, and limits to confidentiality
9. Invite discussion of patient's previous experience with CV, current beliefs/attitudes about CV, and questions he/she might have regarding the modality
10. Orient patient to the basic features of the CV equipment, remote control, and additional relevant features if using web-based CV software
11. Discuss the merits and potential benefits of receiving CV treatment
12. Clearly communicate that treatment via CV is not a second-rate treatment option, but instead represents a state-of-the-art approach to treatment delivery
13. Communicate a team approach for coordinating patient's care, noting collaborative working relations with staff at patient site
14. If applicable, normalize patient's experience of uncertainty or unease with CV
15. At the conclusion of the encounter, inquire about patient's experience with CV during the visit

have the potential to influence alliance in treatment [90]. Some patients may already have experience with videoconferencing either in a clinical setting or through personal use via Skype or FaceTime. In this case, it is useful to inquire about the patient's experience in terms of successes, satisfaction, and dislikes regarding treatment through videoconferencing.

Orienting patients to the CV equipment can help overcome initial discomfort and increase confidence regarding use of the equipment; this is the first behaviorally collaborative task in CV mediated treatment and so time and care should be taken to set the stage for future collaborations and success. In this sense, being able to collaborate off the bat on something tangible may be advantageous in establishing therapeutic alliance. *In other words, we suggest not rushing through or minimizing CV orientation but using it as therapeutic tool.* Many CV devices are fairly similar to a standard television monitor and remote. It may be helpful to describe the CV equipment in this way and, if available, orient patients to the basic features on the remote control (e.g., on/off button; volume control, camera pan). Other videoconferencing set-ups, such as those through a PC, may have additional features and controls that can be reviewed together. Some patients may have more experience and familiarity with web-based videoconferencing software than providers and in these situations may be able to assist in navigating the CV equipment and providers should be open to looking for, utilizing, and reinforcing such patient competencies.

As with any technological device, technical difficulties with equipment do occur from time to time. These include visual pixilation, audio delay, frozen images, and/or dropped calls. While these challenges are infrequent, especially with higher-end equipment and sufficient bandwidth, providers should inform patients near the beginning of the first CV encounter of the procedures in place if a problem with the equipment were to occur. For example, in the event of a dropped call, the provider should attempt to reconnect and if unable to reconnect, attempt to contact the patient on his/her cell phone or the office phone located in the patient-site room, or alert appropriate staff at patient-site for assistance. Anecdotally, some providers have found that connectivity problems with some CV devices can be quickly and easily resolved by unplugging and then reconnecting the CV equipment to the power outlet. Preemptively discussing these procedures with patients can further limit patients' uncertainty and concern with the modality. Being able to follow-through on a back-up plan, and verbally noting the success of that plan, is another opportunity to reinforce teamwork and alliance. The provider's confidence and flexibility in managing these challenges in treatment through CV has the potential to promote positive patient attitudes in treatment. See Appendix 8.A for a provider-oriented checklist of tasks to complete during an initial CV encounter.

In the first session, it is also important to inform the patient about the limits to confidentiality relevant to the clinical service (see Chap. 7). Along these lines, it is helpful to inform the patient that no one else is in the provider's office as some patients may have fleeting concerns about this possibility but may not feel comfortable asking about it during the first session. Some providers even use their CV camera to pan/scan their office to show that there are no other individuals in the room. If others are present (e.g., trainee, etc.), it is important to obtain consent beforehand and to make appropriate introductions. It is good practice to have persons present in either the patient's or provider's office to be in view and visible through the CV camera. Inquiring if others are present in the room at patient-site is recommended as, on occasion, CV providers have been surprised to learn well into an appointment that a patient's significant other or relative has been sitting just off camera for the duration of the appointment.

10.7.3   Procedures to Address Patient Concerns

Some patients may experience ambivalence or trepidation about commencing treatment through CV. Therefore, it is essential that providers inquire about and discuss patient concerns regarding CV, openly, during the initial appointment and revisit throughout the treatment. Providers can assist patients by reflecting their concerns and normalizing their experience. It is possible and helpful to validate feelings without necessarily validating the concerns. There may also be several potential solutions to specific patient concerns, so it is imperative that providers take the time to understand exactly what the patient's worries are.

It may be helpful for patients to know that, most often, trepidation disappears within the first few CV appointments as patients feel more comfortable with the

Table 10.7 Procedures for when patients express concerns about CV modality

1. Reflect the patient's concerns nondefensively and normalize their experience

2. Find out specifically what patient is reacting to; it could be modifiable (e.g., audio volume, starkness of CV room, etc.)

3. Invite patient to collaboratively solve the problem

4. Use the opportunity to get to know the patient

5. Attempt to validate the patient's feelings and yet offer information that may assist in alleviating their concerns

   a. Convey that most patients feel very comfortable with the modality after the first few encounters

   b. Offer your own experience with CV in positive terms focused on services not modality, that is, "I really enjoy interacting with patients with CV because I found I can help many more people"

   c. Clearly communicate that CV is not a second-rate treatment option

   d. Relate findings from research suggesting that outcomes from treatment through CV are comparable to that achieved with in-person treatment

   e. Discuss specific and unique benefits that treatment through CV may offer patients

6. Emphasize information regarding steps to ensure patient privacy and security

7. Convey sense of collaboration through a team approach to coordinating patient's care, noting collaborative working relations with staff at patient site

8. Communicate confidence and positive expectancies regarding patient's comfort with the CV modality and the usefulness of the modality

9. Ground the conversation in the reason for episode of care

10. Ground the conversation in patient's choice; that is, provide alternatives for face to face care and discuss, pros and cons

11. Know when to stop; passively expressed concerns should be discussed but don't make concerns whole focus of session unless necessary. Checklist points should be chosen based on clinical need

modality. It should be clearly communicated that treatment via CV is not a second-rate treatment option, but instead represents a state-of-the-art approach to treatment delivery [91]. Providers can offer their own experience with CV and relate findings from research suggesting that outcomes from treatment through CV are comparable to those achieved with in-person treatment. Additionally, it can be helpful to identify specific and unique benefits that treatment through CV may offer. For example, many patients find that CV increases access to specialty services, which otherwise may not be available to them. There is likely added benefit associated with reduced travel time, reduced leave taken from work, lessened impact on childcare needs, and a reduced wait time for clinical services. In certain populations such as with patients in rural areas or in small communities, they may prefer meeting with a provider through CV due the anonymity it provides. Similarly, some patients report reduced stigma associated with engaging in treatment through CV. In general, the idea should be conveyed that CV is being offered for patient-centered reasons, rather than provider- or hospital-centered reasons. In many instances, patients are more open to the idea of CV after considering this perspective and the many potential benefits associated with the modality. Table 10.7 denotes specific procedures to address when patients express concerns regarding the CV modality. Note, patient refusal of CV is a relatively low base rate event (though it does occur from time to time), clinical techniques to address concerns are aimed at building teamwork and understanding, rather than building a case or convincing. Initial patient reticence can be viewed as a clinical "gift," an opportunity to demonstrate provider responsiveness, openness, flexibility, and eagerness to assist the patient. The conversation provides an immediate venue to instill hope that the patient can get better or be successful in addressing health concerns.

Conclusion

The majority of what we know regarding alliance in CV services is related to providing services on a one-to-one basis with a patient and provider in separate mental health or medical facilities. Even so, this chapter has summarized findings and provided recommendations for techniques and procedures relevant to a wide variety of CV services.

The field of telehealth is exploring the limits and boundaries of CV use; CV is now being used in war zones, in the homes of providers and patients, in group settings, and with portable mobile phones and tablets. As technology and creativity broadens the contexts in which services are possible, it will be important to continue to examine potential developing threats to therapeutic alliance. Doing so will allow practitioners to address possible problems using their therapeutic creativity and the development of new clinical techniques for use alongside of new technologies. Regardless, the current state of the literature indicates that CV is easily adopted with high levels of alliance and satisfaction, on par with in-person services. Even so, what we do as clinicians matters. Indeed, there is more variability in therapeutic alliance related to different providers than to these different modalities of care. As the saying goes, "it's a poor craftsman who blames his tools." Expanding services to include CV-based care provides new opportunities for individual clinicians to think about and expand their clinical skill sets, techniques, and how they conceive clinical engagement in the information age.

References

1. Freud S. The dynamics of transference. In: Starchey J, et al., editors. The standard edition of the complete psychological works of Sigmund Freud. London: Hogarth Press; 1958. pp. 99–100. (Original work published 1912).
2. Freud S. On the beginning of treatment: further recommendations on the techniques of psychoanalysis. In: Starchey J, et al., editors. The standard edition of the complete psychological works of Sigmund Freud. London: Hogarth Press; 1958. pp. 122–44. (Original work published 1913).
3. Bordin ES. The generalizability of the psychoanalytic concept of working alliance. Psychother Theory Res Pract. 1979;16:252–60.
4. Maddux JE, Rogers RW. Protection motivation and self-efficacy: a revised theory of fear appeals and attitude change. J Exp Soc Psychol. 1983;19(5):469–79.
5. Horvath AO, Del Re A, Fluckiger C, Symonds, DB. Alliance in individual psychotherapy. Psychotherapy. 2011;48:9–16.

6. Horvath AO, Symonds DB. Relation between working alliance and outcome in psychotherapy: a meta-analysis. J Couns Psychol. 1991;38:139–49.
7. Martin DJ, Garske JP, Davis MK. Relation of therapeutic alliance with outcome and other variables: a meta-analytic review. J Consult Clin Psychol. 2000;68(3):438–50.
8. Horvath AO. The alliance. Psychotherapy. 2001;38(4):365–72.
9. Shirk SR, Karver M. Prediction of treatment outcome from relationship variables in child and adolescent therapy: a meta-analytic review. J Consult Clin Psychol. 2003;71(3):452–64.
10. Kivlighan DM Jr, Patton MJ, Foote D. Moderating effects of client attachment on the counselor experience-working alliance relationship. J Couns Psychol. 1998;45(3):274–8.
11. Gunderson JG, Najavits LM, Leonhard C, Sullivan CN, Sabo AN. Ontogeny of the therapeutic alliance in borderline patients. Psychother Res. 1997;7:301–9.
12. Mallinckrodt B, Coble HM, Gantt DL. Working alliance, attachment memories, and social competencies of women in brief therapy. J Couns Psychol. 1995;42:79–84.
13. Baldwin SA, Wampold BE, Imel ZE. Untangling the alliance-outcome correlation: exploring the relative importance of therapist and patient variability in the alliance. J Consult Clin Psychol. 2007;75:842–52.
14. Zuroff DC, Kelly AC, Leybman MJ, Blatt SJ, Wampold BE. Between-therapist and within-therapist differences in the quality of the therapeutic relationship: effects of maladjustment and self-critical perfectionism. J Clin Psychol. 2010;66:681–97.
15. Del Re AC, Fluckiger C, Horvath AO, Symonds D, Wampold BE. Therapist effects in the therapeutic alliance-outcome relationship: a restricted-maximum likelihood meta-analysis. Clin Psychol Rev. 2012;32:642–9.
16. Ackerman SJ, Hilsenroth MJ. A review of therapist characteristics and techniques positively impacting the therapeutic alliance. Clin Psychol Rev. 2003;23:1–33.
17. Thompson SJ, Bender K, Lantry J, Flynn, PM. Treatment engagement: building therapeutic alliance in home-based treatment with adolescents and their families. Contemp Fam Ther. 2007;29:39–55.
18. Rees CS, Stone S. Therapeutic alliance in face-to-face versus videoconferenced psychotherapy. Prof Psychol Res Pract. 2005;36(6):649–53.
19. Backhaus A, Agha Z, Maglione ML, Repp A, Ross B, Zuest D, Rice-Thorp NM, Lohr J, Thorp SR. Videoconferencing psychotherapy: a systematic review. Psychol Serv. 2012;9(2):111–31.
20. Steel K, Cox D, Garry H. Therapeutic videoconferencing interventions for the treatment of long-term conditions. J Telemed Telecare. 2011;17:109–17.
21. O'Reilley R, Bishop J, Maddox K, Hutchinson L, Fisman M, Takhar J. Is telepsychiatry equivalent to face-to-face psychiatry? Results from a randomized controlled equivalence trial. Psychiatr Serv. 2007;58(6):836–43.
22. Bouchard S, Payeur R, Rivard V, et al. Cognitive behavior therapy for panic disorder with agoraphobia in videoconference: preliminary results. Cyberpsychol Behav. 2000;3:999–1008.
23. Bouchard S, Paquin BR, Payeur R, et al. Delivering cognitive-behavior therapy for panic disorder with agoraphobia in videoconference. Telemed J E Health. 2004;10:13–25.
24. Morgan RD, Patrick AR, Magaletta PR. Does the use of telemental health alter the treatment experience? Inmates' perception of telemental health versus face-to-face treatment modalities. J Consult Clin Psychol. 2008;76:158–62.
25. Simpson S. The provision of a psychology service to Shetland via teleconferencing: patient/therapist satisfaction and ability to develop a therapeutic alliance. J Telemed Telecare. 2001;7(Suppl 1):34–6.
26. Day SX, Schneider PL. Psychotherapy using distance technology: a comparison of face-to-face, video, and audio treatment. J Couns Psychol. 2002;49(4):499–503.
27. Germain V, Marchand A, Bouchard S, Guay S, Drouin M. Assessment of the therapeutic alliance in face-to-face or videoconference treatment for posttraumatic stress disorder. Cyberpsychol Behav Soc Netw. 2010;13:29–35.
28. Bischoff RJ, Hollist CS, Smith CW, Flack P. Addressing the mental health needs of the rural underserved: findings from a multiple case study of a behavioral telehealth project. Contemp Fam Ther. 2004;26:179–98.

29. Wade SL, Wolfe CR, Pestian JP. A web-based family problem-solving intervention for families of children with traumatic brain injury. Behav Res Methods. 2004;36(2):261–9.
30. Glueckauf RL, Fritz SP, Ecklund-Johnson EP, Liss HJ, Dages P, Carney P. Videoconferencing-based family counseling for rural teenagers with epilepsy: phase 1 findings. Rehabil Psychol. 2002;47:49–72.
31. Hufford BJ, Glueckauf RL, Webb PM. Home-based, interactive videoconferencing for adolescents with epilepsy and their families. Rehabil Psychol. 1999;44(2):176–93.
32. Frueh BC, Monnier J, Grubaugh AL, Elhai JD, Yim E, Knapp R. Therapist adherence and competence with manualized cognitive-behavioral therapy for PTSD delivered via videoconferencing technology. Behav Modif. 2007;31(6):856–66.
33. Himle JA, Fischer DJ, Muroff JR, et al. Videoconferencing-based cognitive-behavioral therapy for obsessive-compulsive disorder. Behav Res Ther. 2006;44:1821–9.
34. Greene CJ, Morland LA, Macdonald A, Frueh BC, Grubbs KM, Rosen CS. How does telemental health affect group therapy process? Secondary analysis of a noninferiority trial. J Consult Clin Psychol. 2010;78(5):746–50.
35. Porcari CE, Amdur, RL, Koch EI, et al. Assessment of post-traumatic stress disorder in veterans by videoconferencing and by face-to-face methods. J Telemed Telecare. 2009;15:89–94.
36. Simpson S, Bell L, Knox J, Mitchell D. Therapy via videoconferencing: a route to client empowerment? Clin Psychol Psychother. 2005;12:156–65.
37. Whitten P, Kuwahara E. A multi-phase telepsychiatry programme in Michigan: organizational factors affecting utilization and user perception. J Telemed Telecare. 2004;10:254–61.
38. Thorp SR, Fidler J, Moreno L, Floto E, Agha Z. Lessons learned from studies of psychotherapy for posttraumatic stress disorder via video teleconferencing. Psychol Serv. 2012;9(2):197–9.
39. Bratton RL, Short TM. Patient satisfaction with telemedicine: a comparison study of geriatric patients. J Telemed Telecare. 2001;7(Suppl 2):85–6.
40. Cluver JS, Schuyler D, Frueh BC, Brescia F, Arana GW. Remote psychotherapy for terminally ill cancer patients. J Telemed Telecare. 2005;11:157–9.
41. Constantinescu GA, Theodoros DG, Russell TG, Ward EC, Wilson SJ, Wootton R. Home-based speech treatment for Parkinson's disease delivered remotely: a case report. J Telemed Telecare. 2010;16:100–4.
42. Constantinescu GA. Satisfaction with telemedicine for teaching listening and spoken language to children with hearing loss. J Telemed Telecare. 2012;18:267–72.
43. Earles J, Folen RA, James LC. Biofeedback using telemedicine: clinical applications and case illustrations. Behav Med. 2001;27:77–82.
44. Frueh BC, Henderson S, Myrick H. Telehealth service delivery for persons with alcoholism. J Telemed Telecare. 2005;11:372–5.
45. Gustke SS, Balch DC, West VL, Rogers LO. Patient satisfaction with telemedicine. Telemed J. 2000;6:5–13.
46. Harvey-Berino J. Changing health behavior via telecommunications technology: using interactive television to treat obesity. Behav Ther. 1998;29:505–19.
47. Hui E, Lee PSC, Woo J. Management of urinary incontinence in older women using videoconferencing versus conventional management: a randomized controlled trial. J Telemed Telecare. 2006;12(7):343–7.
48. Karagiannis GE, Stamatopoulos VG, Roussos G, Kotis T, Gatzoulis MA. Health and lifestyle management via interactive TV in patients with severe chronic cardiovascular diseases. J Telemed Telecare. 2006;12(Suppl 1):17–9.
49. King VL, Stoller KB, Kidorf M, et al. Assessing the effectiveness of an internet-based videoconferencing platform for delivering intensified substance abuse counseling. J Subst Abuse Treat. 2009;36:331–8.
50. Lingley-Pottie P, McGrath PJ. A paediatric therapeutic alliance occurs with distance intervention. J Telemed Telecare. 2008;14:236–40.
51. Loane SE, Bloomer R, Corbett D, et al. Patient satisfaction with realtime teledermatology in northern Ireland. J Telemed Telecare. 1998;4:36–40.

52. Lowitt MH, Kessler II, Kauffman CL, Hooper FJ, Siegel E, Burnett JW. Teledermatology and in-person examinations: a comparison of patient and physician perceptions and diagnostic agreement. Arch Dermatol. 1998;134(4):471–6.

53. Mashima PA, Birkmire-Peters DP, Syms MJ, Holtel MR, Burgess LP, Peters LJ. Telehealth: voice therapy using telecommunications technology. Am J Speech Lang Pathol. 2003;12(4):432–9.

54. Mucic D. Transcultural telepsychiatry and its impact on patient satisfaction. J Telemed Telecare. 2010;16:237–42.

55. Sanford JA, Griffiths PC, Richardson P, Hargraves K, Butterfield T, Hoenig H. The effects of in-home rehabilitation on task self-efficacy in mobility-impaired adults: a randomized clinical trial. J Am Geriatr Soc. 2006;54(11):1641–8.

56. Shepherd L, Goldstein D, Whitford H, Thewes B, Brummell V, Hicks M. The utility of videoconferencing to provide innovative delivery of psychological treatment for rural cancer patients: results of a pilot study. J Pain Symptom Manage. 2006;32(5):453–61.

57. Sicotte C, Lehoux P, Fortier-Blanc J, Leblanc Y. Feasibility and outcome evaluation of a telemedicine application in speech-language pathology. J Telemed Telecare. 2003;9:253–8.

58. Shore P, Goranson A, Ward M, Lu MW. Meeting Veterans Where They're @: a VA Home-Based Telemental Health (HBTMH) Pilot Program. Department of Veterans Affairs. In Press 2013.

59. Ward E, Crombie J, Trickey M, Hill A, Theodoros D, Russell T. Assessment of communication and swallowing post-laryngectomy: a telerehabilitation trial. J Telemed Telecare. 2009;15:232–7.

60. Weatherburn GC, Lister AG, Findley LJ. The feasibility of reviewing chronic fatigue syndrome clients at a distance: a teleconference pilot study. J Chron Fatigue Syndr. 2007;14:23–32.

61. Whitten P, Mickus M. Home telecare for COPD/CHF patients: outcomes and perceptions. J Telemed Telecare. 2007;13:69–73.

62. Rees C, Haythornthwaite SC. Telepsychology and videoconferencing: issues, opportunities, and guidelines for psychologists. Aust Psychol. 2004;39(3):212–20.

63. Fenton JJ, Jerant AF, Bertakis KD, Franks P. The cost of satisfaction: a national study of patient satisfaction, health care utilization, expenditures, and mortality. Arch Intern Med. 2012;172(5):405–11. doi:10.1001/archinternmed.2011.1662.

64. Kairy D, Lehoux P, Vincent C, Visintin M. A systematic review of clinical outcomes, clinical process, healthcare utilization and costs associated with telerehabilitation. Disabil Rehabil. 2009;31(6):427–47.

65. Polisena J, Tran K, Cimon K, Hutton B, McGill S, Palmer K. Home telehealth for diabetes management: a systematic review and meta-analysis. Diabetes Obes Metab. 2009;11:913–30.

66. Mair F, Whitten P. Systematic review of studies of patient satisfaction with telemedicine. BMJ. 2000;320:1517–20.

67. Williams TL, May CR, Esmail A. Limitations of patient satisfaction studies in telehealthcare: a systematic review of the literature. Telemed J E Health. 2001;7(4):293–316.

68. Mair FS, Goldstein P, May C, et al. Patient and provider perspectives on home telecare: preliminary results from a randomized controlled trial. J Telemed Telecare. 2005;11(Suppl 1):95–7.

69. Kleiner KD, Akers R, Burke BL, Werner E J. Parent and physician attitudes regarding electronic communication in pediatric practices. Pediatrics. 2002;109:740–4.

70. Schopp LH, Johnstone BJ, Merrell D. Telehealth and neuropsychological assessment: new opportunities for psychologists. Prof Psychol Res Pract. 2000;31:179–83.

71. Ackerman SJ, Hilsenroth MJ. A review of therapist characteristics and techniques negatively impacting the therapeutic alliance. Psychotherapy. 2001;38:171–85.

72. Gibson K, O'Donnell S, Coulson H, Kakepetum-Schultz T. Mental health professionals' perspectives of telemental health with remote and rural First Nations communities. J Telemed Telecare. 2011;17:263–7.

73. Hopp F, Whitten P, Subramanian U, Woodbridge P, Mackert M, Lowery J. Perspectives from the Veterans Health Administration about opportunities and barriers in telemedicine. J Telemed Telecare. 2006;12:404–9.
74. Simms DC, Gibson K, O'Donnell S. To use or not to use: clinicians' perceptions of telemental health. Can Psychol. 2011;52:41–51.
75. Richardson LK, Frueh BC, Grubaugh AL, Egede L, Elhai JD. Current directions in videoconferencing tele-mental health research. Clin Psychol. 2009;16(3):323–38.
76. Starling J, Foley S. From pilot to permanent service: ten years of paediatric telepsychiatry. J Telemed Telecare. 2006;12(Suppl 3):80–2.
77. Mitchell JE, Myers T, Swan-Kremeier L, Wonderlich S. Psychotherapy for bulimia nervosa delivered via telemedicine. Eur Eat Disord Rev. 2003;11:222–30.
78. Gagnon M, Godin G, Gagné C, et al. An adaptation of the theory of interpersonal behaviour to the study of telemedicine adoption by physicians. Int J Med Inform. 2003;71:103–15.
79. Tuerk PW, Hontoria EG, Rauch SAM, Hall B, Yoder M, Nagae N. Collaborative international mental health response to disasters: establishing community programming & evidence-based therapy training. The 26th annual update in psychiatry: disaster, trauma & recovery, Medical University of South Carolina.https://drive.google.com/file/d/0B9hm_OnfRj1FUFgtb1dZbjJ-jdXM/edit?usp=sharing. 2013.
80. Dowell NM, Berman JS. Therapist nonverbal behavior and perceptions of empathy, alliance, and treatment credibility. J Psychother Integr. 2013;23(2):158–65.
81. Chen M. Leveraging the asymmetric sensitivity of eye contact for videoconference. In: Proceedings of the SIGCHI conference on human factors in computing systems. New York: ACM Press; 2002. pp. 49–56.
82. Tam T, Cafazzo JA, Seto E, Salenieks ME, Rossos PG. Perception of eye contact in video teleconsultation. J Telemed Telecare. 2007;13:35–9.
83. Graham LE, McGimpsey S, Wright S, et al. Could a low-cost audio-visual link be useful in rheumatology? J Telemed Telecare. 2000;6(Suppl 1):35–7.
84. Lovell K, Cox D, Haddock G, et al. Telephone administered cognitive behaviour therapy for treatment of obsessive compulsive disorder: a randomised controlled non-inferiority trial. BMJ. 2006;333:883.
85. Lovell K, Fullalove K, Garvey R, Brooker C. Telephone treatment of obsessive-compulsive disorder. Behav Cogn Psychother. 2000;28:87–91.
86. Taylor S, Thordarson D, Spring T, et al. Telephone-administered cognitive behavior therapy for obsessive compulsive disorder. Cogn Behav Ther. 2003;32:13–25.
87. Tachakra S, Rajani R. Social presence in telemedicine. J Telemed Telecare. 2002;8:226–30.
88. Sharpley CF, Jeffrey AM, Mcmah T. Counselor facial expression and client-perceived rapport. Couns Psychol Q. 2006;19(4):343–56.
89. Rubino G, Barker C, Roth T, Fearon P. Therapist empathy and depth of interpretation in response to potential alliance ruptures: the role of therapist and patient attachment styles. Psychother Res. 2000;10(4):408–20.
90. Shore JH, Savin D, Novins D, Manson SP. Cultural aspects of telepsychiatry. J Telemed Telecare. 2006;12:116–21.
91. Tuerk PW, Yoder M, Ruggiero KJ, Gros DF, Acierno R. A pilot study of prolonged exposure therapy for posttraumatic stress disorder delivered via telehealth technology. J Trauma Stress. 2010;23:116–23.

Index

© Springer International Publishing Switzerland 2015   253
P. W. Tuerk, P. Shore (eds.), *Clinical Videoconferencing in Telehealth*,
Behavioral Telehealth, DOI 10.1007/978-3-319-08765-8

CPSIA information can be obtained at www.ICGtesting.com
Printed in the USA
LVOW04*1656191214

419645LV00007B/154/P

9 783319 087641